Allenby

Also by Brian Gardner

THE BIG PUSH (Cassell)

GERMAN EAST (Cassell)

THE WASTED HOUR (Cassell)

UP THE LINE TO DEATH (Methuen)

Allenby

by

BRIAN GARDNER

CASSELL · LONDON

CASSELL & COMPANY LTD
35 Red Lion Square, London WC1
Melbourne, Sydney, Toronto
Johannesburg, Cape Town, Auckland

Printed in Great Britain by
Cox & Wyman Ltd.,
London, Fakenham and Reading
F.165

Contents

Illustrations

Meinertzhagen and Lloyd (later Lord Lloyd) at Advanced Intelligence H.Q. in the Sinai Desert, 1917. (*Col. R. Meinertzhagen.*)

British Intelligence photograph of the Commission of Liman von Sanders, signed by the Kaiser.

The Hejaz Railway. (*Imperial War Museum.*)

Lawrence and bodyguard. (*Imperial War Museum.*)

Lt.-Colonels Lawrence (*left*) and Alan Dawnay (*right*). A contrast in military dress as well as in guerrilla tactics.

'El Aurens'. (*Imperial War Museum.*)

Newcombe – the unsung hero of the Desert Campaign. (*Imperial War Museum.*)

Joyce – front seat, near-side – in his Rolls. (*Imperial War Museum.*)

Wavell as a Staff Officer, 1915.

Following page 140

The Mayor of Jerusalem offering the surrender of the Holy City to Sergeant Sedgewick (*left*) and Sergeant Hurcombe, just before 9.0 a.m. on the 9th of December, 1917. (*Col. R. Meinertzhagen.*)

Allenby just prior to his official entry into Jerusalem; photograph taken by Lt.-Colonel Davis, the U.S. Military Attaché.

Allenby listening to his Proclamation, ending four centuries of Turkish control of Jerusalem, from the steps below the Tower of David, the 11th of December, 1917. Lawrence and Wavell are among the officers present. (*Imperial War Museum.*)

Holding the line, before the final offensive of 1918. A Lewis Gun section of the 2nd Leicestershire Regiment. (*Imperial War Museum.*)

The bridge over the Yarmuk valley which Lawrence never succeeded in destroying. (*Imperial War Museum.*)

Lowell Thomas (back to the camera) meets Feisal. Lawrence stands between them. (*Imperial War Museum.*)

Part of Capt. Pisani's French Contingent, under Allenby's command, on the march. (*Imperial War Museum.*)

Allenby arrives in Damascus on the 3rd of October, 1918. (*Imperial War Museum.*)

Feisal leaving the Hotel Victoria in Damascus after his first meeting with Allenby on the 3rd of October, 1918. He had just been informed of the limitations to Arab influence in the territories beyond Damascus. (*Imperial War Museum.*)

Arrival at Alexandria as Special High Commissioner, the 10th of November, 1919.

At the Residency, Cairo. The stork and his friend 'the Bull'.

Allenby, Feisal, Lloyd George and Lady Allenby, in London, 1919. (*P. A. Photos Ltd.*)

Following page 188

The Prince of Wales and the High Commissioner in Cairo, June 1922.

Lord and Lady Allenby at the first opening of the Egyptian Parliament.

Following page 204

Lord Allenby, Lord Balfour and Sir Herbert Samuel in Jerusalem, March, 1925.

Reviewing French Dragoons at Reims after the war.

The War Memorial at Wallasey.

Maps

Allenby was morally so great that the comprehension of our littleness came slow to him.

This dreamlike confidence and decision and kindness which were Allenby. What an idol the man was to us.

T. E. Lawrence

Introduction

One of the several strange things about the study of the First World War is that those people who seem to need from it a hero figure have relentlessly fastened their attentions and loyalties elsewhere than on Edmund Allenby, one of the most interesting military personalities of the war, and a real-life hero-figure if ever there was one. He has waited in the wings. This book, however, is not intended as the kind of partial tribute with which, for instance, Douglas Haig's reputation has been saddled; in which a blind eye is turned to the defects that any mere human must possess. Such well-meaning eulogies serve temporarily to confuse history, and even in the end may have the opposite effect to that intended by the author. I therefore approached Allenby with some, but not many, preconceived ideas, and a determination to be objective. But I must gladly admit that before long I had gained more respect and admiration for my subject than I had foreseen. It has been easier to detect mistakes in Allenby's career than it has been to notice flaws in his character.

Nor is this book intended as a conventional biography; that task has already been done supremely well by Lord Wavell, who was outstandingly qualified for it. It is intended as a study of a man in his times, primarily based on his own writings; a fascinating but neglected soldier and statesman, who was a worthy descendant of his ancestor Oliver Cromwell. Allenby was a man whose life, like the lives of all great men, had a profound influence on the lives of others. I have gone into his relationship with others whose careers touched his in greater detail than hitherto. A man's life on its own tells only part of the story. I have attempted to portray Allenby as the dominating figure on a stage where other important actors also play their parts.

Allenby had a strange knack of drawing to him men of destiny: Cecil Rhodes, Oates of the Antarctic, Baden-Powell, Milner, Henry Wilson, Lawrence and Wavell were among his admirers and friends. Owing to the relevance of Lawrence to the Allenby story, I have included my own assessment of Lawrence—humbly in the face of the many that have gone before—and quote, I believe for the first time, some writings of his that have remained practically unnoticed since they first appeared anonymously in 1918. It has also seemed relevant to tell the story, in very brief outline, of events which affected Britain in the Middle East between 1914 and 1945, and British policy, or lack of it, in that area. If Allenby was able (almost alone) to act in that area for many years without being either Zionist or Arabist, it should be possible to write of that schism, particularly in regard to Lawrence, with similar detachment.

From an early date the basis of Allenby's military thinking was, as he said, that 'The principles of war are eternal, but there are no rigid rules for their application.' One must beware of labels in writing history, but I have found it best to distinguish between two broad schools of thought in British military affairs: the progressives and the conservatives. One of the objects of the book is to reveal Allenby as a progressive in influence, and usually, if not invariably, in action; to show him as a valuable cornerstone in the progressives' edifice. Although Allenby died before the Second World War began, he had some positive influence on its conduct. The fact that the British Army has been dominated for some decades now by the progressives should not blind us to the fact that it has not always been so.

Allenby's reputation has been something of a puzzle. It has been difficult to reconcile the picture of an ill-tempered, repugnant, and inadequate general that some have described, with the man whom we know gained, among some of those who worked with him closely, a veneration that has not been accorded to any commander this century, except to Wavell, MacArthur and Slim. Wavell's book, written very much from the latter standpoint, did not entirely solve the riddle. An examination of Allenby's letters, however, does provide a clue; for there, behind the formidable exterior, lurks a cultured, perceptive and generous human being, which not everyone would have suspected (Allenby was not known as 'the Bull' for nothing). A man can be forgiven being a commander who sometimes makes mistakes; no general has been entirely free of them, such is the frailty of human nature. He can be forgiven especially if he has enough of the basic virtues, and Allenby was basically a fine type of Englishman: honourable, compassionate, and frank. What makes him doubly interesting is that not all suspected it at the time. His imperious, intimidating manner, explosive temper and total inability to suffer either fools or sycophants made him enemies as well as friends.

That Allenby has been somewhat neglected is due neither to T. E. Lawrence, who heaped praises upon him, nor to the most authoritative writer on the war, Liddell Hart, who has always written of the man and his campaigns in high terms; nor, indeed, to the dramatists and film-makers, who from time to time have recognized in Allenby a truly dramatic figure. A careful portrayal has been given in Terence Rattigan's *Ross*, and another in the film *Lawrence of Arabia*. Robert Bolt, who with the American writer Michael Wilson did the screenplay for that film, has said that he considered Allenby the greatest man portrayed in it. Lowell Thomas, who in America after the war started the Lawrence legend, found to his dismay that the demand was for more of Lawrence and less of Allenby; as is well known, he supplied the demand. Allenby, indeed, has always been overshadowed by Lawrence; he is remembered, if at all, as a character in the cast of the Lawrence story. The perspective of history may well reverse the roles.

*   *   *

I have been fortunate in being given, by the present Lord Allenby, the use of all the papers and documents in his possession, well preserved in a large trunk and two boxes. In his biography, Wavell said that Allenby 'left no papers'. Certainly, he did not keep a diary, or conscientiously collect papers and copies of his own letters in the same way as did some of his contemporaries; nevertheless, there are some thousands of memoranda, notes, telegrams, speeches, and letters in Lord Allenby's collection, the vast majority hitherto unpublished. Allenby was a prolific letter-writer. During the height of his career he wrote four or five pages nearly every night to the two women who dominated his life. His letters to his wife *alone* during the South African War amounted to about a quarter of a million words of detailed description of the campaign. They may be the best from the war which exist. When the affectionate parts had been excised, they were copied out and sent to various members of the family; the originals all survive. The majority of his papers seem to have been preserved more by his mother and his wife—Allenby was fortunate that in nearly all his career he was served and loved by these two truly remarkable women—than by the man himself; there are also letters to his sisters, his nephew and others.

Occasionally, however, Allenby took care to preserve certain letters or documents which had an important bearing on his career or reputation. Having been summoned to the Foreign Office, and (literally) presented with the Official Secrets Act, it has not been possible for me, at this time, to publish all of these. This is more inconvenient for the reputation of Allenby than it is for that of others. Further to these, there are some important papers collected by Wavell himself; these he passed on to the present Lord Allenby so that they should be kept, and if necessary consulted, together with Allenby's own papers, retaining only the right of their use during his lifetime. These throw some light especially on the clash of personalities on the Western Front, although Wavell, owing to one of those concerned being still alive, was not himself able to make full use of them. This entire collection, that of both Wavell and the Allenby family, I have designated in the text and the Notes—'A.P.' I also quote from a number of papers, and letters from some of Allenby's surviving staff, that I have collected myself. So far as Ypres and Palestine are concerned some familiarity with the scene of action (in calmer times) may have assisted me.

Except where I thought them of particular interest, I have not reproduced again letters already quoted by Wavell. Where I have relied heavily on Wavell, and on the excellent but over-respectful Savage (a previous biography not mentioned by Wavell), I have endeavoured to add previously unquoted material, or fresh biographical material. My debt to Wavell's book is great. One naturally feels a proper sense of humility and respect at following in the footsteps of one who was himself a great man, and a far better writer on military history than is sometimes appreciated today.

I have quoted some previously unpublished extracts from the diaries of Sir Henry Wilson; for permission to do so I am grateful to Major C. J. Wilson. Much of the material on Egyptian politics is based on the very extensive private notes, by Reuter's Cairo correspondent of that time, which have been deposited in the Allenby Papers.

The Lawrence articles referred to above appeared anonymously in *The Times* on the 26th, 27th and 28th of November, 1918, and amount to some six thousand words. They give a colourful and fairly complete picture of the Arab rising and Feisal's campaign, and are Lawrence's first public writings on it. I can discover no details of them in Lawrence's other writings or published letters, and *The Times* will not reveal their authorship. They are not included in *Oriental Assembly*, which is said to contain 'practically all the author's miscellaneous writings'. However, the stylish writing is unmistakably that of Lawrence, and although one or two others would have been able to write much of the same story, no one but Lawrence could have written of the Akaba raid in the first person. Professor A. W. Lawrence, who did not know of the articles, is confident that they are by his brother, and so is one

of the bibliographers. Lawrence was in London at the time
the articles appeared, as he was at a meeting of the Eastern
Committee of the Cabinet some days before. He was, however, still in the Army at that date, and was thus required not
to publish reports of his service without permission; this no
doubt explains why the articles have remained so little known
for so long. Lawrence once wrote, in a letter to Ronald
Storrs, 'I know how rare fugitive writings become in time.
Once I did three or four columns in *The Times*, but I have
never seen them since.' Anonymous articles in the same newspaper, August, 1920, are also, Professor Lawrence agrees,
'probably' by Lawrence.

I am indebted to *The Times* for allowing me to quote these
articles. I am also indebted to the following for allowing me
to quote at length passages from sources which are acknow-
ledged in the Notes at the rear of the book: The Controller of
H.M. Stationery Office, The Australian War Memorial,
Messrs. Ernest Benn, Chapman & Hall, Constable, Eyre &
Spottiswoode, Harrap, Hodder & Stoughton, The Executors
of the T. E. Lawrence Estate and Jonathan Cape, Weidenfeld
& Nicolson, Sir Ronald Wingate, Major-General J. F. C.
Fuller, and the 2nd Earl Haig and the Trustees of the late
Field-Marshal Earl Haig.

To Lord Allenby goes my sincere gratitude for his generosity and understanding throughout; for the historian he is
indeed the ideal custodian; his papers were in my possession
for as long as I wished, with unrestricted use, but, of course,
with total independence in writing the book. I am indebted
to him for the use of photographs.

My thanks are also given to Colonel R. Meinertzhagen,
Colonel P. C. Joyce, Lt.-Colonel F. W. Young, Major R. H.
Brodie, Captain B. H. Liddell Hart, Professor A. W. Lawrence and Mr C. S. Forester. I also acknowledge the advice
of the late Colonel R. H. Andrew. I am alone responsible for
expressions of fact and opinion in the book.

CHAPTER 1

Early Life

Edmund Allenby was born on the 23rd April, 1861, at Brackenhurst Hall, near Southwell, in Nottinghamshire. A pleasant but unexceptional country house on the road to Nottingham, it had been the home of his mother's family for about fifty years. The bedroom windows at one side looked down a gentle slope to the small country town of Southwell, dominated by its majestic, squat-towered Minster, one of the most beautiful of Britain's buildings.

It was St. George's Day. The flag of England, no doubt, flew from the Minster tower; the ripe, melodious peals of bells would certainly have been clearly heard at Brackenhurst. To the other side of the house could be seen, in the distance, the smoke and factory chimneys of Nottingham, dimly observed over low, rolling hills which were decorated with large fields and clumps of trees. Oak and elm clustered around the elegant iron-work gates. Perhaps the most notable feature of Brackenhurst was the beauty of its gardens and rockeries, well known in the county. Roses, clematis and ivy luxuriated in the surrounds of the house, with its great bow windows and iron balustrade. It would have been difficult to have been born in a more representative English setting.*

In his early years there were a number of clues to Edmund Allenby which, despite other appearances to the contrary,

* Today, Brackenhurst is the home of the Nottinghamshire Farm Institute; there is no memorial or plaque.

might have revealed to the particularly discerning observer the promise of a determined and powerful maturity.

Allenby's mother, Catherine Anne Allenby, was the daughter of the Rev. Thomas Coats Cane, vicar of the ancient Church of Halloughton, within close walking distance of Brackenhurst Hall. A woman with a pronounced strength of will, Catherine Anne Cane had married into the Allenby family in 1859. Two of her forebears lay buried in the nave of the Minster below; she was distantly related to the Coats of the cotton empire.[1]

The Allenbys had lived in Lincolnshire since at least the fifteenth century, and probably longer. The first record of an Allenby in that county (there are earlier traces of the same family in Cumberland) is the institution of Henry Allenby as rector of Thorganby. The Allenbys appear to have been stolid members of the Lincolnshire squirearchy for the next three and a half centuries, caring for their land and livestock, but seldom venturing beyond Lincolnshire and Nottinghamshire. In the eighteenth century some powerful blood was injected into the family when a direct descendant of Oliver Cromwell, also an Eastern Counties man, married Hynman Allenby (Hynman had been, and remains, the predominant male Christian name of the family since 1672). Occasionally a daughter or son would settle farther south in East Anglia, and from time to time an Allenby went as far afield as Sicily or Australia, but for the main part the family, never prolific, kept close to the family home of Kenwick Hall, near Louth. They were, as Wavell has said, 'typical of that lesser landed gentry who have been the backbone of the English race and the principal source of its greatest names.'[2] The Allenbys have always been, and still are, country people; one of the few people in the mainstream of the family ever to have lived in London was Edmund Allenby himself. Allenby's father, it appears, had made some attempt to shake off the lack of ambition inherent in this quiet, modest family for so long. He had gone to Corpus Christi College, Cambridge, but left without a degree. He had decided to become a doctor, and began the study of medicine, but soon dropped it. He had some musical talent. But eventually he found himself leading the life of a country squire, as his forebears had since the Conquest. There are, however, indications that he was not entirely satisfied with this fate; shooting, riding, fishing and sailing—these were more than acceptable; but the up-keep of land, the husbanding of property, the intricacies of finance, these were not only extremely boring, they were also hardly matters to concern a gentleman. In Hynman Allenby there was no exception to the influence of the Industrial Revolution on the social system; to be middle-class, invaded by money-making men of commerce, was no longer satis-factory. It was the marriage of this man to Catherine Anne Cane that sparked greatness from the Allenbys who had lived and died practically unnoticed to the rest of the world for four centuries.

Their second child, and eldest son, was christened Edmund Henry Hynman.* Allenby's father bought a house at Felix-stowe, an estate in Norfolk, and a 28-ton yacht. He lived for sport, and went as far as Norway, an enterprising journey for that time, in order to fish. He tended to live beyond his means, and only the wisdom and character of his formidable wife kept the family from the disaster which threatened from time to time. Allenby *père* became friendly with the eccentric Edward Fitzgerald, translator of *The Rubáiyát*, who lived near by, and they yachted together at Harwich. A friend from his Cambridge days, and a frequent visitor to Felixstowe House, was Prof. Edward Cavell, a keen botanist.

Such was the background in which the young Allenby developed as a boy; woods full of birds, which he watched and listened to with fascination; trees with birds' nests; the wind slapping in sails; the barking of gun dogs; a stream with trout; a pool for swimming. He always considered him-self a Suffolk man, and took the greatest interest in the

* There were six children of the marriage. The second son was Capt. Frederick Claude Hynman Allenby, C.B.E., R.N., who had a dis-tinguished naval career, and it is his eldest son, a former Lt.-Colonel of the Derbyshire Yeomanry, who is the present Viscount.

3

county; he later recalled hearing often the old Anglo-Saxon plurals in his Suffolk childhood—words like 'meezen' (mice) and 'reezen' (nests). Allenby was on a donkey's back before he was a year old, and rode a horse as a small boy as a matter of course. A hefty child, he knew little physical fear, but beneath the ruddy-faced exterior of a typical, healthy country boy was hidden a sensitivity not perhaps suspected by either his elders or his playmates. He later wrote:

I remember, when I was a small boy, being horribly frightened of anyone with a painted face, or a mask on. Guy Fawkes' Day was a horror to me especially.[3]

From time to time he would, with his mother and brothers and sisters, visit Kenwick, or other places in Lincolnshire, where most of the family were still living. (Kenwick belonged to the Allenbys until well into this century.) At the age of ten he was sent to a small private school at Ashbocking, near Ipswich. One who later remembered the young Allenby at this time has recalled: 'He was always painstaking and thoroughgoing. He was a quiet, strong, manly, conscientious boy, of singular modesty, who never put himself forward.'[4]

From there he went to Haileybury in 1875. Haileybury, a new public school which had already won some notoriety through a run of scholarships to Oxford and Cambridge, had been founded only thirteen years previously by a group of Hertfordshire and East Anglian landowners who wished to make some use of the noble and substantial buildings of the old East India College. The first 'Master' (i.e. Headmaster) had left to become Dean of Oriel College, Oxford, and when Allenby went to Haileybury the Master was E. H. Bradby, one of the outstanding headmasters of the time; under him the fledgeling school gained a reputation which has scarcely been surpassed since.* Bradby collected round him a small group of young, talented men from the universities. Although the academic standard was high, discipline, it appears, was

* After fifteen years Bradby left Haileybury to work in the East End of London; a remarkable action for a Victorian headmaster.

4

not. Some of the rowdy traditions of the old East India College had remained, and the school had an individual character of its own among schools of the time; conformity was less the rule than elsewhere. Conditions were rough and rigorous; but for those who wanted to learn, the opportunities were excellent. There was still a strong link with India, and Bradby insisted on a code of religious fervour mixed with loyalty to the monarchy. Sir Reginald Blomfield, the architect, and a senior boy in Allenby's time, wrote of Bradby: 'He was a man of singular indifference to popularity and current reputation. He had his own standard of duty and his own ideals to aim at, and he went for these with a characteristic directness of purpose which sometimes led to misinterpretation, but seldom failed to be justified by the result . . . . Above all, he taught us to hate sham and pretence, and to aim at being thorough.'[5]

Allenby was in the house named after Bartle Frere, who had been at Haileybury in the East India Company days, and who, after a distinguished career in India, became a controversial High Commissioner and Governor in South Africa; it is likely that the pupils were probably expected to study Frere, and there is little doubt that Allenby was made to ponder on that unfortunate man's trials as High Commissioner. Allenby was a large boy, although not at all athletic in organized games, and was thus not worried by bullying. His best subject was Greek, and he was also more than average in Latin and French. He was a rather quiet, withdrawn, thoughtful child, with a wry sense of humour that gave him the appearance of being older than his years. He was merely satisfactory in work. Allenby rose to the Lower Sixth, and Bradby, apparently impressed by his steadfast but puzzling character, made him a prefect in his third year, an unusual distinction. A contemporary remembered: 'He was sane, simple, and direct in all he did.'[6] The housemaster, one learns, was not a strong man either physically or in character (he was drowned swimming in the Thames a year after Allenby left), and leant to some extent on his most capable prefect. It seems that Allenby had developed a natural authority at this time.

5

Among his contemporaries were five future generals; but Bradby's talents as an educationalist lay elsewhere than in training for the services. Also at Haileybury with Allenby were a future Keeper of Printed Books at the British Museum, an Oxford historian, an artist, an editor of the *Cambridge Review*, a Regius Professor of Divinity at Cambridge, two Newdigate Prizewinners, a housemaster at Repton, a headmaster at King Edward's, Birmingham, a poet and a Professor of Latin (to say nothing of a large number of tea planters, Indian Civil Servants and obscure country vicars).[7]

In 1878 Allenby's father died, the Norfolk estate was sold, and the young Allenby left Haileybury a year early. Two influences on his life had thus played their parts: the rather gay and charming countryman who had tried to come to terms with new social trends by efforts to make a career or to become a sporting grandee, and Bradby's patriotic fervour and respect for books, learning and the intellect.

It had been decided that Allenby should go, like so many of his school friends, into the Indian Civil Service—a rather novel idea for the Allenby family. This was considered at the time an outstanding prospect for a boy with above-average capabilities. Together with his school friend Henry McMahon, Allenby was sent off to a crammer's in Bayswater. He stood for the examination twice, and twice he failed. The subjects offered by him were Greek, Latin, English Composition, French, Mathematics, Chemistry, Mechanics and Astronomy. This failure was a grave disappointment to Mrs. Allenby; it was decided the boy would have to go into the Army, as the days of being a country gentleman on a small income were clearly numbered.

Not particularly interested in becoming a soldier, Allenby nevertheless sat for the Royal Military College at Sandhurst in 1880. He was placed fifth out of 110 successful candidates.

Allenby arrived at Sandhurst to start his military career, with no more than modest ambitions, on the 10th of February, 1881. He was with his best friend, McMahon, who had also failed to enter the Indian Civil Service. It is likely that Allenby was influenced in attempting to join both the Indian Civil Service and then the Army by this friend.*

Allenby did well at Sandhurst, but not exceptionally so. Being a big, hardy young man, and having come from a school notorious at that time for its toughness, he took easily to the disciplinary life. As at school, he was picked out for command, both because of his natural but quiet authority and his rather mature attitude; he soon became an 'under-officer'. He was a popular cadet, his best friends being McMahon and H. A. Lawrence (later General Sir Herbert Lawrence). He was not, however, the typical cadet, who confined his interests to women and the Army. He had already, under the influence of Edward Cavell, become interested in botany. He was fond of drawing and adept at quick pen-and-ink sketches. And he had developed a passion—it was to last him his life—for travel. Between leaving school and leaving Sandhurst, he visited Belgium, Germany and Switzerland with the family. He had also been to Rome with Herbert Lawrence, and had spent two months living with a family in provincial France in order to improve his French. (From that date there was not a year of his life in which he was not abroad.) This sudden bursting forth from the narrow bounds of East Anglia to new lands and experiences quickly broadened (although it did not at this date sharpen) his mind and added to the growing maturity that was marking him out from his contemporaries. As Wavell said: 'Many young men who joined the Army in those days of unhurried country life had similar qualities [to Allenby]. But few had learned to study books also, as Allenby had, and few had his experience of foreign travel, and could actually speak to those queer foreigners in their own language.'[8]

After ten months at Sandhurst, Allenby passed out twelfth and was gazetted to a commission in the 6th Inniskilling Dragoons. As is the case with so much of his early life, there was no obvious reason for this choice. He had no Irish

* Remarkably enough, Allenby closely followed on Sir Henry Mc-Mahon as High Commissioner for Egypt.

connections, and no family connections with the regiment (nor, indeed, with any regiment). It was, however, an inexpensive one, and this may well have influenced Allenby, as his private income—in those days essential for an officer—was inconsiderable. It was also the choice of one of his best friends at Sandhurst, and we have already seen how easily swayed the young Allenby was by his friends.

The Army in which Allenby found himself as a very junior officer owed much to the reforming zeal of Edward Cardwell; a military life was still considered a fairly light-hearted affair, despite the experiences of the Crimean War, but since Cardwell it had become quite possible, even acceptable, for a young man to take his duties seriously.

Cardwell was a retiring, precise, hard-working lawyer. Even at the height of his influence, which was considerable, he was not well known out of military and political circles. Somewhat colourless, not a little prim, he had become Secretary for War in Gladstone's Government in 1868.

For some years prior to this he had been formulating views about the British Army, as had other people with inquiring minds. But with Cardwell the matter was almost personal. He was the complete antithesis of the typical officer of the time, who was a gay, nonchalant, lisping blade priding himself on his ignorance of affairs apart from riding, gambling and women. Cardwell had previously been Colonial Secretary. During this time he had concentrated the Army at home from its far-flung commitments by insisting that colonial governments must henceforth pay, or help to pay, for the military on their territories. The Maori Wars alone had been costing the British taxpayer £1 million a year. His first reform as War Minister had been to abolish the purchase of commissions; not without a bitter fight. Gladstone had backed Cardwell, but the Commander-in-Chief, the Duke of Cambridge, had been outraged at the idea, and Queen Victoria herself had been most dubious. Many British families had been buying commissions for years; it had become a kind of right. Cardwell's bill had been called 'wicked, wanton, costly and crotchety'. The Lords had turned it down, but

Gladstone had got round them by appealing to the Queen. Officers had petitioned parliament, but the bill had become law. Even Lord John Russell had been aghast at such a blow to mid-Victorian life.

Cardwell had also abolished flogging (but only in peace-time); had restricted royal power in the Army; had changed the system of recruiting; and had reorganized the regimental grouping of the infantry on a county basis. All these had been fought by the conservatives and traditionalists with the use of every parliamentary device. But by reorganizing the infantry Cardwell had strengthened the cavalry, which had been powerful enough to resist most of his efforts at reform (as had the artillery). The cavalry, by the date of Allenby's commission, represented the original Army of the 'good old days' before the confounded meddler, who knew nothing about these things, had got his way with the Queen.

Cardwell had been a paper worker. He had seldom gone to have a look at his soldiers. He had known little more about real conditions in his Army, which were appalling, than did any other politician. He had been able to do little about pay, and not much about leave. In the first case there was still far too little, and in the latter far too much. The low pay hampered recruitment: the long leave made the Army grossly inefficient. Officers were accustomed in some regiments to as much as six months' leave every year. They kept town houses. They spent much time travelling on the Continent. No social event was too small to shirk a duty.

But gradually, after Cardwell's reforms, those who would normally have purchased a commission started turning away to other pursuits where a gay life was promised. Instead, young men were contemplating making a career of the thing. Most of them had failed at Oxford or Cambridge, or both, they were not very bright, there was not much else to be done with them, and so they went into Cardwell's army. They took part in the antics of the pre-Cardwell men; swung from chandeliers, kept horses as best their finances would allow, learnt about wenches, and longed for a 'punitive' war where they could gain a medal or two and have some fun. These

were the men whom Allenby now mostly found as his contemporaries.

The Inniskillings were stationed in South Africa, and
Allenby, aged twenty-one, joined them at camp seventeen
miles from Durban. For much of the next twenty years, with
only a few years in England, Allenby was to serve in South
Africa. Alone of nearly all his contemporaries who rose to
high command, he never served in India (ironically enough,
considering his schooling and earlier intentions), which was
the forge on which great British military reputations were
expected to be shaped.

South Africa was in political ferment. The struggle between
Boer and Briton, with all its bitterness, was clearly heading
for an inevitable climax. The Transvaal had, the year before,
regained its independence from Britain; an independence
already prized and asserted by the Orange Free State. There
were continual squabbles between the Boers and the British
authorities as to which should control, annexe or 'protect' the
remaining native territories, especially Zululand. The
Inniskillings were a major part of the tiny force that the
British government thought fit to station there.

It was, perhaps, the most enjoyable time of Allenby's life.
The rough, tough, open-air life of a regiment on ceaseless
patrol suited him well. The native life of the country, the
animals, and the flora and fauna, all totally new to him,
fascinated him. The constant air of hardly suppressed ten-
sion, and the possibility of action, with a cavalry charge at
any time, could not but have thrilled any young man of action.
He enjoyed, especially, the sport. There was a good deal of
polo, but Allenby was too big ever to be a first-rate rider; his
proficiency on horseback, one gathers, was only just up to the
standard required by a cavalry regiment, but this was com-
pensated for by his popularity and his well-balanced but reserved amiability. At this time Allenby tipped the scales at
13 st. 4 lb., and one can find some sympathy for his horse.
His ill-advised audacity in polo, not always very skilfully
executed, involved him on a number of occasions in serious
accidents owing to the force of his falls; on one occasion he

was unconscious for several days. On the whole, Allenby enjoyed the lonelier sports away from the crowd; in all circumstances, not only in sport, the smaller the group the more comfortable he felt. He did a great deal of game-hunting, in which he developed a keen interest for a few years, but which left him as suddenly as it had taken hold of him; his love of wild life no doubt winning a painful battle. One can summon up an accurate picture, in those distant years in South Africa, of this large, rather ungainly, but good-looking young officer struggling to find his place in the regiment, and when off duty collecting rare ferns and flowers from the coasts, plains and mountains, which were then pressed and sent home to Felixstowe.* There was also fishing in shark-infested waters in Natal, crocodile hunting, sailing and turtle hunting.[9]

But these were interludes in what was, after all, a predominantly military life, most of it spent on active service. From 1883 to 1885 the regiment made expeditions to Zululand and Bechuanaland. On the latter, Allenby met, and apparently got on very well with, Cecil Rhodes, who accompanied the Inniskillings. The officers of the regiment were disconcerted to find Rhodes talking for hours on end to a very junior subaltern. During these peaceful but dangerous expeditions the young officer learnt the minor but highly relevant aspects of war: patrols, mounting of outposts, protection of camps and convoys, the importance of supplies. Edmund Allenby, who had joined the Army almost by accident, and who at first would vastly have preferred to have been travelling about in Europe, became aware that the life of a professional soldier was not so dull after all. He no doubt found, during those years of interesting and complicated police work, that a soldier's duties, as distinct from his sporting pleasures, were occasionally of some interest.

After four years in South Africa, Allenby was sent home for the normal tour of regimental duty at the cavalry depot.

---

* These do not always seem to have received the attention he hoped for. Some of them are still in their original envelopes among the Allenby papers.

There he learnt more of the regimental side of the Army, the necessities and obsessions with 'spit and polish' for which he had not previously cared. But now that he felt more seriously about his commission, he was more easily able to accept that side of Army life; as a cadet it had not unduly disturbed him, and he now saw no reason why his men should not similarly be prepared to show a high standard in turn-out and unquestioning respect of discipline. Before returning to the regiment, which had moved its headquarters from the camp near Durban to Pietermaritzburg, he was promoted Captain. The town, clearly, was a more comfortable place than the camp, for not only were there proper quarters, there were dances, races and parties, as well as the usual sporting activities which continued as unabated as before. Despite his slightly more serious attitude to his career, his basic style remained unchanged.

A brother officer wrote of Allenby at this time: 'Whatever may have been his own secret thoughts and ambitions, Allenby carried out all his military duties with complete efficiency . . . but all with rather an air of *insouciance*, so that many thought of him as one constitutionally easy-going who took nothing seriously. He was popular with all ranks; he had a strong sense of humour, with just a touch of irony. . . . A great reader on all manner of subjects unconnected with his profession, he could hold his own in conversation with older men . . . he held original ideas on many subjects, military and civil, and did not hesitate to give expression to them, however contrary they may have been to accepted standards. He was always a little detached in manner, and did not court familiarity.'[10]

One can, however, discern a trend to lay aside the easy-going attitude which he had inherited from his father. After seven years in the Army, Allenby was made Adjutant of his regiment. During the period of his adjutancy, the humour was to become more dry and more hidden, the keen, professional soldier more in evidence. He was strict, demanded work before pleasure, and was, it seems, the terror of the subalterns. He had never been a great talker, preferring to

Brackenhurst, Allenby's birthplace, drawn in 1878 by his sister Kitty.

Captain Allenby about 1890.

The Staff College, 1896. Allenby is second from the left in the second to last row. Haig is last officer on the right, three rows from the back.

listen, and this, combined with his apparent distance and formidable appearance, did not make a very popular Adjutant. Allenby was given the nickname of 'Apple-pie', which was not only a play on his name but also indicated his insistence on neatness and order. Allenby's apparent severity appears to have been, at first, entirely simulated, to make up for the basic amiability of his nature. He was not the first, nor the last, officer—commissioned or non-commissioned—to discover that for good discipline a reputation for severity is very helpful. (In later years there are signs that the simulation had become so habitual that it was a real part of the man; it became allied to an evil temper. But many a petrified young officer—not least T. E. Lawrence—was to be so taken aback by the sudden, deep, kindly glance, or the gentle phrase which, almost mischievously, emitted from 'the Bull' when apparently in one of his most thunderous moods, that, instantaneously, they were captivated for life. No one has ever accused Allenby of bearing a grudge; his explosions were considerable, but they were soon over.)

Thus the whole attitude of the man, but not the character, had changed in a very short while. Allenby had discovered his role in life, and for the first time his rivals started to look at him seriously as a contender for high honours: probably the regiment, perhaps even a brigade. His own ambitions, however, extended no farther than the regiment.

*   *   *

In 1890 the Inniskillings returned to Britain and had the pleasant posting of Brighton. There was a great deal of training and irksome peace-time regimental duties, and the standard of 'spit and polish' demanded by the Adjutant was higher than it had been in South Africa; nevertheless, as was customary at the time, there was generous leave for officers, and plenty of time for polo, hunting, shooting and fishing. At this time Allenby began making regular trips to Scotland during the season. He was unfortunate, however, in having a commanding officer who contrived to be away from his regiment for most of the year, responsibility and virtual command of the regiment thus falling upon the Adjutant. When his adjutancy came to an end in 1893, one suspects that it was to the general relief of the regiment, which shortly returned to more carefree days. Allenby himself, however, had been fired with the desire to discover more about what was now his profession; during this period he was seeing a good deal of his mother, and she urged him to make use of his talents and accept all the challenges of his career.

At that time the Staff College was not considered very seriously by the average young officer or his commander; having passed the course there did not compare, for instance, with a large private income or an expertise at polo, both of which were more useful assets to a good regiment. There were thirty-two vacancies each year, but only about twice that number of candidates competed for places. Allenby decided to take the almost unique step, in the Inniskillings, of sitting for the examination.

His general education was sound, and his knowledge and interests unusually wide for a young cavalry officer, but his knowledge of military theory was very little. He sat first in 1894, and failed to qualify; the regiment was not surprised. But it was a surprise when Allenby, not at all deterred, took the positively eccentric step of sitting again the following year, and of passing. He was the only cavalry officer to enter the Staff College by competition, in January, 1896, and the first officer from his regiment who had ever done so. He passed in twenty-first.

Another cavalry officer who entered the Staff College on the same day as Allenby was Captain D. Haig, of the 7th Hussars. The two men had similarities of background. They were practically of the same age, Haig being less than two months the younger. They came from similar county families, had been to new Victorian public schools, had no family influence or connections in the Army, had both lost their fathers early and owed much to their mothers. They had both travelled (Haig had toured the United States). But there the resemblance ended. Haig was a serious, trim young officer, with steadfast eyes and determined jaw; he was devoid of a sense of humour, and impatient of all pastimes that tended to distract from his work. Allenby was large, rather distant in manner, and with soft, rather big eyes; although he enjoyed the conviviality of the mess little more than did Douglas Haig, it was for different reasons: he was not so much irritated by the antics as bored. Haig was extremely religious; Allenby, although he enjoyed biblical studies, was not. Both men worked harder than was customary during the course, but, despite this, Allenby, at least, retained popularity with his colleagues; so much so, indeed, that he was elected Master of the Staff College Draghounds, in succession to his friend Herbert Lawrence. It is worth noting, perhaps, that Haig had also failed his examination to enter the College at his first attempt, but, unlike Allenby, he had not sat for it again. Haig had been fortunate to come across some useful contacts, among them Colonel John French, the Duke of Cambridge (Commander-in-Chief), and Field-Marshal Sir Evelyn Wood, who, particularly, pushed forward Haig's claims on several occasions. Every senior officer who met Douglas Haig appears to have been highly impressed with him. There was, however, inclined to be an atmosphere at Camberley between those officers who had entered through competition and those who had not.

Both men applied themselves to their studies with diligence; Haig to such an extent that some of his contemporaries took it for granted that he would reach the top of the profession, for at the time an officer who took an Army career seriously, to the detriment of his social life, was considered a bore with a Field-Marshal's baton on the brain. Haig, far more studious, became a rather lonely figure. Allenby appears to have been chiefly remembered at the College for his steady but undistinguished work, his remarkable appetite, his dry wit, and his handling of the hounds. He continued to broaden his interests and, reacting no doubt to the experience of adjutancy, relaxed a little and led a full and enjoyable social life. Haig, already dedicated to a military career, had few if any interests outside military affairs and his family. Allenby, however, had added a love of poetry (which he enjoyed learning by heart), rose-growing (at Felixstowe) and, above all, ornithology, to his passions of travel and botany. He continued to travel abroad while at the College, and spoke French fluently enough to qualify as an Army interpreter in the language; he was also fairly fluent in German. Haig's previous experience of travel is revealing; he visited France and Germany. On the first occasion he had, while on leave, observed and written a long account of the French manœuvres of 1893—one imagines to the astonishment of his seniors and the awe of his contemporaries. The following year he had been to Germany and studied the German army. Perhaps the most academic of the instructors at the College at that time was G. F. R. Henderson, an expert on the American Civil War. But a prolonged study of a new weapon, the machine-gun, which was already being considered by thoughtful civilians, and which had been first presented as a practical proposition nearly two decades before, was not much in evidence in the course.

Another of Allenby's contemporaries at the Staff College was Captain J. E. Edmonds, later to be the Official Military Historian of the Great War. Edmonds had a poor opinion of both Allenby and Haig. He later wrote: 'Allenby was curiously taciturn; rather out of his depth in the very medium company of 1896-7; we elected him Master of the Drag because we did not want Douglas Haig.' Of Allenby's notorious unpunctuality at the College, he said: 'A cavalryman who had actually passed in by competition could take liberties!' One of those at the College, Captain G. Barrow, who was later to serve under both Allenby and Haig in the First World War, later compared the two men, with some benefit to Allenby.* He recalled that Allenby never objected

* Later General Sir George Barrow. Edmonds became Brig.-General Sir James Edmonds. Capper (see next page) became Major-General Sir Thompson Capper; he died of wounds received at Loos, 1915.

to an opinion which did not coincide with his own. This was in marked contrast to Haig, who was as a rule intolerant of any opinion that differed from his own. Even Haig's concentration was confined to one side only. His study and interest were almost entirely devoted to the general staff, and operations and staff duties branches. He was not a good judge of men, and made some 'blobs' in his selections. Barrow added that Allenby, on the contrary, where the choice was left to him, invariably chose capable assistants, and fitted square men into square holes. More than once Allenby said to him, 'Haig was always so infernally jealous of me.' He well remembered his first sight of Allenby. Allenby came into the ante-room one day dressed in hunting kit. Barrow thought he had seldom seen a more striking figure. He thought the majority of the students, if not the instructors, would have placed Capper at least as high as Haig. Capper, he recalled, was full of imagination and originality, was quicker on the uptake and a student of his profession. 'The difference between the two can be put this way. If I commanded an army and was opposed by Haig, I should always know what he would do; if I was opposed by Capper I would never know what he was going to do, and would always be fearful of being surprised. As an instance of Haig's unpopularity at Camberley, no one would sit next him at mess if there was a place vacant elsewhere.'[11]

Allenby's Staff College report contained the following assessment: 'This officer has sufficiently good abilities and much practical common sense. In all his work the practical bearing of the subject dealt with is always kept in view; and so long as the subject or situation falls within his knowledge, it is rapidly and thoroughly dealt with. In matters with which he is not so conversant he is not very good at working into details. He has energy, good judgement and rapid decision, and is a clear thinker and writer. He is active and a good soldier, and has the power of exerting influence on others and getting good work out of them.'[12]

Before leaving Camberley, Allenby was promoted Major, whereas Haig left as a Captain: although this had nothing to do with performance at Staff College. Later in their careers neither man had a high opinion of the capabilities of the other; relations between the two were usually cordial, if a little reticent

Inscribed on the wooden panels at the Staff College, Camberley, are the names of those who have passed the course there since the foundation of the College. On the panel recording the students who passed out in 1897 are the names of Major E. H. H. Allenby, 6th Dragoons, and Captain D. Haig, 7th Hussars. They are placed next to each other.

*   *   *

While at Staff College, Allenby had married. At the house of sporting friends in Scotland he had met Miss Mabel Chapman, the daughter of a landowner from Salisbury, Wiltshire; her mother had been the daughter of the marriage of Sir Henry Fletcher, Bt., grandson of a Chairman of the East India Company, and Emily Maria Browne, also of a well-known Indian Civil Service family.*[13] They knew each other for a few days only on that occasion, but when Allenby returned to the same house party the following year, he was thrilled to find her there again. Having made up his mind, he was not a man to delay, and within a week of the second meeting they were engaged. It was, by all accounts, a genuine and immediate case of a love-match. Despite strong objections from Miss Chapman's father, who considered Allenby, without substantial private means, no better a prospect than any other young officer, they were married the following December. She, too, was fascinated by birds and flowers, and until his death she shared and cultivated his various interests, and devoted her life to his. It is clear from his letters that their

---

* She was distantly related to Fletcher Christian, the mutineer of the *Bounty*; her niece married Michael Sadleir, the author and publisher.

marriage was a particularly happy one. She was a quiet, peaceful, very feminine woman—something of a contrast to Allenby's strong-willed mother—consumed with a tremendous admiration for her 'loving Edmund'. The only child, Horace Michael Hynman, whom Allenby adored, was born thirteen months later.

In his last year at the College, Allenby was sent with a party of officers to study the battlefields of Belgium, including Waterloo; a study which he found irksome, although he discovered some distractions. He wrote to his wife from Brussels:

I went tonight to a magnificent music-hall, the Palais d'Été, an enormous place. Metz was a very interesting town, barring the battlefields. There was a fair, however, to which I went one evening. It had a delightful collection of waxwork horrors which you would have loved to shudder at.[14]

Soon after leaving the Staff College, Allenby was posted to Ireland as Brigade-Major of the 3rd Cavalry Brigade in Ireland. Nothing could have pleased him more, and, with his charming, gentle bride, he took up his appointment in March, 1898. There was excellent, cheap hunting and good fishing; it is probable that this aspect of Irish life appealed to him more than did his staff duties, but he appears to have been a conscientious and adequate staff officer. It was the only staff appointment of his career, and it ended after eighteen months.

Haig, too, had got the very posting he desired on leaving Camberley. Allenby's appointment would certainly have horrified him had it come his way; he had no desire to kick his heels in a sportsman's paradise, for there was fighting to be done, and in fighting there lay experience. Through the good offices of Sir Evelyn Wood, he was sent to the one place where fighting was taking place—one of the very few officers to be sent out for the final stages of Kitchener's campaign against the Dervishes of the Sudan. Thus, while Edmund Allenby was fishing in Kildare, Douglas Haig was with the Egyptian Cavalry in the awful holocaust of Omdurman. From his tent,

Haig despatched long and irritable letters to his Field-Marshal patron at home, detailing everything he thought wrong with the conduct of the campaign—which was considerable; unusual, but in the circumstances justifiable, conduct for a junior officer. In that same year a Pole named Bloch, not a soldier but a banker who had studied modern weapons, wrote a book called *Is War Impossible?* In it he wrote: 'War will become a kind of stalemate. . . . Everybody will be entrenched. It will be a great war of entrenchments. The spade will be as indispensable to the soldier as his rifle. . . . It will of necessity partake of the character of siege operations. . . . Your soldiers may fight as they please; the ultimate decision is in the hands of famine . . . that is the future of war.'[15]

Shortly the catching of fish and the slaughtering of half-armed Arabs was to be finished. The recalcitrant Boers were causing more trouble in South Africa. From the Curragh to Khartoum and beyond, the British Army prepared to do battle. Allenby was returned to his regiment, which was almost immediately ordered to the theatre of war.

Less than three weeks after the outbreak of war, the Inniskillings embarked at Queenstown for South Africa. Major Allenby telegraphed twice to his wife, from whom he had been so suddenly parted, in this reminder that he was once more a professional soldier, at five o'clock and half-past midnight:

All on board safely. Start in about an hour. Good-bye. Take care of yourself and Michael.

Anchored tonight near Queenstown. Very comfortable. Sail early tomorrow. Queenstown illuminated and very pretty with fireworks, etc. God bless you. Best love.[16]

It was not much to say, but then there was not a great deal to be said. It was war, and perhaps for the first time in his life Allenby, as he gazed at the lights across the water, fully realized that his business was the waging of war. Unlike the vast majority of his contemporaries who had been in action in some remote corner of the Empire, Edmund Allenby, approaching his fortieth year, had never fired a shot in action.

CHAPTER 2

War: South Africa

Soldiers don't make wars. Politicians make war, soldiers end it.
ALLENBY

The letters of Edmund Allenby from the South African War contain possibly the most interesting and detailed accounts of that war, written at the actual time, that exist; they have been carefully preserved by the family, but are little known outside it. Sensible, down-to-earth and utterly frank about the hazards involved in the duties of a regimental officer, they set down at length the exact things which those at home wished to know (with the exception, perhaps, of some lengthy treatises on South African bird life). Remarkably devoid of the clichés of the period (apart from continually calling his wife 'my old woman'), they were sent off complete with maps, sketches and the writer's own illustrations. ('This is something like what I can see through my glasses.') Many of the letters, in fact, amounted to diaries, as each night or early morning a little more was contributed to the growing letter before it was despatched—usually once a week, but depending on the mail (but invariably as frequently as possible). The first words of his first South African War letter were: 'I think I'll start a letter now and finish it gradually before sending it off.' He kept to the method for the entire campaign. His wife wrote to him every night throughout the war. Unlike the diaries and letters of some of his contemporaries, personalities very rarely figure in his outpourings. But, as well as an account of the war, they do give the best picture of this professional soldier at that time; compassionate, impatient, absorbed in the mysteries of wild-life and flowers, hating war but rapidly turning his mind towards the problems of waging it. His troops, one imagines, would have been astonished to read the fluent letters of the stern, uncommunicative 'Apple-pie'.

From the start Allenby was wretchedly homesick; on the ship out his misery was increased by an uncomfortable set of new false teeth (Allenby was bothered by teeth trouble for many years), and by a terrible bout of sea-sickness. He wrote:

> I am coming to the conclusion that I have too happy a life at home to make a really good soldier. I catch myself often half-hoping that the war may be won by the time we arrive, so that I may get back quick.[1]

It was a ghastly journey, and by the time it approached the Cape Verde Islands the little transport, 3,500 tons, had broken a propeller shaft. With horses, men and crew all exhausted by the rough weather she drifted helplessly before high wind and an angry sea. Allenby was the senior officer aboard. It was an unpleasant experience, especially as forty-six years before most of the regiment had perished at sea when *en route* to the Crimea. While the ship drifted towards the cliffs of the Isle of Sao Antonio, Allenby drilled his men in lifebelts. At almost the last moment, by sheer good fortune, they were confronted by the remarkable and unexpected sight of a Liverpool tug appearing round the lee of the island, accompanied by a Royal Navy cruiser, smoke belching, band playing and men cheering encouragement.

After a considerable delay, Allenby reached Cape Town on the 11th of December. On passing Madeira, impressed by the climate and scenery, he had written:

> We must come and stay here for a month next winter.

And despite the bad news and depression which greeted him

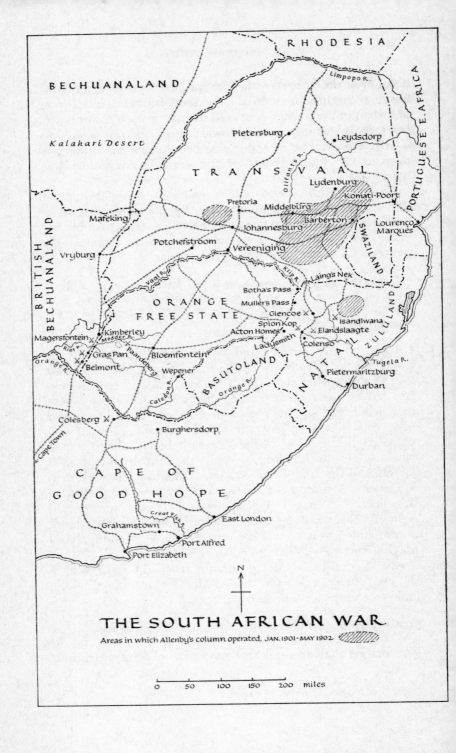

BECHUANALAND

Kalahari Desert

RHODESIA

Limpopo R.

PORTUGUESE E. AFRICA

BRITISH BECHUANALAND

Mafeking

Pietersburg

Leydsdorp

T R A N S V A A L

Olifants R.

Lydenburg

Komati-Poort

Pretoria

Middelburg

Barberton

Lourenço Marques

Johannesburg

Potchefstroom

Vereeniging

SWAZILAND

Vryburg

Vaal R.

Klip R.

Laing's Nek

O R A N G E

F R E E S T A T E

Botha's Pass

Muller's Pass

Spion Kop

Glencoe ×

Isandlwana ×

Acton Homes

× Elandslaagte

Magersfontein

× Kimberley

Modder

Riet

Paardeberg

Ladysmith

Colenso

Z U L U L A N D

Orange R.

× Gras Pan

Bloemfontein

Belmont

Wepener

BASUTOLAND

Caledon R.

Orange R.

Tugela R.

N A T A L

Pietermaritzburg

Durban

Colesberg ×

Burghersdorp

C A P E   O F

G O O D   H O P E

Cape Town

Great Fish

East London

Grahamstown

Port Alfred

Port Elizabeth

N

THE SOUTH AFRICAN WAR

Areas in which Allenby's column operated, JAN. 1901–MAY 1902

```
0      50     100    150    200   miles
```

in the Cape, Allenby, as most others, still believed the affair might be over well before the following Christmas.

It was admitted that the Boers had started well, but then they everywhere had the advantage. Only in Natal were the British in any strength; but it was not expected that the ill-organized Boer irregulars would give much trouble to the Empire as soon as the Army Corps and the Cavalry Division (of which Allenby's regiment was part) were ready for operations. Direct advances would be made on Bloemfontein and Pretoria, the capitals respectively of the Boer republics of the Orange Free State and the Transvaal. The hearty, imposing, but none-too-quick-witted Sir Redvers Buller was to command the operation.

Things, however, worked out rather differently. The Army Corps abandoned, for the time being, all thought of victorious marches on the capitals and split up into two columns: one, under Buller, to relieve Ladysmith, the other, under Lord Methuen, to relieve Kimberley. The Cavalry Division was sent to a position roughly half-way between the two columns, near the Orange Free State border, with the mission of preventing any further Boer advances into the Cape Colony; it was confronted by a large force of irregulars excellently placed along a ridge of hills.

It was there that Major Allenby, second-in-command of the Inniskilling Dragoons, found himself at Christmas, 1899. In command of the Cavalry Division was Major-General John French, who was 'providing the only gleam of comfort to British pride at this moment'.[2] Together with his well-thought-of and busy principal staff officer, Major Douglas Haig, French had just escaped from Ladysmith in the nick of time on the last train. Allenby found the long wait on the plain before those hills extremely irksome:

Matters don't seem to be going on well elsewhere. However, it can't be helped; we must see it out now we are here. I am always thinking of you, my love, and like to imagine you doing things at the time I am thinking of you. You are always in my thoughts and prayers, as I know I am in yours. I don't think the war will be over as soon as we expected at first, but I long for the day when I shall see you again.[3]

It's nice of you all to be making Tam O'Shanters for the men. I am sure they will appreciate them; though most of them have knitted woollen nightcaps that are served out to them on board ship and that they are allowed to keep. I always sleep in the one we bought in Dublin. One wants them these cold nights.[4]

Allenby was not always impressed by the handling of the Cavalry Division in the small operations that took place all the time. On one occasion a squadron of the Inniskillings was despatched to the aid of the Suffolk Regiment, which had attempted to penetrate a gorge of the hills.

There was about half a battalion of the Suffolk Regiment (about 12 officers and 400 men). We could hear the firing and see the flashes of the Boer rifles, which began a tremendous fusillade at about 3.30 a.m., which lasted till daylight. Then our guns began to shell the hill, but soon stopped as the rifle-fire ceased. We then got a signal that 200 infantry had come back, and that the rest of the attackers had been cut off. Fincastle's squadron was sent out to find out what had happened. He went out, as gallantly as he would, across a great plain between hills full of Boers, and worked round the position the infantry had attacked. The enemy let him past, without firing, till he was close to the position, and then let him have a *feu d'enfer* from all sides. He turned and came back under an awful hail of bullets at full gallop; his squadron well scattered to make as little target as possible; and, by a miracle, not a man or horse was hit. It was quite true; the Suffolks were captured. We stayed there, shelling the Boer positions until about mid-day, when fire ceased. It was a bad business. The old tale of attacking a position of unknown strength with too few men. The Suffolks were half-way up the hill when fired on. They went on to nearly the top, when they came to a great ditch with a wall behind it held by Boers in the ditch and behind the wall. The whole of the leading company was knocked over, then they were surrounded and forced to surrender. The Colonel, the Adjutant, two subalterns and about 30 men were killed, and 170 men and 11 officers in all are killed, wounded and missing, out of a total of 12 officers and 400 men.

The prisoners were put together on a hill, by the Boers, where they stood all morning (we could see them), holding up a Geneva Cross flag. The Boers treated them well and allowed our own doctor to go out to them. They (the Boers) said to him: 'We admire your men's courage, but we are surprised that you go on making these foolish attacks.' For that matter, so am I. I was not surprised at the result of the attempt, only disgusted. The fact is that we have not enough men to turn these fellows out, and we ought to play a waiting game until we have got really enough to make something like a certainty of it. The Boers are as stubborn as mules and as brave as lions in defending their positions. They have spies everywhere, and I believe they knew the exact moment the Suffolks left their camp for the attack, though it was kept so secret that the regiment only got the order 15 minutes before they fell in. The Boers said they had full information of it all.[5]

Allenby was quick to learn the surprising lesson that war with modern weapons, as distinct from that against half-armed natives, required intelligence and the use of the brain more than courage and flamboyance. He was given command of one of the squadrons, a position very much more suited to his nature than that of second-in-command, in which he had not been a great success.

I rode over [to H.Q.] this a.m. General French was very affable when I reported myself. He said that owing to the range the squadron must be kept detached, but that he would make it a special-duty squadron, for anything he might wish, and especially wished to have me near him as he heard I was a reliable officer. That was nice of him, wasn't it? . . . I think that the lessons of the war have been learnt now by our generals, and that they will sit tight till reinforcements come. We shall dance around the Boers, shell them and bother them, in fact play their game, but not bang our heads any more against brick walls. . . . All our disasters have been caused, hitherto, by our contempt of the enemy.[6]

This showed a fair appreciation, and an uncluttered mind, for a regimental officer with little knowledge of staff work.

Allenby was making a name for himself as a determined but very safe cavalry leader, and French (on Haig's recommendation) turned to him more and more for special assignments.* Allenby's exceptional knowledge of the terrain, and of the enemy, from his early years in South Africa, served him well. He loved pitting his wits against the ruses and feints of the Boers, but by following a number of his own simple rules to avoid ambush his column was never once involved in a disaster; in fact, he carried out French's policy of harassing the enemy more frequently and more efficiently than any other squadron commander. His exploits were not only well known in the Army, but he became mentioned in the despatches of the war correspondents to the London newspapers. No junior officer was better known to the public. Meanwhile Lord Roberts, who had served his country for over forty years in India, had arrived to take command from Buller; with him was his Chief of Staff, Lord Kitchener.

I'm just up, 5.30 a.m. Guns are firing in the distance, but I hope we shall be peaceful today. Our General [French] thought he'd try to frighten the Boers a bit. . . . At 3.0 a.m. yesterday I started, with my squadron and two guns of John [Powis's?] battery, to try and hammer a 15-pounder gun on the front of the main Boer position, while the rest of the troops made wide turning movements against his flanks. It was pitch dark and I went on a luminous-compass bearing till light, when I found myself about three miles from my object. The Boers were having breakfast, as we could see by their smoke, but they sniped at my advance scouts. The guns came into action against the hill where the enemy's gun was supposed to be. He soon answered us with shrapnel, but it was some 15 minutes before he got the right range. Then we found that we had four guns against us. In the next 20 minutes the place became distinctly unhealthy. The Boer guns were well hidden; and our 23-pounder R.H.A. guns, though they fired steadily and most accurately, could not silence them. The Boers fired splendidly, especially with the automatic guns, nasty

---

* A letter from the Earl of Athlone in the A.P. confirms that this was Haig's doing. Athlone served in the Inniskillings during the war.

South Africa: Allenby, third from the right, parleys with a Boer scout.

A page from a letter written by Allenby during the South African War.

Extempore Cavalry Corps conference, near Ypres, November, 1914. From left to right: Colonel Seely, and Generals Bingham, Vaughan, de Lisle, Allenby. Seely, recently War Minister, had resigned over the Curragh incident.

Lady Allenby, on the right, July, 1915.

spiteful things that go 'Pop, pop, pop, pop, pop' faster than you can count, and hammered our guns savagely. I withdrew the guns. We got well shelled with shrapnel and cannon shell as we withdrew. We had to draw back two miles before they stopped shelling. Their last shell, at nearly four miles range, blew the helmet off one of my men; but, luckily, didn't burst. Our loss was two gunners wounded and 17 artillery horses killed and wounded. It was a miracle to me that we lost no more, as we were right in the open without a stick of cover. Quite a hopeless job. We stayed out in the plain till about 10 p.m., when the G.O.C., French, came up. He told us we had done excellently.[7]

Our guns shell the Boer positions every day for some hours. I don't think we do them much damage, but it, no doubt, annoys them. We know hardly anything of what is going on in the other columns, and really not much of what occurs in our own. . . . I wish this business was over and that we were back at the old Curragh.[8]

We shell them leisurely all day and every day. There is some fighting, too, most days, on the flanks of our long line, but we don't get much forwarder. I hope, now that Roberts has come, he will concentrate all his force on one line, either here, Modder River or Natal, and drive through while the rest sit tight. It's no use trying to be strong everywhere. The Boer positions are too strong to take unless by an overwhelming force, and, with weak forces like ours, one cannot turn their flank and get behind them. Also, though we are still in Cape Colony, we are practically in a hostile country, as nearly all the farmers are disloyal and most of them have already left their farms and joined the Boers; while those who remain act as spies. So all our movements are reported, while we can get very little reliable information from the inhabitants.[9]

Despite urgings from several impatient officers, French was prepared to continue these badly planned, minor engagements indefinitely, rather than launch a full-scale attack on the strongly defended heights; an attack which, as Major Allenby saw, was bound to end in disaster. In due course French's Chief of Staff, Douglas Haig, was replaced. (He returned later.)

Our present tactics are Boer tactics, and we worry, worry, worry them; I think we are right, as we are not strong enough here yet. I believe Roberts approves thoroughly of what French has been doing. The Suffolks' disaster was his only major mistake.[10]

We want heaps more artillery. Without them one fights in the dark. The Boers occupy extended positions; we shell them more or less; then directly our infantry attack a tremendous fire breaks out, but one can't see a puff, or a flash, or a man, as they, like ourselves, use smokeless powder. So our people get shot down without seeing an enemy to fire at. With a huge force of artillery we might be able to so smother all the positions with shell that none of the enemy dare put up his head to fire.[11]

Edmund Allenby, in fact, was learning more of the military art before the hills of Colesberg than he had learned in all the rest of his years put together. There, in miniature, were similar problems to the ones he would have to face as a general fifteen years later. Meanwhile, there were other irritations to war:

I hear that Kitchener thinks we have too many luxuries and too much baggage at the port; and there are rumours that he is going to cut it all down. You might, therefore, send me out an occasional box of cigarettes as, later, they may be difficult to come by.*[12]

By now Lord Roberts had summed up the situation. He decided that the relief of Kimberley was his most urgent task; besieged in the town was an extremely irate Cecil Rhodes. The move towards Kimberley, which, owing to a continuous stream of British reinforcements coming into the Cape, could now be undertaken, was to be the first part of a thrust to Bloemfontein. Under cover of the existing Methuen column, Roberts assembled a large force at the Modder River, about twenty miles from Kimberley. Part of French's Cavalry

* After the war Allenby, for a time, conquered the smoking habit; he feared it was affecting his eyesight, and thus his ornithology. He also, for the sake of his health, reduced his remarkable appetite.

Division were ordered to leave the Colesberg area and congregate there. Meanwhile the unfortunate Sir Redvers Buller was left to his own devices in relieving Ladysmith as best he could.

We are massing guns in huge quantities, also Cavalry and Mounted Infantry, and I hear there are to be four Divisions of infantry besides. Roberts will, I believe, come in person. . . . Lord Fincastle [posted to the Inniskillings] has left us and rejoined his regiment, the 16th. I dined with them last night, in great luxury; they have brought their Indian tents with them.[13]

We, the Cavalry, are off tomorrow, at 3 a.m., on a wild enterprise into the Free State, which should be a success. . . . Thank you, my sweet, for sending me the Eau de Cologne. It has not yet arrived, but may do so. Last mail but one has gone drifting round the country somewhere. My teeth have not bothered me since I first came out.[14]

Roberts's plan to relieve Kimberley was a simple, bold and wise one, but it demanded a great deal of his troops. A long flanking movement involved the rapid movement of troops over parched ground; it was possibly the largest and most difficult way of getting from the Modder camp to Kimberley. It worked very well. Allenby's squadron was in the advance guard. It was the hottest month of the year, and water was scarce. After six days the exhausted Cavalry rode into Kimberley after sunset; horses whitened in caked mud and dust, men black-lipped from thirst. The Diamond City was saved as it began its fifth month of seige. Allenby's squadron had been heavily engaged with the enemy practically the entire way:

We got in here after a very hard week. . . . We are in a beastly bivouac, tentless, blanketless, unwashed and dusty. . . . We lost about 10 officers killed and wounded and I think about 30 men. . . . My property now consists of the dirty clothes I live and sleep

in day and night, a cloak, a saddle blanket, a toothbrush, a box
of cigarettes and a tube of lanoline. On the march I lived chiefly
on biscuit and beef tongues. The horses are half starved. Rhodes
is behaving very well. He sent our men soup, firewood, etc. I
dined with him last night. He's much the same as I remember him
15 years ago.* . . . The town has not suffered severely from shell-
fire, but most houses and many people have had narrow escapes.
Everyone has a splinter-proof shelter in his garden or veranda.
The poorest people lived down the mines for three days before we
turned up. . . . Last week was the longest week I ever have spent.
It feels like six months. Lord Roberts told us, before we started,
that we should remember it all our lives.[15]

Roberts's prediction was certainly true in Allenby's case.
He never forgot the comparative ease with which Kimberley
had been relieved from a strong and determined foe by the
use of ruthless speed and a deceptive flanking movement.
After a few days' rest the depleted Cavalry Brigade, re-
assembled under French, set off to invest a Boer force under
Cronje, while their own supplies were cut off by a daring raid
of De Wet. Roberts's arrival in South Africa had transformed
the situation, and Allenby took careful note of the Commander-in-Chief's preference for flanking movements and
surprise rather than 'the bull-headed frontal attacks' that had
been employed hitherto, and which were, as Roberts's biographer has written, 'of the same school as Haig in 1917 and
of Western Europe in 1944', whereas Roberts was 'the pro-
genitor of Allenby in the First World War and of Churchill's
strategy, overruled by the Americans, in the second.'[16]
    At this time the New South Wales Lancers were joined to
Allenby's squadron and placed under his command; a situation which was likely to cause some unhappiness. In fact, the
two units worked very well together under Allenby's command. An Australian newspaper reported: 'The squadron of
Lancers is now attached to the 6th Inniskilling Dragoons
under the command of Major Allenby. This officer is almost

* The two men saw a good deal of each other during the next few days.
This did not endear Allenby to some of the senior officers.

worshipped by his men, who would go anywhere and do anything under him. He has the reputation of being able to handle cavalry with any other man in the British Army. His promptness in tight corners and coolness under fire have not a little to do with the spirit of hero-worship which prevails. . . . They now call themselves "Allenby's Own".[17]

With the relief of Kimberley, and shortly afterwards of Ladysmith, the initiative of offensive had changed; now it was the British who were preparing to invade Boer territory rather than the reverse. Many of the Dutch townsfolk, indeed, were ready to come to terms with the British, and a fine opportunity was presented to Roberts for quickly finishing off the war. Unfortunately, however, his clumsily organized force was in poor shape; most of it was on short rations, and the problem of supply was now more important and difficult than the problem of the enemy. Allenby noted all this with some impatience. He told a staff officer* that the whole organization of the Army was utterly out of date, and blandly outlined what was required: a properly trained staff; the peace-time Army to bear some resemblance to a war-time Army; promotion above the rank of Captain to be by selection; uniform organization of the Imperial military forces. The young staff officer later wrote: 'All this sounded revolutionary in March, 1900, and I was deeply impressed.'[18]

The exhausted, hungry force of Lord Roberts pushed on to Bloemfontein:

I believe our objective is Bloemfontein. When we get there, as I suppose we shall one day, I hear the idea is to wait six weeks and reorganize the Army before having a go at the Transvaal, so if I eat my Christmas dinner at Donhead [his wife's family home] I shall be lucky, it seems. I hope, though, that the Boer will sicken a bit soon, when he finds he has to go back after each fight, instead of forward as has been his wont hitherto.[19]

* Captain F. B. Maurice; later Major-General Sir Frederick Maurice, military historian.

Allenby was one of the first men into Bloemfontein, in March, 1900. With the fall of the Free State capital, many people thought the war was as good as won; a general relaxation took place, and efforts were made to disentangle the problems of supply and to repair the railways. As far as the cavalry was concerned, the most pressing need was for remounts. Meanwhile the Boers, gladly accepting the unexpected respite, recuperated and regained some confidence.

Major Allenby spent two months with his squadron in bivouac, uncomfortable and discontented, just outside the town. He was on frequent missions and special duties, still being called upon by French as his most reliable squadron commander. On one occasion he had eleven consecutive days of active campaigning; on another he, with a junior officer, was sent on a dangerous night ride to Colesberg with a despatch from French. His major interests were the hold-ups in his parcels sent out from home, the size of which, predominantly of underwear, cakes, puddings and cigarettes, were the astonishment of his fellow officers. Allenby's appetite and heavy smoking were notorious. A pair of boots was ordered from Morrison's of Dublin; enteric was suffered by almost the entire squadron apart from its commanding officer; visitors and sightseers flocked into the town, including Lady Roberts and her daughters, somewhat to the annoyance of Allenby; poems of an officer in the New South Wales Lancers, who was encouraged and fostered by Allenby, were sent home to the family. And week after week, in skirmishes and on patrol, casualties bit away at the regiment:

Every evening an infantry band plays in the market place and Bloemfontein is quite peaceful. The only mark of war is the herd of khaki-coloured and bearded ruffians that are really British officers. Personally I don't wear a beard, but shave about every third day. My clothes are getting a bit ragged, but I mend them myself very skilfully. . . . Most people think the war's nearly over. I fancy the Free Staters will oppose us in the north when we go in, and that the Transvaal will make a fight. . . .
. . . As usual, the poor old Inniskillings were sent out to clear up the situation. [We] searched diligently for Boers all the afternoon.

34

As I suspected, the alarm was caused merely by a Boer patrol, who fired a few shots at my advanced scouts. I came back cross, and talked severely to my superiors on their methods of outposts, which, instead of securing our repose, ensure that we will be disturbed every day. . . . The Boers are full of activity again now. I suppose that they think that our long stay here implies weakness ; and they have had one or two small successes of late, which has hardened the hearts of those who were wavering. I am sick of this show.

. . . Do you see in the papers that Milner and Roberts are objecting to the number of grass widows at the Cape? I should not mind you being there though, my sweet, if I could be there with you. . . . I am not surprised to hear that you were all disgusted at the loss of 7 guns of Broadwood's Brigade. He's a personal friend of mine, and, as you say, it's hard to form an opinion unless you were there ; but I can't excuse any man who is caught napping. One is always liable to be smashed up by superior force, but one should never be caught unprepared to do one's best. However, I hate criticizing, and I hate war; so I'll change the subject. Bloemfontein gardens are now full of chrysanthemums and roses. . . .[20]

During this period the commander of the Inniskillings fell ill and lay in hospital, assuring Allenby that he was about to die, although the doctors said his condition was not serious. Before long he was sent home, and Allenby received the acting command of the regiment. There was no other practical candidate, and it seems that the regiment as a whole was delighted to have its best-known serving officers in command.

On the 3rd of May, 1900, the Army began its advance from Bloemfontein to Pretoria. The advance consisted of a great number of minor engagements, but no major battle; on a broad front Roberts's force moved relentlessly forward, vastly superior in numbers but continually harassed by a clever and mobile foe.

In the first week the Inniskillings were involved in their worst fighting of the war up till that time. A squadron, under a relative of Haig, were sent on by G.H.Q. without support, much to Allenby's disgust. They were badly cut up, and the strength of the regiment was further whittled away after the losses from enteric and skirmishing around Bloemfontein: eight killed, eleven wounded, and eleven missing. There were some further desperate engagements on the way to Pretoria.

Two Vickers maxim guns have arrived for our brigade, much to our great satisfaction. The Boers dislike them intensely. . . . We crossed the Vaal River into the Transvaal; the country was mountainous, but brother Boer was compassionate and did not shoot. I think he has had nearly enough. But there have been a great many Germans and Irish in the lot we have been lately fighting; I fancy the burghers prefer sniping at a distance. . . . Roberts occupied Johannesburg yesterday. No opposition. I rode in to look at the town, which is really a very fine one, and made myself ill with an enormous lunch at Frascati's Restaurant. . . . Last Sunday I rode into Pretoria to look at the place. It's a fine town, with some good buildings and shops, and well planted with trees. Mrs. Kruger is still in the town. We have a guard on her palace, which is quite an unassuming cottage. . . . News is very scarce and unreliable. We've had no letters or papers for five weeks, and don't really know what is going on. We hope soon, though, to have mails, and also to hear that Buller has shaken off dull sloth and is bestirring himself. . . . It appears that De Wet has collared 3 weeks of our mails, besides a lot of clothing. It's a nuisance. I am beginning to dislike De Wet. He is keeping the war alive.[21]

Most people believed that the surrender of Pretoria, after little fighting, was virtually the end of the war. For a time Allenby himself was inclined to this view. But, despite tentative negotiations between Roberts and Botha, small but desperately fierce battles continued to flare up from time to time over a wide area. The Transvaal Government had successfully evacuated the capital, together with its bullion, and Botha now retreated eastwards along the railway to the coast. President Kruger, meanwhile, left for Holland, still confident of bringing about European intervention on the Boers' behalf.

The weeks went by with continued inactivity, as once again the cavalry waited for its remounts and the Boers recouped themselves. Allenby—his expertise as a cavalry leader who seldom suffered heavy losses now fully recognized—was appointed to a Committee of Cavalry Reorganization; a General and a brigade commander being the other two members. Allenby wrote home: 'It is not so much reorganization that the cavalry want as a little common sense.' He endeavoured to supply such sense to the committee's meetings, and before long the cavalry was, indeed, reorganized with common sense.

They have started a newspaper here now, in which we can see Reuter's telegrams and exaggerated accounts of our latest successes. Lord Downe* and his attachés have gone back home, as they think that all big operations are over, as I suppose they are. I fear, however, that brother Boer is not absolutely defeated, and that he'll give trouble yet. . . . Met one or two of Mahon's people who relieved Mafeking. They had a sharp fight before they got there, and are a little sore as they say that Baden-Powell thinks he did it all himself. . . . No one knows where anyone is. Lord Bobs publishes no moves, as the whole place is full of Boer spies and Boer sympathizers.[22]

Eventually the cavalry moved on, advancing in the general direction of Middelburg. The weather was unusually severe; an officer and several men of Allenby's regiment died from exposure in one hailstorm.

We left rather suddenly on July 9th. . . . The Boers are burning all the grass as they retire, to spoil our grazing; but we can get on without it. I fancy we are to join hands with Buller's cavalry soon, then I think we shall have a general advance North and East and perhaps settle the show. . . . We (First Cav. Bde.) are under Curly Hutton.† Luckily he's getting well known now and I don't think he can do anything with us without leave from

---

* Brigadier-General H. Dawnay, Viscount Downe, a veteran of the Zulu War of 1879.

† Later Lt.-General Sir Edward Hutton, who organized the Australian Army.

Pretoria. He wanted to have us out on a reconnaissance today, a quite unnecessary one; but did not get leave.

Roberts thinks the war will end in two or three weeks; I think he is optimistic, but hope for the best. . . . The fighting is mainly long-range shelling, as directly we get close off they go, and we can't catch them. . . . [Today] we are in a good bivouac, in a nice grassy place, with a good stream running below. It's better than having to use dam water, which is, as you will naturally suppose, 'dam' bad.[23]

Things are going on very slowly. They are guerrillaring all over the place, and I don't see where it will end. I often dream at nights that I am back at home with you, sweetheart, but I wake up and find the beastly veldt still around me. French came round my outposts and was very complimentary. He is always kind and appreciative.[24]

I am sending in, tomorrow, a farm full of women and children. They are getting short of grub, and Roberts is sending all destitute families to Botha. I'm sorry for a poor woman. She has seven children, two of them ill. I gave them a shilling, and they said 'Dankge'. Appearances point to the likelihood of an eighth soon, but the lady tells me she has not seen or heard of her husband, who is fighting, for ten months. Let us hope she is not telling the truth. [An officer] has left an order with a wine merchant at Cape Town to send the mess a bottle of whisky a day by parcel post. Eight bottles arrived yesterday, just in time as we were getting run out.[25]

Think of it—grouse shooting beginning tomorrow, and everyone in Scotland sharpening their muskets. I am convinced that I was not made for a long campaign; I feel too homesick. . . . Don't get too fond of yachting. It is more costly than hunting, and I can't afford it.* . . . I fancy we are likely to remain holding this position till Buller comes up from the South and joins hands. No one knows much about his movements. I see *The Times* is annoyed about the mess-up at Zilikat's neck. I don't wonder. I've been through the pass, which, properly guarded, should have been impregnable.[26]

* He once wrote of yachting: 'All very well on a warm day, when the sea is flat; at other times it is an overrated sport.'

Allenby's regiment was the first of French's force to make contact with the unhappy Buller, who had slowly progressed north from Natal.

Today we have got in touch with Buller. I got orders to march early with my force towards Carolina, to get connection with him tomorrow, and was preparing for battle when a staff officer and escort rode in from him. He is some eight miles hence, with 15,000 odd men—mostly consisting of the late garrison of Ladysmith.

Buller came over and lunched with me, and I rode back with him to look at his camp. . . . They are all fat and fit, and have plenty of stores. Buller thinks the Boers will give in about the 15th October, as the climate gets too bad by then in the bush veldt where they are.

We get *Country Life*, when we do get papers, and it is a most refreshing paper on the barren veldt; such charming pictures of trees and gardens, etc. My men are in quite indecent rags.[27]

Yesterday French rode round our outposts again. When he had finished mine he went on to the Carabiniers on my right. Dear old Sprot [?] was showing him round, mistook his bearing, and had us all close to a Boer picquet. Brother Boer began to loose off briskly, and we all had to ride ignominiously for safety. French lost his helmet, which was gallantly retrieved by one of his staff. It was rather funny.[28]

While the main British Army struggled on up the railway to the Portuguese border, the cavalry turned south towards Swaziland. Allenby's Inniskillings were now selected for one of the most difficult cavalry tasks of the war—to lead the flanking movement that captured Barberton. The movement had to take place over precipitous mountain heights, but Allenby, who also had the Carabiniers regiment and a light gun, appeared, much to their astonishment, behind the Boers, who were defending an almost perpendicular defile.

We started into an awful country, like Switzerland for mountains. . . . Thick fog. Boers sniping. The country is lovely for a peaceful tourist to visit, but impossible, almost, for cavalry. . . . I am pretty well dog-tired. You have no idea what the country is

39

like to go over. Unless we had done it, I would have sworn that cavalry could not move in it.[29]

Allenby lost one of his best officers, and suffered other casualties. French was very much impressed, however, and asked Allenby to lead the advance into Barberton as a mark of honour. Allenby declined, saying that he and his men needed rest.

I saw rather a curious incident the other day. A hare got up in front of my horse and raced off full tilt. It was so scared that it ran into a wagon rut, turned a somersault, and broke its neck. At the present moment I am King of Sheba, so I suppose you are the Queen of Sheba.* . . . French came up yesterday. He and his staff seemed to think that the fighting was pretty well over. . . . My coat just keeps going, but it was badly eaten by white ants a fortnight ago, and is now very well ventilated. My servant has patched it here and there with what looks like parts of a brown sock. . . . Personally I'm dead off all fighting, and I never want to see another shot fired. I feel more deadly sick of the war every day. My martial ardour, which was always a somewhat feeble flicker, has quite burnt out. . . . You all seem to think the war is over; I wish I was as confident.[30]

The Cavalry Division left the Barberton area in October, 1900, and was ordered to return to Pretoria, clearing the south-east Transvaal on the way. As usual, the Inniskillings were selected for vanguard duties. On the first day of the move they were involved in a heavy engagement, due to the staff having omitted to inform the advance guard that the Division had stopped and was setting up bivouac. The Inniskillings, unaware of this, proceeded on their own and were soon engaged by a large Boer commando, which was aware that they had become isolated from the main body. Prompt action by Allenby averted a disaster, but he suffered twenty-

* Allenby had been sent by French, from Barberton, to take the important Sheba gold mine at Eureka City. He garrisoned the area for a month, during which time he was able to return to some plant collecting.

five casualties, including Captain Yardley, his best friend in the regiment, wounded.

The Boers are as unyielding as they ever were; and I don't see what can stop this guerrilla fighting for a long time. Some day, I suppose, they'll run out of ammunition. . . . I can't help thinking I've had great luck. I'm the only one of the original officers who has not been killed, wounded, sick or prisoner. . . . The picture papers are more grotesquely inaccurate than ever. Our people who have been prisoners say the Boers are intensely amused by them. [31]

Pretoria: *7th November, 1900*. My dear Michael, I hope it will not be very long now before I come home to see you. You will be quite a big boy then. What fun we will have. You and I will ride and play cricket and go fishing and sail boats on the pond. . . . [32]

It was now decided that, while much of the Army returned to England, the Cavalry Division would be split up into mobile columns in order to subdue the many wandering Boer commandos and pockets of resistance that showed no signs of recognizing that the war was over—greatly to the annoyance and frustration of G.H.Q. Allenby was informed that, after his excellent handling of the Inniskillings, he was not to be confirmed in his command after all. Another officer of the regiment, Col. Rimington,* who had hitherto been employed with a special force of scouts, was to take over. Rimington was, in fact, senior to Allenby, but the appointment was received by the regiment with some surprise. Allenby's exploits, however, had gained him a widespread reputation, and there was some jealousy at G.H.Q. Before being broken up, the Division had to return to Johannesburg, where Boer resistance was regrouping. Allenby, however, had to leave his regiment to receive urgent dental treatment in Johannesburg:

French told me the other day that he was sorry I had not been given command of the Inniskillings. I don't trouble myself about my prospects. I might possibly get offered command of some

* Later Lt.-General M. F. Rimington, Commander of the Indian Cavalry Corps, 1914.

other regiment. In that case it might mean India or remaining out here. I doubt if you would be very pleased at that; neither should I, as I want badly to come home.

When we get near Johannesburg, I hope to get my teeth looked at. Most of my false ones have been broken by hard biscuits, and the others want a bit of tightening up.

I can't get home [because of] the abominable obstinacy of the Boers. At the same time, I admire their obstinacy greatly. . . . I had a long dream about you and Michael last night, and, on awakening, thought I was in England, not having slept in a bed for so long.[33]

[The brigade] wired me to return today, but as the dental expert had got my teeth still in his pocket, I refused to go. I went and saw Col. Haig, who said : 'Certainly you can't go'; so I got the medical officer to give me a certificate. . . .[34]

Yesterday I lunched with Douglas Haig at French's house; a palatial mansion belonging to a refugee millionaire. French is away just now.[35]

I am rather glad Roberts has gone.* He is not looking well, and I fear that this campaign has about worn him threadbare. I don't wonder at it. Poor old man! I was amused today on being told that I was one of the few people who had not visibly aged during the war.

Rimington's a great friend of mine, but I don't think the job of 2nd in command is much of a catch, especially after having commanded a regiment in the Field for eight months.

Kitchener is back in these parts, and is said to be fairly confident of finishing the show in a month or two. I hope and suppose he knows more than I do, otherwise I fear he is over sanguine.[36]

Allenby was promoted brevet Lt.-Col. in November, and the regiment refitted in Pretoria. Among the new subalterns who joined the regiment, now much under strength through

---

* Roberts left for England in November, 1900, to become Commander-in-Chief of the Army in succession to Wolseley. Kitchener took over command.

casualties, was Lawrence Edward Oates. On patrol on the 6th of March, soon after his arrival, he remained with some wounded soldiers and, with two men, held off the enemy until nightfall, when help came. He was severely wounded. Some fellow officers considered Oates's gallantry the most courageous that had occurred in the regiment since its arrival in South Africa. He was recommended for the Victoria Cross. As the regimental history cryptically put it in 1909: 'Oates's bravery was acknowledged, one cannot say rewarded, with a mention in despatches.' (Oates finished the war with Queen's Medal and two clasps.) Thus started a career that was to end twelve years later in an Antarctic blizzard. After being invalided home, Oates returned to active service before the war's end, one of the few who did so. Allenby and Oates, both East Anglians, were impressed with each other, and it is reasonable to suppose that the young officer took some note of the character of his popular and strongly principled C.O. Oates remained with the regiment after the war and, following in Allenby's path, became Adjutant in 1909, before going to the Antarctic with Scott.[37]

Early in 1901, Allenby's doubts as to his future were temporarily settled when he was selected to lead one of the columns being formed to clear the country of resistance. His command ('quite a nice little force') consisted of the Scots Greys, the Carabiniers, a detachment of infantry, and some horse artillery.* Many months of weary and wretched trekking followed; an elusive enemy was chased, but seldom brought to battle. As Allenby said: 'We flit backwards and forwards like snipe on a bog.' The Inniskillings went to another column, which was to be commanded by Rimington.†

Douglas Haig was also given command of a column in the comparatively quiet, but important, area of the Cape, British territory. As well as his column, Haig was given command of a regiment, the 17th Lancers. It had been widely

* At the end of 1901 the Scots Greys were replaced by the 13th Hussars.

† Wavell served as a subaltern in Rimington's column.

expected that this appointment would be given to Herbert
Lawrence, who was himself a 17th Lancer. In protest, Lawrence, Allenby's close friend since Sandhurst days, resigned
from the Army.*

The 'column period' of the South African War fell into two
phases. At first it was hoped that the British mobile columns
would so harass the many remaining Boer forces that they
would sue for peace. The enormity of this task, however, had
not been appreciated by G.H.Q.; the areas from which the
Boers operated contained few settlements and communications were practically nil; the whole British effort depended
on one vulnerable railway line, from which the mobile
columns had to be supplied; the terrain admirably suited the
hunted, whereas the hunters, mostly exhausted and dispirited
by the long-drawn-out campaign, had few, if any, advantages. With the failure of this method, it was decided that the
only way of concluding the war was to deprive the stubborn
Boer of means of subsistence; farms and crops were to be
burnt and destroyed, and cattle and sheep driven off or
slaughtered. Such duties were described by Allenby as
'beastly work'.

In general, Allenby agreed with the column strategy, but
he was alternately angered and bemused at the way it was
carried out. He saw little point in having mobile columns
unless they were to some extent independent of G.H.Q. He
believed Kitchener tended to live in a false world, relying on
his own great self-confidence and the advice of staff officers
who were mostly ignorant of conditions. He also found it extremely difficult to make worth-while co-operation with some
of the other column commanders. Of all the column commanders fully engaged, he was almost alone throughout this
period in avoiding ambush, disaster or unnecessary attacks of
superior forces. Although under Kitchener he no longer got
most of the difficult and dangerous tasks, as when directly

---

* He returned to the Army in 1914, became General Sir Herbert
Lawrence, and was to work well with Haig in 1918. Meanwhile he devoted himself to finance, and made a considerable fortune in the City.

under French, his assignments were as dangerous and important as any.

By this time, however, there were rumours among the staff, and among Allenby's superiors, that he was over-cautious, and it was certainly true that Allenby was more respectful and thoughtful of human life than some of his contemporaries. Despite the importance of his command, which in fact almost amounted to a Brigade, Allenby remained a Lt.-Colonel; the difficult situation arose by which the commanders of the regiments in his column were sometimes senior to himself.

No doubt, unless I make a mess of it, they will confirm me in the rank when the war ends, if it ever does end. [38]

Whether we shall do any good or not I don't know, but it appears to be the best plan of doing things. . . . We left our tents behind, but I am trying to smuggle one with me under the guise of an office tent. [39]

French told me yesterday that he was very much pleased with the way my Brigade worked in the fight on the day before. The cavalry have all got long rifles now, and it gives them a lot of confidence. . . . As French says, we hustle them well. I'm tired of hustling Boers, though, and should like to get back to England and your dear love. We caught one of Botha's staff officers yesterday. He said the war would last another year at *least*. [40]

I should rather like some of those fashionable warriors who went home at 'the End of the War' to come out and see what the war looks like now that it is at an end. It might give them a few new ideas. As far as my experience goes, the 'War' was the easiest part of the campaign. We've had more fighting since the 'War' ended, more trekking, and much more discomfort. . . . I've lost 32 horses in nine days, only two of which were lost in action. The rest have died from exhaustion and short food. There's no help for it. Isolated like we are, we must patrol a lot to keep Brother Boer at a distance, as well as collect grub. I've told French, but he can't, of course, help it. [41]

Why the Boers keep on, beats me. Those about here are as sick of it as we are, and, in many cases, very hard up. A nice old gentleman of 69 came in to surrender yesterday (a very cold and

wet day) with bare feet, having neither boots nor socks left. . . .
I have got a bit balder and greyer, but my Brigade Major com-
plains that I don't look old enough to be in command of a
column. . . . [The Chaplain] recommends me a book—*L'Art du
Croire, ou Préparation Philosophique à la Foi Chrétienne*, by A. Nicholas
Majestrat. You might send it to me if you can get it.* Don't be
afraid of my apostatizing. It is *à propos* of great religious arguments
I used to have with him. I am reading Winston Churchill's book
on Ian Hamilton's march. It is better than I expected.†[42]

I can't help thinking that our diplomacy during the whole
campaign has been below contempt. We have been severe when
we should have acted leniently, and lenient when we should have
been stern. We have, besides, always treated the Boer, when cor-
responding with him, as one outside the pale of civilization;
though, if taken the right way, he is a very decent fellow. I know
that very few of my countrymen agree with me, but I have always
liked and admired the Boer, and always shall. I have seen nothing
in this campaign to change my previous opinion of him. . . . I am
quite out of touch now with anyone of our people, and far ahead
of them all. I am giving the men 2 lbs. of meat a day, besides that,
they only get 1¼ biscuits! All the commanders of the units under
me are really my seniors.[43]

I console myself in thinking that one column is only one pawn
in the game, and that the man with the chess board in front of
him has a bigger view than I who can only see one square on the
board, or, at the utmost, the next. . . . I always try to state in my
reports exactly what happened, without any ornamentation; so I
am not responsible for the exaggerated form of the official
version.[44]

The Boers call the district that we are now going to 'Hell', and
I'm told that is a flattering name for it. Kitchener wired me to
start today, but I told him it was not possible.[45]

It's quite absurd the way we are hurrying through this work.
There's a good month's police work to be done in these fastnesses;

* The Chaplain, a Catholic priest named Knapp, became one of
Allenby's close personal friends. The friendship continued till Father
Knapp's death during the First World War.
† *Ian Hamilton's March*, by Winston S. Churchill (1900).

and I am bound to be back on the railways in three days from now. . . . They won't even give one a chance of finishing up a job; either of fighting or police work. I presume it is to throw dust in the eyes of the British public.[46]

I am getting frightfully sick of this incessant trek. . . . I've not been well for more than a week, but was loath to leave the column.[47]

This was the first time in the campaign, after a tremendous spell of active service, without a day's break for months on end, that Allenby had gone sick. He must have been one of the last to do so—with influenza and exhaustion. His first day in hospital at Pretoria, the 25th of May, 1901, was his first day away from active service since landing at Cape Town on the 11th of December, 1899. After two weeks, spent mostly sitting contemplating in the luxuriant gardens of the hospital, he rejoined his column. Shortly afterwards, in one of his long diary-letters, he wrote to his wife:

Unless I get knocked out, or go sick, I cannot ever ask for leave. The war has to be fought to a finish, and I flatter myself that I am doing some good. I should, anyway, after the way they have pushed me on, be ashamed to ask for a holiday. Of course, lots of people have wriggled home somehow, but their example is not to be followed by everyone. But every hour of the day, and a great deal of the night, I am thinking of how much I want to be with you. I feel, like you, often, that the war is absolutely unbearable, and I have to harden my heart, very sternly, to keep me from getting hysterical.[48]

I got helio communication with 'Ghazi' Hamilton,* but can get no orders out of the lunatic. . . . *L'Art du Croire* has arrived; only two small volumes, so I shall be able to carry it. Kitchener sent me a charming telegram last night; we were all very pleased to get it. . . . [The Boers] have bolted where I can't get at them;

---

* For a time Allenby's column came under Brig.-General G. H. C. Hamilton, C.B., commanding the 4th Cavalry Brigade. He retired after the war, and died in 1933.

especially as a dear old fossil who is supposed to be co-operating with me, some miles E., won't come up.

The Boer idea, now, is to get South; to raise the Cape Colony. It is a fine strategic idea. They seem to have given up all intention of peace. They are misguided fools, but good patriots. They know that England is spending a million and a half a week on the war, and that we can't do that for ever. What annoys me is that some of our own officers say the same. . . . As you will suppose, it hurts me to burn out nice scenery, but I can't help it, and I fear, tomorrow, I shall have to burn some very good farms.[49]

Before I left my old camp, I put a company of the Inniskilling Fusiliers in ambush. About 9.0 a.m. about 150 Boers came on to our old ground. This is the second time we gave John Boer a lesson not to be in too great a hurry after us. . . . Kitchener helios to me to move about here [Zeekohoek area]; to draw the Boer fire, and to make them waste ammunition. Great fun. [50]

Just in to camp, at 10.0 p.m., after marching all day. I am being rushed off, on some wild-cat show, after nothing. These tom-fool orders have killed 20 or more of my oxen today, and more will die tomorrow. . . . This morning we heard, as I had expected, that our prey has moved round our right flank. He is now at a place which I ought to have been sent to; and he'll get away from us. I suppose I shall still have to carry out my original orders; so I shall, as usual, walk over the deserted Boer camps. This sort of thing makes one rather sick and tired. Lord K. of K tries to run the whole show from Pretoria—a quite impossible job—and fails. District Commanders, with several columns under them, are the only people who could bring the show to a speedy finish.[51]

Methuen has moved N.W. and thereby left a big gap in the ring we were drawing round them. It is rather disgusting, as I really think that, with a little management, we ought to have got a lot of them. There are a good many co-operating columns; quite enough if they were properly worked in unison. It is the old story. No one in command locally; but an odd-jobbing general trying to run the show with any column he can scrape together, and all the while being interfered with from Pretoria.[52]

I dined with Lord K. [in Pretoria] last night. His Lordship was beaming with good humour. I had an interview with him in the a.m. He told me he thought he would give my column a week or so of rest. I thanked him. They have had none since January [eight months previously].

Kitchener, however, either forgot or ignored his promise, for the following day 'Allenby's Column' was back in the field.

I am so glad the new yacht [his father-in-law's] has been such a success, and that everyone has so enjoyed the summer season.

Lord K. has been very genial to me. I don't know whether he is a great man or not. I think he is hampered by the Government which, so far as I can gather, is weak. Joe Chamberlain appears to be the only stiffbacked man in the lot. The Boers don't believe any of our proclamations; nor do I.

Gough's Mounted Infantry have been cut up by 800 or 1,000 Boers, and have lost three companies and two 15-pounder guns with their ammunition. A nice, cheering thing to hear in the middle of the night.[53]

Gough's column, which had achieved some notoriety for daring escapades, had been somewhat impetuously led to defeat by its dashing commander; Colonel Hubert Gough was captured, but escaped. It was, perhaps, unfortunate that it was Allenby's column which was sent to his rescue, and which, in fact, picked up Gough himself; for the two men did not get on together. Hubert Gough, later the First World War General and commander of the Fifth Army, and Douglas Haig, were already friendly; neither man was comfortable with Allenby, but with Gough in particular there was, from this occasion, some coldness. If Allenby thought a contemporary had behaved foolishly, he was not the man to hide his opinion.

People have been saying: 'I wish these Dutchmen would concentrate and give us a show.' Now they have done so, have mopped up a column, taken two field guns, and we are not in a position to hit them back. At this rate the war will go on for years.

I am feeling more than ever inclined to go sick and come home. Futile job after futile job creates disgust. The more I see of our great generals, the more they sicken me. Every man for himself. I am beginning to think I am one of the few commanders out here that do not play to the gallery and tell lies to push themselves. But this is blasphemous! To change the subject— beautiful scenery, and a quick-running river full of fish. . . .

I have lost 70 horses in two days. All for no use. I am absolutely sick of the show. This man Hamilton has a reputation. He is, as a consequence, playing to the gallery, with the result that he has absolutely destroyed my column, and done no good by it. I had better change the subject. I saw, yesterday, the most beautiful fell-heather; the bells were coral pink in colour, growing in clusters, each bell about two inches long. . . .[54]

Allenby's letters home became increasingly and justifiably bitter about the conduct of the war; they are possibly the most critical accounts of the war to have been written at the time by a serving officer, and are an extraordinary indictment of Kitchener and his generals. In a letter to his father-in-law, Allenby stated:

One is always at high pressure, always coming under a series of difficult generals. They don't care a straw about the horses, as one is probably only under the same general for about a month at a time. When he has played about, and knocked one's column to rags, he goes off with some other columns somewhere else. There is no system of keeping anything in reserve. The object being, I suppose, to make the British public think that the Boers are being pressed everywhere—which they are *not*. I have thought, for the last year, that we have not enough troops. These Yeomen are useless. After being some months in the field, they learn a bit; but by the time they are any use, they have probably been captured two or three times; presenting the Boers, on each occasion, with a horse, rifle and 150 rounds of ammunition per man.[55]

Allenby's column now came under the orders of Major-General Bruce Hamilton,* brother of Brig.-General G. H. C.

* Later General Sir Bruce Hamilton; he was promoted and knighted for his part in the campaign; died in 1936.

Hamilton; Allenby had scant respect for either as a commander. They were typical of those who seemed to him—an
ex-Staff College man—to be 'Generals with no more brains or
backbone than a bran doll'.

We conducted the most ill-arranged night march I have ever
seen. . . . a monumentally futile operation. Yesterday Bruce
Hamilton heard of a party of Boers, from 30 to 90, who were
vaguely supposed to have been at some farms about 20 miles from
here. He therefore ordered 300 men per column—900 in all—for
a night surprise. He took command, but the column commanders
had to come too. The result was 1 General, 3 column commanders, and 5 or 6 regimental commanders to run this band of 900.
We sallied forth at 7 p.m.; luckily, a lovely night with a $\frac{3}{4}$ moon.
We marched on, steadily, till 3 a.m. Then we began to try farm
after farm. At 6 a.m., having seen no signs of a Boer, we off-
saddled for two hours, had some breakfast, and came back here
[Bethal], having done 50 miles in 12 hours fruitlessly and foolishly. The Dutchmen had gone 30 hours before; naturally, seeing
that columns were all around their haunts. If it had been ad-
visable to send out, one regiment under its own C.O. could have
done the job quite as effectively. And yet you people at home
wonder why the war goes on. I trust I may get away by myself
for a while, soon. I have no use for these modern Major-Generals.[56]

I always believe in recommending one's best men, even
though one loses, temporarily, by it. No one is indispensable; I
find that the old idea is still true—the headman goes, but the
understudy (if the headman has been really good) does as well, or
perhaps better.[57]

On the 20th of December, 1901, Lt.-Colonel Allenby, after
many months of ceaseless and most frustrating campaigning,
finally collapsed. He entered a military hospital in Pretoria,
once a girls' school, the same evening, with an attack of 'low
fever', made severe by sheer physical exhaustion and exposure. After a few days' recuperation, he was sent to Durban
by Kitchener, who at last appreciated that Allenby could
continue no longer without a break. At the Ocean View
Hotel, Allenby had an enjoyable and much-needed week's

leave. He visited friends made during his former years in South Africa; walked beside the sea; chatted on the veranda with families from England who had come to be near their menfolk in the Army; above all, he studied the plants at the Botanical Gardens. He returned, for further duty, to Johannesburg.

I was walking, this afternoon, in the public gardens. I saw a little 6-year-old girl trying to catch goldfish in a pond. I began to talk to her, and she borrowed my stick to hunt them with. After a time she said: 'Do you hate the Dutch?' I said: 'No—do you?' 'No,' she answered, 'I can't be expected to hate my own people.' I said: 'Why should you? I like them.' But it was a long time before I could get her to shake hands with me when I said goodbye. There you have a little irreconcilable; brought up in the belief that the English hate the Dutch and that it is the duty of the Dutch to hate the English.

I was rather amused this a.m.; Lord K. said: 'Well, you didn't take very long leave!' I felt like saying: 'Well, I can do with a bit more, if you like to give it me.'[57]

Soon Allenby was back with his column; the latest book from home in his kit; engaging in a long correspondence with the mother of one of his officers who had been killed; taking tea with, and arguing with, some lonely missionary which his enormous column—its transport alone stretching two or three miles—occasionally enveloped; and always chasing, and evading ambush by, the elusive Boer. Would the war ever end? The tramping, dusty, footsore and wretched infantrymen were almost past caring; the cavalrymen, sick and tired of it all, did not know.

Owing to the lack of success of both the 'hustling' and the 'burning' strategies, it was decided to build a series of blockhouse lines, against which the remaining Boers would be driven; a sensible idea in the circumstances, but one which had taken a great deal of time to occur to Kitchener and his staff.

Meanwhile Mrs. Allenby, thoroughly alarmed by the tone of her husband's letters, more bitter than anything she had known in him before, determined to go to South Africa in the hope of seeing him. For most of the war she had been living with her family near Salisbury, but had also spent a short stay at Felixstowe, and much time beside the sea. She arrived at Durban in March, 1902, and went to the Ocean View Hotel. By that time, however, at long last, it seemed that the war might be nearing its conclusion; even the pessi- mistic Allenby was inclined to think so:

Things are very different now, I am glad to say. Where there is one Boer now, there were 100 then; and their spirit is much tamer. My three guides were fighting me in those days. They are such good, charming fellows.

The peace rumours are very conflicting. Myself, I am rather hopeful.

It seems to me incredible that I may be within a day or two of seeing you. I can't at all realize it.[58]

Peace was declared seventeen days later, on the 31st of May, 1902.

Allenby finished the war with a much enhanced reputa- tion; whereas before it he was an unknown Major in an un- fashionable cavalry regiment, at its end he was known throughout the Army as a highly competent, reliable com- mander, who welcomed responsibility, carried out his tasks with thoroughness and vigour and had strong and interesting views of his own.

Allenby was, indeed, transformed by the war. He started it a serious but by no means dedicated soldier; he finished it depressed and astounded by the incompetence of his superiors, and convinced that he had to try to put matters right. He had enjoyed command, preferring to be out in the wilds with no one's orders but his own; he was fired, a little late in his career, to rise as fast as he could in the Army in order to enjoy further responsibility and to get things done the way he felt they should be. He had discovered that he had an innate dislike of being a subordinate—especially as he recognized that the majority, if not all, of his superiors had an inferior intelligence to his own. Although he kept his criticisms entirely to himself and his family, and did not at any time further himself by reporting on his superiors to their superiors, he had learnt more from the war than most; the importance of well-organized methods of supplies, the desirability of leaving local tactics to local commanders, the vital advantages of superior mobility, the uselessness of frontal attacks against an enemy in superior positions (as at Colesberg). He had also discovered that while not being a born soldier, he was undoubtedly a born leader; this he had not before suspected. 'Allenby's Column' was renowned for the loyalty with which its men regarded their chief. For the rest of his career he was to have the style, developed in the South African War, that was to bring him countless admirers, including men, such as Lawrence and Wavell, as great or greater than himself: long silences broken by unexpected and sometimes learned comment, dry humour, universal inquisitiveness, undisciplined temper, a somewhat Olympian aloofness, and flashes of a deep gentleness—the more effective in a man so large and of such military appearance and bearing.

His Chaplain wrote: 'He is always bright and cheerful, but in his heart he is dreadfully homesick; undoubtedly one of the most capable and brilliant officers in the service; one, I believe, unlimited in his capacities, and capable of conducting the whole of the operations in South Africa.'

Another friend wrote: 'He is always keeping cheery under the most trying circumstances. Everyone looks up to him and he always does magnificently. It annoys me that his good deeds are not more published.'[59] Another of his officers said: 'During the temporary lulls of an action he used to display his well-known power of detachment, and would talk with animation on any and every subject, quite divorced from the business in hand, from the Descent of Man to the habits of insectivorous birds. . . . It was this power, coupled with the ability to pick up the thread in a moment, which, with his never-failing sense of dry humour, kept him always cheerful and free from the outward appearance of worry which, in the South African War, showed itself in so many commanders of less ability. . . . During the many hours we used to spend during an advance sitting by our horses awaiting the order to move on, he liked nothing better than to study the habits of the termites whose small mounds covered the ground everywhere, and I have seen him so engrossed in a fight between rival parties of these creatures, or in a raid on them by black ants, that one would imagine he had nothing else in the world to think about.'[60]

Allenby, indeed, who was in perpetual wonder at all things, increased his interests still further during the war. Political magazines like the *Spectator* and *Truth* (with its somewhat sensational criticisms of the war), were sent out to him from home, and no matter how rough he was living, he was seldom without a book. A passion for birds, well advanced before the war, now equalled his interest in botany. On at least one occasion his knowledge of birds served him well. Riding ahead with another officer to reconnoitre a farm, he saw through his field-glasses a number of ducks perched on a wall. Knowing that ducks did not perch on walls, he immediately rode back and ordered another route, thus avoiding a dangerous ambush for his small party; it later transpired that the Boers had placed the ducks on the wall, behind which they were hiding, hoping that Allenby's men would go directly to the farm for poultry and eggs.

Allenby was made a substantive Colonel (in the same *Gazette* as Douglas Haig). He received a Companionship of the Bath and appointment to the command of another Irish regiment, the 5th Lancers. Three months later he returned to England, a chastened but very determined professional soldier of forty-one.

CHAPTER 3

Peace: Cavalry

What is the use of cavalry in modern warfare?
Well, I suppose to give tone to what otherwise would be a mere vulgar brawl.

PUNCH, 1891

Allenby took over command of the 5th Lancers at Colchester, in Essex, in August, 1902. He was a stern and distant regimental commander. His experiences in South Africa had convinced him that the Army was inept and lackadaisical, and that in its present state it constituted a grave weakness in the security of the nation. This thought haunted him, and dominated all his thought and action, in the years that led up to the First World War.

The 5th (Royal Irish) Lancers was a somewhat gay regiment, where military matters had not been allowed to take precedence over social affairs; it was notorious for the dashing escapades of its officers, and it was thought that Allenby would be the man to bring it up to a normal standard of efficiency. This he succeeded in doing, but he was probably not in command long enough to make a permanent contribution. The 5th Lancers improved their efficiency for a while under their demanding C.O., and a real respect was accorded Allenby by officers and men. During manœuvres on Salisbury Plain, he surrounded the headquarters and transport of an opposing division, much to the astonishment of the 'captured' General concerned. He found manœuvres and exercises enjoyable and easy, and on several other occasions took wry enjoyment in embarrassing his superiors. Field-Marshal Sir Evelyn Wood is known to have been well pleased with the 5th Lancers in both the August and September manœuvres of 1904.[1] In return for a high standard of efficiency, Allenby delegated considerable responsibility to his squadron commanders. A favourite expression of his at this time was Confucius's 'My people become good of themselves'.

Exactly three years after taking up command of the 5th Lancers, Allenby, having survived the war, nearly lost his life in a sailing accident at Cowes. He was a guest on his father-in-law's yacht. Among other guests was a young lady, Cecily Papillon. She has left an excellent account of this near-disaster: 'On the morning of August 10th, I went sailing with Colonel Allenby, the yacht's mate, and one other hand, in the yacht's cutter—an open boat about 18 feet long. By a most merciful providence, as events turned out, Mrs. Allenby did not accompany us, as she thought it was too rough for her to enjoy the sail. The sea was choppy and there was a good bit of wind. Beyond the big yachts that were racing, we saw no other small craft out except a fishing yawl. We sailed nearly to Ryde, then turned and came back. We were shipping a certain amount of water all the time, and were never on an even keel. When we were off Norris Castle, about ½ mile out, the mate, who had the tiller and the sheet, took advantage of a sudden calm to order the other sailor to bail out the water. Whilst he was in the act of doing this, a sudden squall burst upon us—the boat keeled right over, and water rushed in, and she went down in less than a minute. I had only once been in the sea before, and that was bathing from the shore, and could not swim a stroke. The mate could not swim either, but had some notion of treading water. The other sailor could swim, but had the greatest difficulty in keeping himself afloat, owing to a bad attack of cramp. He was handicapped also by being in oilskins. Colonel Allenby and I had both got greatcoats on. When the boat sank, I came up to find Colonel Allenby a little way off on my left, beyond the mast and rigging, which were slowly sinking; the mate on my right, and the other sailor in front of me. For a few seconds my skirts no doubt buoyed me up before they became saturated. Colonel Allenby, who was swimming strongly, called to me to try and get clear of the rigging, coming quickly to my assistance. I think it was his confidence and the masterly way in which he at once took command of the situation which enabled me to obey him; otherwise I should not be here, as I must have been drawn down immediately by the ropes of the sinking mast. He told me I must get *under* the ropes to get clear of them, and I made a plunge towards him. Of course I was soon going through all the horrible sensation of drowning. I came round making a noise like whooping cough, to find myself being supported in the water by Colonel Allenby, who was saying everything he could to encourage myself and the others, and giving orders to each of us what we were to do. He had pushed an oar to the mate. For 20 minutes he was able to make three people in such great peril obey him in every detail. I was several times under water, and it always felt like taking gas and coming round in the sea instead of in the dentist's chair. Colonel Allenby, in holding me up, was practically holding the mate up too. No one had seen our cutter go under, but after a bit we saw one of the big racing yachts go by a little way off, but she was keeled over on the side away from us, and we were afraid she would not see us. However, there were boats coming to our rescue. The boats of the Red Eagle Yacht picked us up. The mate was just going down to his dinner, and he had a look round first and felt sure that he saw two heads above the water some way off. They had a long row to get to us, though. [Our] mate is still suffering from being so nearly drowned, and I am only just recovering from my long subsequent illness. Colonel Allenby has been the means of thus saving my life, and I think the lives of all three of us, because if the two men had not been enabled by his encouragement and directions to keep their heads, they, too, must have been drowned. The sea was very rough, and it was a wonderful performance on his part, both morally and physically.'[2]

For this affair Allenby received a testimonial for the saving of life from the Royal Humane Society.

A year later he was promoted to Brigadier-General, in command of the 4th Cavalry Brigade, with headquarters also at Colchester. In the world of cavalrymen at that time there was only one more worth-while step up the ladder for Edmund Allenby: command of the Cavalry Division itself, a post infinitely more desirable than that of, say, Prime Minister, Foreign Secretary, or even—many agreed—than that of the Commander-in-Chief himself.

Shortly after Allenby left them, the 5th Lancers were in the news again; three Majors and two Captains were placed on half-pay, a scandal about which one newspaper wrote: 'The fact is that the authorities were perfectly well aware that some drastic measures had to be taken. This is not the first time that this regiment has earned the unenviable notoriety that it now basks in before the public gaze. Every effort has been made to try and bring it up to a normal standard. Men of the best have been taken from elsewhere to command it. Was not the present colonel's predecessor no less a person than Brig.-General E. H. H. Allenby, C.B., who now commands one of our Cavalry Brigades? He came from the Inniskilling Dragoons. No middle course would now suffice, therefore they had, reluctantly, to call a spade a spade and do what they have done.'*[3]

It was not customary for brigade commanders to meddle too much with age-old traditions of cavalry regiments, but Allenby had ideas of his own as to the training of cavalry and the amount of time that his officers should be expected to spend with his three regiments. He was also determined to see that his innovations were carried out. Allenby was not a popular Brigadier; the only friend he made at this time was Colonel Sir Philip Chetwode, one of his regimental commanders. As Wavell has written: 'It cannot be denied that in

---

* Allenby always maintained a fond recollection of the 5th Lancers, and took an interest in them. The regimental history (of 1922) was dedicated to him, although it spelt his name incorrectly.

Allenby increasing authority brought increasing asperity. He who had been a noticeably easy-going young officer and a good-humoured squadron commander was a strict colonel, an irascible brigadier, and an explosive general.'[4]

Concurrent with this picture of a peppery senior officer was Allenby's continued and increasing interest in flowers and birds, in foreign travel, and his tender and happy family life. Michael was growing into an unspoilt, active, intelligent boy of good looks; a son after Allenby's own heart, and in whom he took the greatest pride and delight. Watching Michael grow, over the years, into a fine, forthright young man was a continual joy to his father. Baden-Powell, a friend of Allenby's in South Africa, and now Inspector-General of Cavalry, was impressed by the boy, and was first inspired and prompted to write his book *Scouting for Boys* by an incident concerning Michael Allenby, who, therefore, has a place in the history of the Boy Scouts. It occurred when Allenby, riding home after a field day, suddenly heard from above: 'Father, you are dead . . . always look upwards as well as around you.' The startled Allenby looked up to see not only his son in the foliage of a tree, but also the formidable young governess he had recently engaged. The woman told Allenby that she was teaching his son observation and character-training from a little handbook for soldiers she had discovered. This booklet for Army scouts had been written by Baden-Powell, a South African war hero. Allenby told 'B-P' what had happened, and the founder of the scouting movement wrote: 'My eyes were opened to the fact that there could be an educative value underlying the principles of scout training.'[5] Not long afterwards he resigned from the Army to launch the Boy Scouts.*

In due course Michael went to a small school for boys, and

---

* On the outbreak of war, Baden-Powell, younger than some of the Generals, tried to get back in the Army, but was somewhat coldly turned down. Kitchener told him, with evident glee, that the nation could not spare him from his Boy Scout activities. Allenby remained one of his friends.

in 1911 entered Combermere House at Wellington College, which was the accepted school for future Army officers. It seems to have been taken for granted that Michael would follow his father in a military career, although his intellectual interests and a fair academic record might well have suggested a different course. Allenby had been concerned as to how he would be able to afford to educate his son, as his Army salary was barely enough to provide for the standard of living expected of a senior officer, and his private income was negligible; this problem, however, had been solved by the South African War, during which his pay, accumulating in a London bank, had been wisely invested in securities. As he had written:

There is one good thing about the war. The son will have some savings laid by, wherewith he will get the schooling that, in the old days, seemed beyond his reach.[6]

Colchester is only thirty miles from Felixstowe, and Allenby was often able to meet his mother, who took the closest interest in his career, and who listened to, and commented on, all his dissatisfactions and ambitions. With his wife, Allenby visited Seville, Paris and other European cities, and in 1908 they took a long leave in a trip to Lake Victoria Nyanza. Everywhere he went enormous descriptive letters were sent to the old lady in Felixstowe House.

At home, he became a keen and proficient fisherman, and he took up the unusual hobby of boomerang throwing, in which he became expert. He could not afford to hunt. By this time he had completely given up the cavalryman's major occupation, polo, considering it too expensive to find a horse that could cope with his substantial weight and his vigorous play; he had never been very interested in the game.

By 1910 Allenby had been promoted Major-General, at the age of forty-eight, and was appointed Inspector of Cavalry in the spring of that year. His Chief Staff Officer was Hubert Gough, who also commanded the 3rd Brigade. No two men could have been less alike than Allenby and Gough, who was a jolly, slight, volatile Irishman. Gough, who had served under Haig, wrote: 'Haig always knew exactly what he wanted. Allenby was not always sure of what he did want. . . . He never suggested anything. . . . He had a great regard for regulations and every sort of detail. . . . When inspecting some unit, if he noticed some small neglect of detail or non-compliance with an order, however trivial, he got excited and sometimes began to shout, and I have seen him rush at an offending officer and threaten him with a stick . . . mentally somewhat lazy.'[7] This unhappy relationship continued for two years. With headquarters in London, Allenby had to travel the nation, including Ireland, visiting various cavalry stations. Now, at last, he was able to achieve some of the reforms he had wished for. They turned out to be reforms based on sound common sense, but not fired with imagination. For years Allenby had been appalled at the way cavalrymen, on manœuvres, had ignored orders to use their chin-straps; he had watched as caps flew off in all directions, and all proceedings were brought to a halt while headgear was recovered. He now insisted on the observance of this order, and the result was a painful and bitter war between almost the entire cavalry and the Inspector-General, a well-known 'affair' at the time. The Inspector-General won, but in the process lost such little popularity as he had previously enjoyed. Nothing infuriated Allenby more than plain silliness in fighting men, especially as since South Africa he took soldiering as a most serious occupation. Allenby's explosions soon became legendary, and were widely feared; the matter was not eased by the tradition that cavalrymen should not be asked to undergo the same rigours and discipline as infantrymen. Captain B. H. Liddell Hart has written: 'It was commonly felt among his contemporaries that he had changed for the worse after becoming a general officer. In his pursuit of efficiency he seemed to them to show evidence of being unduly intolerant, and they were inclined to think that the rarefied air of the general officer's plane had gone to his head. His impatience with diverging views, and in sweeping aside reasonable explanations, not infrequently created among his subordinates a sense of injustice.'8

Allenby saw the role of modern cavalry as mobile riflemen who could also be used for reconnaissance, screening and the traditional shock tactics when the opportunity arose. Because of his insistence that the latter role was still valid, much time was spent in massed charges and sword play; his handling of the Division in the manœuvres of 1912 did not find favour everywhere. (Haig was even more against the idea of mounted infantry; his performance on the 1912 manœuvres was disastrous, having been completely out-manœuvred by an opponent who made intelligent use of the new air arm.) Allenby continually demanded the study and practice of cavalry in retreat, which gained him a reputation as an 'alarmist'. This problem had seldom been considered worth serious thought before. He was certain that war with Germany was coming, and in 1911 he ordered a remarkable exercise for the cavalry, which exactly foresaw the conditions of 1914, with Germany invading France through Belgium and Britain landing an Expeditionary Force on the French coast. In an important discussion on cavalry at the Royal United Service Institution in November, 1910, he said:

The question of machine-guns might be studied by the cavalry nowadays, because I do not think we make sufficient use of them. The weapon is not properly understood, and I think that, whether in fire tactics or in the tactical use of the weapon, we have hardly yet made a beginning. Personally I believe it is going to have an enormous future before it. . . .9

In 1914 the Cuban Army possessed a greater proportion of machine-guns per man than did the British. The role of the cavalry in modern war had already been questioned in a book by Erskine Childers, and the role of artillery was also being questioned; in 1909 an article appeared in a German military periodical which predicted a form of siege warfare in which 'an artillery duel may ensue, but any decisive effect to a strife of that kind is not highly probable, and may only result in an enormous waste of energy and ammunition. . . .

Should we, placing blind faith in the effects of artillery, let slip from our hands all the latest technical inventions?'[10] The article received some learned attention in Italy and Britain.

Allenby was somewhat distantly associated with those who, under Haldane, reformed the Army. Through the work of Haldane and his supporters, the Army was ready in 1914 with one cavalry division and six infantry divisions, in a tightly knit, highly efficient Expeditionary Force that was superior to any force of its size in the world. Haldane's main achievement was to build up and reorganize the nation's reserve, leaving the line Army free to leave for Europe should the necessity arise. An Officers' Training Corps was established to train schoolboys to officer this reserve Army;* and under Haldane the line Army, although small by Continental standards, became immaculately trained and better disciplined. Allenby's contribution, however, was not as great as that of French, nor that of Smith-Dorrien or Douglas Haig. A year after the South African War, Haig had been sent to India as Inspector-General of Cavalry there, and became a Major-General five years before Allenby. In 1906 he went to the War Office to work under Haldane in the reorganization of the Army. Allenby's other rival from the Boer War, Hubert Gough, still only a Brigadier-General, achieved fame as the senior officer in the Curragh 'mutiny' of 1914. This affair, on the eve of war, caused much bitterness in the Army; a bitterness which did not have time to subside. Allenby did not have much sympathy for the rebellious Irish cavalrymen, who had shown a natural, if overhasty, unwillingness to fight their own countrymen. Allenby was at the Curragh during much of the trouble, but returned to London at its height and reported to Sir John French, who resigned over the affair. From this time Allenby took a close interest in Irish politics. A lesser-known declaration of loyalty to the Ulstermen had occurred at Aldershot, at a meeting called by Haig.[11] On the

---

* Wavell, a junior staff officer at the War Office, was partly responsible for the organization of this scheme.

brink of a European war, the rift between politicians and military was almost complete.

During Allenby's period as Inspector, the cavalry arm had been re-invigorated and given a more realistic outlook towards modern conditions. But there had been serious omissions. The Cavalry Division (scattered in England and Ireland) had, because of draught and for economy reasons, only trained as a division twice since 1910; it had no regular, permanent staff. On mobilization a number of staff officers, some of them strangers to each other, were brought together under Allenby, who had been given command of the division on the outbreak of war. The cavalry was thus commanded by a man who, although respected, was widely unpopular; perhaps, indeed, the most unpopular cavalry commander in memory. Only those closest to him, and who knew his work well, such as Herbert Lawrence, French and Chetwode, perceived that, given a little luck, the commander of the Cavalry Division, fifty-three years of age, heavy, ill-tempered and demanding, embarking for France, might achieve true greatness in the coming war. 'Apple-pie' had become 'the Bull'.*

* Chetwode said that he first heard Allenby described as 'the Bull' in 1909.

CHAPTER 4

War : Retreat

The Great War was a lengthy period of general insanity.
ALLENBY

The story of the First World War is one that is unlikely to be forgotten, or forgiven, as long as men have knowledge of the past. The four years that tore the heart from the Western world, and stained Europe with more blood than it had ever known before, make a terrible comment on human activity; but, of course, there was a kind of glory, too, in what men did, and what they fought and suffered for.

Never before had men's minds been more confused by the complexities of killing their fellow men; there were new weapons; there was a new, vast scale of operations. The Generals of all nations, struggling to wage war, and to protect their reputations, met with varied success: at the best it was only modest. The greatest war the world has ever experienced did not produce its greatest commander; there was no Alexander, no Caesar, no Napoleon, Wellington or even Montgomery in the First World War. On the whole the British Generals met their terrible problems in two ways: there was one group who believed the answer could only be found in accepting conditions and by applying themselves to the resulting logistics with unyielding stubbornness; the other group, though steadfast, attempted to apply themselves to the various pieces of the puzzle to see if they could discover a way of breaking the deadlock. The majority belonged to the latter group, and Allenby was among them. Nearly all of them were, at heart, 'Westerners', and believed that the war could only be won on the Western Front.

But in August, 1914, few believed the war would last long, and most believed that the cavalry would play an important role in a quick victory: either as mobile infantry or in its traditional role. General Allenby was thus watched with particular interest. He received a letter of advice from Lord Roberts, now a very old man, but still thoroughly concerned about his beloved cavalry: 'I shall look forward with intense interest to the doings of the cavalry in the war. May I say how earnestly I hope the men will be made to understand that they should never be on their horses when they can be off them. I issued an order to this effect during the Boer War, and when I was C.-in-C. at home, but I fear the custom still is not to dismount except by order.'[1]

The Cavalry Division, consisting of four brigades and ancillary services, was quickly *en route* for France, with the two infantry Corps, as had long been planned by Haldane and French. Sir John French was reinstated in the Army, and appointed Commander-in-Chief. All bitterness over the Curragh 'mutiny' had apparently—but not in reality—been forgotten. Allenby and his staff sailed on the *Minneapolis* exactly eleven days after the outbreak of war, a remarkable feat of organization. As with the start of the Boer War, he was pestered by teeth trouble. His best set of dentures had been lost in the post a few days earlier. After asking his wife to claim compensation from the Post Office, he wrote:

I shall write when I can; but henceforward my letters will, as you know, probably be few and scrappy. It is a lovely calm day, and the Solent is full of big steam yachts. God bless you, my dear love, and Michael, too.[2]

In fact, Allenby wrote considerably less from France and Flanders than he had from South Africa. His letters display the same respect for the enemy, compassion for his men and awareness of nature; but, not surprisingly, they show

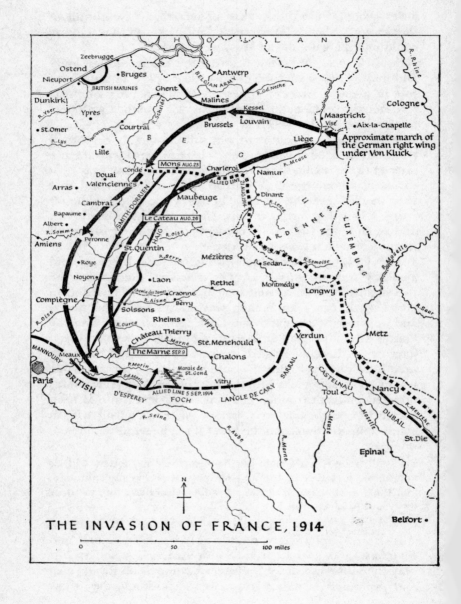

HOLLAND

Zeebrugge
Ostend
Nieuport
Dunkirk
BRITISH MARINES
Ghent
Malines
Antwerp
BELGIAN ARMY
R.Gd.Nethe
Kessel
Louvain
Maastricht
Visé
Cologne
Aix-la-Chapelle
R.Yser
Ypres
St.Omer
Courtrai
R.Schelde
Brussels
Liège
Approximate march of
the German right wing
under Von Kluck
R.Lys
Lille
B
E
L
G
R.Meuse
Mons AUG.23
Charleroi
Namur
Condé
Douai
Valenciennes
Arras
ALLIED LINE AUG.1914
Dinant
R.Lesse
ARDENNES
LUXEMBURG
R.Moselle
Cambrai
Maubeuge
SMITH-DORRIEN
Bapaume
Albert
R.Somme
Le Cateau AUG.26
HAIG
R.OISE
R.Semoise
Peronne
St.Quentin
R.Serre
Mézières
Sedan
Montmédy
Longwy
R.Saar
Amiens
Roye
Noyon
Laon
Rethel
Chemin des Dames
Craonne
R.Aisne
Berry
R.Suippe
Compiègne
Soissons
Rheims
Château Thierry
R.Ource
R.Marne
Ste.Menehould
Verdun
Metz
R.Oise
MANNOURY
Meaux
The Marne SEP.9
Chalons
SARRAIL
CASTELNAU
Paris
BRITISH
R.Morin
Marais de
St.Gond
Gd.Morin
Vitry
R.Meuse
Nancy
D'ESPEREY
ALLIED LINE 5 SEP.1914
FOCH
LANGLE DE CARY
Toul
R.Moselle
DUBAIL
R.Meurthe
R.Seine
R.Aube
R.Marne
St.Die
Epinal

N

THE INVASION OF FRANCE, 1914

0   50   100 miles

Belfort

increasing signs of bewilderment and frustration at the progress of the war. They usually begin 'My Sweetheart', and invariably end with fond endearments. 'You will know, my dear love, that you are always foremost in my thoughts, and that we are together in spirit.'

The country receives us enthusiastically, and they shower flowers on us as we pass through the villages. . . .[3]

And then, quite suddenly, it was war. While the French were putting into action their ill-conceived Plan XVII, the Germans were pouring through Belgium and into France in their carefully worked out vast, sweeping, flanking movement: the Schlieffen Plan. The small British Expeditionary Force, on the left of the French, found themselves facing the brunt of the German advance. Allenby was one of the first to realize what was happening. Two of his staff officers had sat in Mons Railway Station telephoning most of the small towns of Belgium to ascertain where the Germans were, and the direction of their advance.* By this means he discovered that the German right was much farther north and west than had been expected. His report to Sir John French's G.H.Q. was greeted with scepticism: 'The information which you have acquired and conveyed to the C.-in-C. appears to be somewhat exaggerated. It is probable that only mounted troops, perhaps supported by Jäger battalions, are in your immediate neighbourhood. In no circumstances, however, does the C.-in-C. wish the Cavalry Division to be seriously engaged.'[4]

It was the first occasion in which the General Staff was to be proved totally wrong; but it was not to be the last. French's chief of staff at this time was Major-General Archibald Murray, whom most of his contemporaries thought had already risen too high in the Army; French sent him home in

---

* One of them was Major-General G. Barrow, later to be a General under Allenby in Palestine. His own detailed account of the episode is in the Allenby Papers.

January, 1915, but he was promptly made C.I.G.S., the most important position in the Army.

Within twenty hours it had been shown, as might have been suspected all along, that Allenby was in a better position to judge in the matter than G.H.Q. Indeed, it was the role of the Cavalry Division to ascertain such information. To deal with the danger of a possible turning-in of the left flank, Allenby's division was hurriedly moved farther to the left; this involved one of the most difficult night moves made by the cavalry during the war. But it was to no avail. The British line, thinly stretched, clearly could not stem the massive weight of the German divisions, heavily outnumbering them, which was now hurled forward in an apparently irresistible swing south on Paris. The Allies decided to maintain an unbroken front and swing backwards, with a line hinged on Verdun, before the advancing Germans—until a natural barrier or extended German communications gave them the ability to stand and turn back the tide. The great retreat began. It was to be the greatest test of the cavalry in the war, and the only time in Europe that men on horseback were to play a prominent role.

To cover a retreat was one of the traditional and obvious roles of cavalry. For this reason Allenby had insisted on exercises in retreat before the war. But what Allenby had not foreseen was the circumstances that were already creating havoc with all preconceived ideas. In a small action near Valenciennes, at the start of the retreat, the 9th Lancers and 18th Hussars were ordered to charge the flank of massed German infantry. They rode into wires that had been hastily laid by the Germans, and were cut down by machine-gun fire.

The cavalry that were now expected to undertake a vital role in a most dangerous and difficult movement—in the end it turned out to involve nearly a hundred miles of retreat in less than a fortnight—had up till three weeks previously been a collection of totally independent brigades which had practically never come together. The divisional staff had no knowledge of handling a mass of cavalry in the field, and most of them had seldom worked together before. The

Cavalry Commander was widely unpopular, and had failed to gain the confidence of many senior officers, and even of one of his brigade commanders. For the latter defect, an important one, Allenby must take full responsibility; his unwillingness, or inability, to control his wrath in peace-time was now to make his problems in war that much the greater.

As a result of all this, total chaos was only just avoided practically all the way from Mons to the Marne. Allenby lost control of part of the division at a critical period; one of his brigade commanders, sensing disaster, took his brigade off on its own; there was confusion and, on occasions, total misunderstanding. Throughout the retreat, Allenby, as might be expected, remained the most calm and imperturbable General in France. It can only be said that the retreat was successfully accomplished, that total disaster was averted, and that chaos in the German cavalry surpassed even that of the British; and that without the sheer strength of character of Allenby the cavalry could well have been dispersed even more than it was or been involved in catastrophe.

The division was expected to cover the withdrawal of the Second Corps, commanded by General Sir Horace Smith-Dorrien, one of the few contemporaries whom Allenby thoroughly admired and respected. Smith-Dorrien, against the wishes of French, had succeeded General Sir J. M. Grierson, who had died of a heart attack on arrival in France.* Still worried about the length of the German flank, Allenby moved out some miles from Smith-Dorrien. No sooner had he done so than one of Smith-Dorrien's retreating divisions (the 5th) was heavily attacked, and Allenby had to send back quickly part of his force to save the situation. The cavalry, in the next few days, became increasingly entangled in, and hampered by, the vast swarm of French refugees

* The death of Grierson, little remembered now, before the war was two weeks old, may have had a considerable effect on the course of the first part of the war; he was an able and intelligent soldier who had been Military Attaché in Berlin for some years, and had an intimate knowledge of the German Army. He was Haig's successful opponent in the 1912 manœuvres.

fleeing before the German forces. Congestion was further caused by the French Cavalry Corps, which was moving east to west to strengthen the vital left flank behind the British retreat. At G.H.Q. French was, meanwhile, struggling in a maze of suspicions and misunderstandings with the commander of the neighbouring French Army. It was not at all like the Boer War. In a hurried letter to Kitchener, Sir John wrote: 'I may say at once that it will never do to oppose [the Germans] with anything but very highly trained troops led by the best officers. All their movements are marked by extraordinary unity of purpose and mutual support. . . .'[5] French wanted to re-embark the B.E.F., but Kitchener stopped him from doing so.

The difficulty of covering the Second Corps and protecting the left flank were resolved by splitting the Cavalry Corps in two, with Allenby taking command of the larger section primarily covering the flank of the British Army, and the remainder, under General B. de Lisle, attending to the needs of the Second Corps. Instead of helping matters, this made them worse, especially as Allenby's most difficult brigade commander, Gough, was left in his section. Shortly after this reorganization, Gough and the 3rd Cavalry Brigade made off south-east independently of Allenby.* In the following days Gough's division did some good work. Sir John French was in a difficult position, as he had a high opinion of both men, and could not afford to lose either. Gough's brigade never again came under Allenby's command, and was soon attached to the First Corps, under Douglas Haig, of which the Chief-of-Staff was Gough's brother, who also felt a personal animosity towards Allenby.† Gough found this 'very much to my relief . . . gone were the rather casual, vague and impracticable "orders" which I had received so far.'[6]

* Gough later explained his action: 'I felt compelled to safeguard my own brigade.' He died in 1963, aged 92.

† Brig.-General J. E. Gough, V.C., who, like his brother, had played a part in the Curragh 'Mutiny'; killed in 1915. Nephew of General H. H. Gough, V.C., and son of General Sir C. J. S. Gough, V.C., General Sir Hubert Gough did not have the Victoria Cross.

There followed one of the most interesting battles of the war: Le Cateau.

Realizing that much of his cavalry were temporarily out of his control, Allenby went to Smith-Dorrien's H.Q. and warned him that if he continued the retreat immediately the cavalry would not be in a position to give full support, as the other section of the division, under de Lisle, had become separated from the Second Corps. It was a difficult meeting for Allenby, although as it turned out de Lisle was able to provide some aid. However, Smith-Dorrien was a similar type of man to himself, and no words were wasted in recrimination. The infantry were worn out, and some of the commanders believed their troops would be better off fighting than marching; one divisional commander reported that it was physically impossible for his men to march farther that night. Smith-Dorrien decided to stand and fight, and asked Allenby to serve under him; this Allenby immediately accepted without fuss. (When news of this independent decision reached G.H.Q., Murray collapsed, and had to receive medical attention.[7]) After three days and nights of almost continual marching, the Second Corps were thus asked to fight; they were heavily engaged in bitter fighting early the following morning—thus close were the main German forces on the heels of the British. It was the anniversary of Crecy, and the British infantry stood firm. Meanwhile Haig, misunderstanding what was going on, hurriedly marched the First Corps off south-east, thus exposing the right flank of the Second Corps. Heavy casualties resulted. Haig himself, overestimating his own opposition, became 'rattled' and described the situation of the First Corps as 'very critical'. Smith-Dorrien's Corps, engaged against six German divisions and a Cavalry Corps, was actually asked to go to Haig's aid. This it was unable to do. In the general confusion, Haig, who suffered abominably from stomach trouble during the retreat, got lost with his staff car.

It is sometimes suggested that the First World War Generals, blamed for the slaughters of static warfare, would have done much better in a war of movement. The fact is that,

moving or static, they were totally overwhelmed by problems
of which they had no previous experience and for which they
did not have the intellectual capacity or intuition of military
genius to solve on the spot. Allenby, deserted by half his force,
forced to let down a fellow commander when his need was
greatest, was wretched at the whole affair of Le Cateau.
Asked for help from Smith-Dorrien's Fourth Division, Allenby had to reply: 'I am afraid I cannot intervene effectively
in the fight.' He had taken the unusual course of signing the
message himself.

French never forgave Smith-Dorrien for his decision to
fight, and he always believed that Allenby was quite blame-
less in the affair. He believed that the whole retreat had been
jeopardized. He wrote: 'The effect upon the British Army
was to render the subsequent conduct of the retreat more
difficult and arduous.' It was a difficult and trying time, in
which ill-assorted personalities were bound to clash, but
Smith-Dorrien's brave decision would appear to have saved
the B.E.F. from rout.* At the calmest of times, French was
not an unemotional man. The fact is, however, that Smith-
Dorrien, a sensible man, not afraid to make a quick and tremendous decision, had no real alternative.

With difficulty, the Second Corps extricated itself from the
battle of Le Cateau, the companies left to sustain the firing
line fighting to complete extermination. Throughout the
battle the British infantry had fought most courageously, and
the Corps staff handled the delicate movement of dis-
engagement with brilliance. It was one of the very rare
battles on the Western Front, throughout the war, in which
G.H.Q., which normally conducted even minor details, had
no part. The retreat was continued. Three days after the start

---

* Of the many enmities between the Generals during the war, none was
worse than that between French and Smith-Dorrien. Neither man
could stand each other, and in the end Smith-Dorrien was abominably
treated by French. In April, 1915, he suggested a withdrawal
at Ypres. French was so angered that he sent him home and replaced
him by Plumer; when the latter argued the same course, French
agreed.

of the battle, the Cavalry Division, less Gough's brigade, was back under Allenby's command.

After two weeks, the British Army halted. Throughout the retreat, Allenby had tried to cling to the left flank and guard it tenaciously. However, he was bound to come in for a good deal of criticism. The career of a lesser man might well have been finished, but, surprisingly, French's admiration for Allenby was undimmed. He told Kitchener that Allenby had reacted well to a difficult situation. He wrote: 'Allenby handled his cavalry with great vigour and skill.'[9]

French was certainly absurdly over-generous in his praise of Allenby during the retreat, as much of the time Allenby had, in fact, very little cavalry to command. He was, however, similarly generous to Gough. Chetwode, who was in Haig's Corps, later wrote: 'I was sent across to help Smith-Dorrien the day after Le Cateau as Haig had heard he was in great trouble. Half-way across I met Gough in a field and asked him what the devil he was doing there, and he told me he was getting as far away from the Bull as possible. It was a most scandalous affair, and he was almost in open rebellion against Allenby all the time.'[10] During the most confused part of the retreat, Edmonds, later the official historian but at that time a junior staff officer, was sent to ascertain the whereabouts of Allenby's cavalry. On this he wrote: 'I met French, at Vierstraet, who was seeking Allenby. I could only tell him that there was a board in Kemmel village with "Cav. Corps H.Q." on it, but that there was no one there. . . . I spent two years at Camberley with Allenby. He was not dull and slow like Haig, to whom at no time could one explain a matter. I could never get at Allenby's mind. The truth was that Allenby's staff were useless. They never knew where his brigades were.'

Edmonds had been a contemporary of Haig and Allenby, but never rose to high rank. The hopelessly unwieldy organization of the cavalry was recognized by Edmonds. 'I asked Haig in 1913 why there were four brigades in the Cavalry Division, more than any one man could control, as the Germans had discovered. He replied: "But you must have four." "Why?" "*For the charge*. Two brigades in first line, one

in support, and you must have one in reserve"!"[11] Edmonds
thought Rawlinson the best General on the Western Front
during the war. He had a nervous collapse after his first battle
in 1914, and thereafter served at G.H.Q.

During the advance from the Marne, Allenby was again to
be criticized. It was later said that he did not take the opportunity of charging the retreating enemy, and perhaps making
a breakthrough, especially on the 9th of September. But
Allenby's confidence was always disciplined by caution;
moreover, he was already doubting the usefulness of cavalry
in prevailing conditions. Once more his orders were not
always carried out as he had intended; moreover, one of his
chief staff officers was by now added to the list of those who
had 'cracked up' under the strain of the retreat.

For the first time since the retreat had begun, Allenby was
able to write home to his wife:

We've had a strenuous time, and have been fighting every day
for a week; very short of food and sleep. I, personally, have done
well in the way of food, and have had two good nights' sleep, but
the men had a very bad time. Their spirit is splendid, and they
have fought like tigers. . . . These Germans fight, chiefly, so far,
at long range, with artillery.[12]

Three days after writing that, Allenby suffered heavy
casualties, including two friends.

We have had a long period of marching and fighting, but
strategically I believe everything is going well. Today we are
having a halt and rest. . . . I have lost my Burberry waterproof
cloak. Will you send me another, big size, 44 inches in the chest?

Despite being billeted in a splendid château, Allenby had
been in the thick of the fighting on several occasions during
this fluid and confused period of battle. Indeed, at this time
a number of Generals, who were to spend the remainder of
the war in relative comfort, were reminded of the realities of
war. On one occasion Allenby's H.Q. was almost surrounded; he took personal command of the situation and

issued orders 'with, if anything, less concern than most fellows would show at a field day at home'.[13] On another occasion he rode along a line of dismounted men, who were about to break into disorganized retreat, and steadied them by his mere presence. One day Divisional H.Q., established in a barn, came under fire from a German battery. It was soon evident that their whereabouts was known to the enemy, and that the barn was the target of the German artillery. Allenby was reading a newspaper. The staff made hurried preparations to evacuate, but the General read on. At length a senior staff officer approached him and explained that the artillery were certain to find the correct range at any moment. At this, Allenby stood up, removed his reading spectacles, placed them in their case, folded the newspaper with careful deliberation, and walked out. A few seconds after the last of the staff had evacuated, a salvo of shells fell directly on the barn. This true story became well known; thus was 'the Bull' carefully restoring the respect of his staff and commanders, if not of his troops, which had not been his since the South African War.

CHAPTER 5

War: Frustration

After the Marne, G.H.Q. took a firm control over all operations, and divisional corps and Army commanders had to
devote themselves to putting into practice the projected
schemes of the General Staff. Allenby, shocked by his experience during the first month of the war, was glad of the
opportunity to readjust his thoughts on modern warfare, and
to wait his chance to put into practice his own ideas of how to
break the stalemate of the trenches—stretching from Switzerland to the sea—that now ensued. The chance was to come;
meanwhile, as the Army grew from a small expeditionary
force to a vast, unprecedented mass of soldiery, the original
commanders quickly rose in rank. At first Allenby appeared
to have received a jolt to his career when the separation of
the cavalry into two divisions was confirmed; Gough taking
command of the other division. But the B.E.F. was transferred to Ypres, and Allenby received command of both
divisions in the formation of the Cavalry Corps; thus was
French's trust in him confirmed.

During the motley fighting before First Ypres, the so-called
'Race to the Sea', Allenby was able to write home fairly
regularly; short notes, punctuated with terse 'Field Post-
cards' on which he invariably erased everything except 'I am
quite well' and 'I have your letter':

I am very well, but get bored at having to be up at 3.30 a.m.,
or thereabouts, every day—but I am in a house at night, while
most of the infantry are out in trenches.[1]

78

There is perpetual attacking and counter-attacking of local tactical positions, and a tremendous amount of artillery fire. The weather has been wet lately, and chilly, which is very trying for the men at night in the trenches.[2]

Sir J. French said charming things about the cavalry; and the Corps Commanders all have thanked me for the help received from us [in the advance to the Aisne]. I've sent a set of teeth (the old ones) to be repaired. The others are in good trim. Have you received the insurance money, £20, from the P.O. for the set that were lost in the post?[3]

We are very much amazed by the accounts in the papers of purely imaginary flights, and feats of arms, by people who have never seen a shot fired. There is hardly a word of truth in any of the newspaper reports. The great charges, captures of guns, etc., are mostly inventions of the reporters; none of whom have been nearer than Paris. Even the accounts of the German atrocities are nearly all lies. I believe they have behaved very well.[4]

A staff officer comes out twice a day, from Headquarters. Lord Dalmeny acts as his chauffeur. Other noble chauffeurs, e.g. the Duke of Westminster, also drive members of the H.Q. staff. Large numbers of the British nobility and gentry come up, in that sort of way, to see a bit of war.[5]

Winston Churchill turned up today, on a 36-hour visit from England. . . . My mended teeth have arrived, by post, this morning. I have not opened the box, as I am on the march, but I've no doubt they're all right. So now I am well provided.

What the men want most is papers; and, secondly, cigarettes. Pipes mostly, as they get lost.

Don't trouble about Michael. The artillery subalterns don't get killed any more than others. It is no use trying to choose a safe branch of the Army in war. The greatest casualties are always in the junior ranks.*

I am sure that I have the best-trained and most efficient officers and men that have ever taken the field in European war. I have, I think, also, a first-class staff. So I have no excuses if I do badly.[6]

---

* Michael Allenby had left Wellington and was taking the entrance examination for the Royal Military Academy at Woolwich.

The cavalry had hardly arrived at Ypres before it found itself engaged in a furious battle against a much stronger foe. If, at the bloody, but glorious, First Battle of Ypres, the British cavalry had not been trained as mounted infantry, and knew and understood the tasks of infantry, it is probable that the very thin British line would have broken. Allenby's six thousand men, holding a front of six miles, were opposed by an enemy nearly twenty-five thousand strong; in artillery they were outranged and outgunned. Allenby's task at this time was to handle his pitiably small reserves with skill, and this he did; often the line was only held by the arrival of the last squadron in reserve. It was touch and go for many days; it is doubtful whether this desperate affair has ever been surpassed, for valour and tenacity, in British military history. The height of the battle was reached on the 31st of October, when the German force attempted to breach the British line, where it was held by the cavalry, in a massive attack. Allenby reported the situation as 'decidedly critical'. These were such strong words for him that French went himself to Allenby's H.Q., and remained there through the morning while the line was, almost miraculously, held. French later wrote: 'Reviewing the situation as it presented itself on October 31st and November 1st, 1914, I believe that the vital interests of the British Empire were in great danger on both these days. That is to say, the whole coast-line from Le Havre to Ostend was within an ace of falling into the hands of the enemy. . . . The greatest threat of disaster with which we were faced in 1914 was staved off by the devoted bravery and endurance displayed by the Cavalry Corps under a commander, General Allenby, who handled them throughout with consummate skill.'[7]

Thus Edmund Allenby's reputation, severely tarnished during the retreat, was restored; although he would have been the first to admit that his own part in the battle was less than that of many of those struggling to hold on at the front. Even during the worst moments, however, he remained confident and apparently quite unmoved, thus inspiring his staff and commanders. The great heights of discipline which were reached during the battle must be traced back directly to Allenby's tenure of the office of Inspector-General. Another decisive element at First Ypres was the skill of the dismounted cavalryman with the rifle, for which Allenby can also take some credit.

After the First Battle of Ypres, the old B.E.F. was almost annihilated. The expression 'an Old Contemptible' was to remain for over half a century one of the greatest and most respected descriptions of a Briton by his own countrymen; but there were not many remaining.

The bandaged, begrimed, staring-eyed remnants of the Cavalry Corps were relieved from the trenches and put into reserve as reinforcements from England arrived.

On the night of the 31st of October, Allenby wrote to his wife on a tiny scrap of paper torn from his notebook:

Hard and bloody fighting today, but we held off a very fierce attack by the Germans, who were in great strength, with tremendous artillery. My people did wonders.[8]

My poor little A.D.C., Marshall, was killed by a shell today. I'm very sorry. He was a good little lad; and was very kind to me, though I was always pitching into him.[9]

The unsuccessful German efforts to breach the British line at Ypres had resulted in very heavy German casualties; soon the fire of battle began to die down—only occasionally sparked off here and there—into the painfully glowing ember of attrition.

My men have still a lot of trench work, which is very trying and which means great exposure to fire—and consequent losses. It is the regimental officers who suffer. We generals are a long way off; but the regimental officers are always in the thick of it with their men.[10]

Like every other family, the Allenbys had been appalled at the death-rate in the war so far; already many of their acquaintances had been killed (and one close relative—a

81

Cane). On each occasion Allenby wrote to his wife, giving as precise details as he could discover of the man's death, and a bit of a field map on which he had marked with a pencil cross the place where the man had been killed. These details and fragments of maps were then sent on to the wives or mothers by Mrs. Allenby; the maps especially, entirely Allenby's own idea, were of some comfort in trying to envisage the circumstances of a loved one's death.

During the winter months of 1914-15, while the Cavalry Corps were in reserve at Ypres, Allenby began two of the greatest friendships of his life. He was not a man who made deep friendships easily, but when he did they were more often with people outside the narrow confines of professional military life than not.

The château at which he stayed belonged to a most remarkable French widow, the Baroness Ernest de la Grange: aristocratic, witty, cultured, and with much charm. This somewhat unlikely pair, the *chatelaine* and the heavy, ponderous General, quickly became firm friends. They shared a number of interests, including a love of literature, music and natural history, and were able to discuss them, when Allenby's duties allowed, in both French and English (the Baroness had lived some years in America). Rumours about this relationship have naturally been whispered from time to time, but they are quite unfounded. Allenby had a very high sense of personal honour, and was quite devoted to his wife throughout his life. The Baroness was a good deal older than Allenby, who usually only enjoyed the company of women older than himself.

The start of another great friendship was with the G.H.Q. chauffeur, Lord Dalmeny,* who shortly joined his personal staff, first as A.D.C. and then as secretary. He went with Allenby to Palestine, and remained with him in Cairo after the war. A dashing but capable character, Dalmeny, who was unpopular with G.H.Q., had been a Liberal M.P. before the war and a well-known sportsman (captain of the Surrey

* Later the Earl of Rosebery.

cricket XI); despite an age gap of twenty years, the two men got on very well.

Lord Roberts is out here. I suppose he's anxious to qualify for a medal. Most people have been out now, including Lloyd George. I am very glad to hear that we are to have conscription—the idea that it should apply to all unmarried men only appears to me to be very sound. Now is the time to carry it through or never.*[11]

The Prince of Wales called to see me today; but I was out.[12]

I saw Mullens [Brig.-General R. J. Mullens] today. His brigade is just out of the trenches. He says that 48 hours' association with unburied dead Germans made some of his men actually sick; but the opposing trenches are so close that it is impossible to bury them. I spoke to a battalion that had been 31 days in the trenches. They told me that they could stand the cold, but that the mud broke their hearts. I hope to have all my men out of the trenches after next Monday night—but I've hoped this so often, without its coming off, that I don't count too much on it.

I was looking at a map just now. I find that I am only 125 miles, in a straight line, from you. Not far, is it?[13]

Today the King came and inspected two divisions of my Corps. He was very chatty and affable; asked me a lot about Claude,† and told me tales of their adventures together as sub-lieutenants. I delighted the *Baronne* by presenting her to him. . . .[14]

I'm afraid the Kaiser is not very ill; but I'm not sure his death would benefit us. I think his presence hampers his Generals a little.

I hope that we shall soon get a move on . . . the German position is strong and it will be a longer business than some of these [Infantry] Generals thought. I know the ground in the locality well; as well as, or better than, any of them. However, I daresay they'll hit on a plan.

The wetness of the ground makes progress difficult, as the whole country is a mass of mud, and the ground is waterlogged.

* Allenby was being somewhat premature; he seems to have confused the 'Householders' Return', of November, 1914, with full conscription of unmarried men, which did not begin till January, 1916.

† Allenby's brother.

I hear that General Joffre is in great heart and good spirits; which is cheering, as I presume that he is fully informed of the situation.[15]

We have a rumour, tonight, that two German cruisers are bombarding Scarborough. We hope it is true. It will do a lot of good in waking the English public.* . . . it will be the best of tonics for England. A French officer, today, said: 'I regret to see Scarborough bombarded. My compatriots, too, they say "How terrible, how sad." But I condole with the English officers, and they all say—Capital! I do not understand.'

I am glad to see that we have proclaimed a protectorate over Egypt. Sir A. McMahon, the Governor-to-be, was at school with me.[16]

The next abortive attempt to break the line was at Neuve Chapelle, in March, 1915. Allenby was not primarily concerned with this terrible affair, but at a conference at Haig's H.Q. at Merville, on the 26th of February, he suggested that the attack should be on a broader front so as to avoid a bottleneck during the follow-through. His suggestion was turned down rather sharply, although, in the event, it was shown to be wise.

As 1915 dragged on in months of inconclusive and frustrating fighting, so the Army, bloated by further intakes for its greedy needs, swelled to unprecedented proportions. Allenby's Cavalry Corps continued acting as mobile reserve, and in due course the depletions of the First Battle of Ypres were made good. Allenby himself was kept busy with the mainly humdrum tasks of a corps commander, keeping his Divisions ready for battle at the shortest notice; every week two or three letters arrived from acquaintances at home, begging for a place on his staff, all of which he turned down; now and again he visited hospital to have his teeth seen to; he rowed with the War Office over his pay (they eventually

---

* Bombardment of Scarborough and the Hartlepools, the 16th of December, 1914; it did do good in 'waking' the outraged British public to some reality of the war.

agreed to pay him the basic rate for a Lt.-General,
£2,500 p.a.). Allenby found that he did not dislike being
a General; he enjoyed the panoplies of military power. A
mild streak of vanity, not apparent in him before, became
discernible.

By now Allenby was convinced that the cavalry had no
further part to play in the war as mounted troops; he was
one of the first to see that new conditions would demand
totally new approaches. This conclusion had not come to him
as a sudden realization—his background was too deeply
rooted in the cavalry for that—but he had thought about it a
great deal while in reserve. It seemed to him that trenches,
wire, machine-guns and quagmires produced by artillery
barrage had revolutionized war, which indeed they had. It
was a heretical viewpoint for a cavalry General, and the
commander of the Cavalry Corps at that, to hold; but
Allenby made no secret of the fact. Among those who disagreed with him were Douglas Haig, who was told by Brig.-
General H. J. M. Macandrew, of the Indian Cavalry Corps,
that if Allenby and his Chief Staff Officer had their way the
cavalry would cease to exist as such; that in their opinion the
war in France and Flanders would continue and end in
trenches. Haig disagreed, stating that a large force of cavalry
was necessary to reap the fruits of victory.[17] Major-General
J. F. C. Fuller has written, of Haig's obsession with cavalry:
'He was so unimaginative that he could not see that the
tactics of the past were as dead as mutton. We are told he held
that the 'role of cavalry on the battlefield will always go on
increasing', and that he believed bullets had 'little stopping
power against the horse'. This was never true, as an intelligent glance at past battles would have made clear to him.
Yet it had to be true, otherwise how could he employ his
cavalry?'[18]

It was clearly impossible to have as commander of the
Cavalry Corps a man who no longer believed in the role or
usefulness of cavalry in the existing conditions. Thus, on the
6th of May, Allenby was appointed to the command of an
Infantry Corps, the Fifth, in place of General Herbert

Plumer, who, in turn, was succeeding the unfortunate Smith-Dorrien in command of the Second Army.*

* * *

The Fifth Corps was in the thick of the fighting on the Ypres salient, which had once more flared up as the Germans tried, with overwhelmingly superior fire-power, training and equipment, to break the line of fresh British troops that had reinforced or replaced the decimated 'Old Contemptibles'. The Second Battle of Ypres, for sheer wretchedness, bears comparison only with the Third Battle of Ypres (Passchendaele). It had been raging for two weeks when Allenby took over the Corps; and although Allenby had seen the futility of the Cavalry Corps, he had not discovered any methods of breaking the terrible deadlock of trench warfare. His part in the battle was confined to the careful use of his scanty reserves and of seeing that the orders of G.H.Q. were faithfully complied with. These last consisted mostly of counter-attacks, which Allenby vigorously insisted on being carried out. They resulted in much loss of life. The enemy made considerable use of gas against the Fifth Corps, to fatal effect, and also (for the first time against British troops) of flame throwers. All this, but especially the remorseless policy of counter-attack, brought Allenby the greatest unpopularity of his career. His reputation was probably worse than that of any other General in the Army. It seemed that the pre-war soldiers had aptly named him 'the Bull', and in the minds of the troops, and of much of the public, he became the epitome of the bovine brass-hat who was so bemused by the problems of his trade that he could think of nothing better to do than send thousands of men to their deaths. It was a most unhappy period for Allenby, although more unhappy still for his troops; some of his divisional commanders attempted to effect

* Smith-Dorrien was made C.-in-C. of the East African Campaign, but did not take up his command owing to ill-health. He took no further active part in the war.

his removal by secret approaches to G.H.Q. Allenby was continually criticized as not being fully aware of the situation at the front. When the 6th Division was told that it was going to the Fifth Corps, morale so obviously declined that G.H.Q. felt it wise to cancel the order. Only his personal friends, those who had known him in the Army for many years, and his staff, knew of the real man that hid behind the moody, ponderous General who believed his first duty was to carry out orders no matter what he thought of them. One who watched Allenby from a distance was Major A. P. Wavell, a brigade staff officer in the Corps.

During the Battle of Loos, in September, 1915, the Fifth Corps were required to provide a diversionary attack at Ypres to draw the German reserves. For this purpose Allenby and his staff chose a part of the German line, near Hooge, which had previously resisted all efforts to take it. The attack failed, with heavy losses. Earlier in the year the Corps had been involved in a murderous and hopeless action at Bellewaarde (in which Wavell was wounded).

Strategically, Allenby, at this time, had no better ideas on how to win the war than his contemporaries. He had little time for the Gallipoli expedition:

I quite agree with you that it's sickening to see the troops we want here sent to the Dardanelles. [19]

Generals seem to drop out rapidly in these Eastern spheres of action. [20]

However, the lessons of failure at Second Ypres and at Loos were not lost on Allenby. He pondered on them, alone in the evenings, or on long walks, and considered how best the war could break free from its immensely destructive bonds and return to the open movement for which he longed.

While I was near Ypres, I had a visit from one Sir Maurice Fitzmaurice, a great drainage expert; and we discussed a scheme for erecting big pumps near Ypres. [21]

Meanwhile, intrigue and bitterness had spread through the echelons of the British Army as seldom, if ever, before. There was a wide disillusionment at the way things were going, and Sir John French was the obvious target for all dissatisfaction. Douglas Haig, French's likely successor, was convinced that if only Sir John could be removed all would soon be well, or at any rate much better. The man to whom he had once loaned £2,000, and who had helped him in his own career from time to time, was now, he thought, a danger to the British Army; he lobbyed in London, with the King and with Kitchener, for his removal. But Kitchener wanted General Ian Hamilton (who had also been Lord Roberts's favourite) to replace French. The intrigue was furious and bitter.

French had some indication of what was going on and, as his last major appointment as C.-in-C., promoted Allenby to a full General in October, 1915, and gave him command of the Third Army. 'I am lucky,' Allenby wrote, 'as there are not a few senior Generals available.'[22]

CHAPTER 6

War: Arras

Allenby received a very pleasant letter, on his promotion, from his former Army Commander, Plumer: 'No one will send you heartier congratulations than mine, and no one will wish you success in your new command more sincerely than I do. Your departure is a great loss. Please let me thank you warmly for all the support and assistance you have given me. They have been invaluable. Good luck. Herbert Plumer.'[1]

The Third Army held twenty miles of front, from the Somme to near Arras. This was the area which was expected to be the scene of the great British offensive, planned for the summer of 1916 (planned before the Germans had launched their attack on Verdun). It was not a particularly suitable area for an attack, as the German positions, dug in chalk, were strong—on top of a slope and in a number of commanding salients. Nevertheless, the French Commander-in-Chie believed it was a perfect site, and the new British C.-in-C., Douglas Haig (appointed six weeks after Allenby's promotion), neither knew nor greatly cared, as he was obsessed by the idea of attacking yet again at Ypres. However, when the time came to prepare for the attack on the Somme, the Armies were rearranged and the Third Army was moved farther north, so that only its far right wing came into the scene of the coming operations. This was a bitter disappointment to Allenby, who had been keenly planning for the offensive; it was just as well, however, for his reputation. Allenby's most notable contribution to the preparations for the offensive was a network of light railways, with which he had covered the Somme country during the winter of 1915-16, despite early opposition from G.H.Q. If Allenby had commanded at the Somme in 1916, he might well have never been sent to Palestine; indeed, he might well have been sent home, for his already damaged reputation could hardly have stood the massive slaughter that ensued. For Joffre's blithe optimism had led to the choice of a point of attack which was later aptly summed up by Winston Churchill: 'The policy of the French and British Commanders had selected as the point for their offensive what was undoubtedly the strongest and most perfectly defended position in the world.'[2]

The result of Joffre's strategy, if it can be so described, has been widely known ever since.

It is most unlikely that Allenby's Third Army would have fared any better in the impossible task than did General Sir Henry Rawlinson's Fourth Army. But at the time Allenby felt this affair deeply; it seemed to him a personal slight, although Rawlinson was, in point of fact, the senior commander. Allenby's bad reputation with the troops, however, had presumably not escaped the notice of Haig, and Allenby's two closest supporters were gone from the scene: Kitchener dead and French removed from effective power. After this, relations with Haig deteriorated. Although Douglas Haig had not thought highly of Allenby for some time, the latter had no disliking of the new C.-in-C. Shortly after Haig's appointment, he wrote:

I saw Lord French before he went home, and he said many charming things to me. I know D. Haig, the new Commander-in-Chief, well, and like him, too.[3]

From the spring of 1916, however, there was a distinct coldness. Wavell has written of one occasion when the two men met at G.H.Q., on important business, and found themselves alone. After a minute or two, they parted without a word having been said. Wavell wrote: 'At the periodical conferences of Army commanders it was obvious that Allenby's opinions carried little weight, and received scant attention, especially if Gough, commander of the Fifth Army, had a different view. Often Sir Douglas Haig would turn to one of the other Army commanders and ask his opinion on some point while Allenby was still speaking. Such treatment naturally disconcerted Allenby, who was never a very quick debater. . . . Gough had never at any time made a secret of his dislike of Allenby, or of his poor opinion of him as a commander.'[4]

One of Allenby's staff wrote of Allenby and the Commander-in-Chief: 'I believe that the two characters were antagonistic. The Army conferences that I attended with Allenby were completely futile. Haig discussed company or battalion tactics, whether it was best to clear a wood by going into it or round it, etc. I remember Rawly [Rawlinson] saying at one "Certainly go round it" and after a discussion in which the majority favoured going through it Rawly then said, "Certainly I should go through it".'[5]

The role given to the right wing of the Third Army in the Battle of the Somme was to provide a 'diversionary attack' on the Gommecourt salient—an extremely powerful fortress which jutted into the British line on a considerable slope. This was probably the strongest German-held position on the entire British front. Neither Allenby nor his staff (especially Major-General Louis Bols) cared for the idea, and Allenby himself suggested to G.H.Q. that if a diversion was needed to draw the German reserves (a ploy which had met with little success so far in the war, although relentlessly pursued), then a more suitable place would be near Arras: it was farther away from the Somme theatre, and it was more vulnerable. This request was turned down.

In order to deceive the enemy into thinking that the Gommecourt attack was to be the centre of the offensive, the Third Army was ordered to make all its preparations as obvious as possible; these instructions were faithfully carried out.

Major-General S. E. Hollond* described the arrangements

---

* Not to be confused with Lt.-General Sir Arthur Holland, at that time the Third Army's artillery commander.

for the attack as follows : 'Snow's* arrangements for this attack were monstrously bad. He never co-ordinated the plan of his divisions, neither did he supervize their individual arrangements. He went on leave to England for ten days during the preparation and arrived back only a few days before the attack. I thought his supervision so bad that I tried to get Allenby to degommer him, but Allenby wasn't sure of getting G.H.Q. support.'

The VII Corps, which was to undertake the attack, received, in its secondary role, few of the facilities available to Rawlinson's Fourth Army. Lack of pioneer units made necessary the employment of nearly all the attacking troops in digging and other labour work, right up almost to the moment of attack. In one of the two attacking divisions, few, if any, of the front-line troops had a full night's sleep before the battle. The waiting German troops opposite, on the other hand, were living in comparative luxury in deep concrete dug-outs (forty feet deep), supplied with electricity and kitchens.

Four days before the attack, G.H.Q. were delighted to hear from the Corps commander : 'They know we are coming all right.' German records mention the careful preparations for the attack. Three and a half hours before it was launched, they poured down a heavy barrage on the VII Corps' forward trenches. Of the two divisions in the Corps, the 56th (London) Division did perhaps the better on the first day of the Somme battle, the terrible 1st of July, 1916. Despite very heavy losses in struggling across No-Man's Land, remnants of several battalions, weighed down with masses of unnecessary kit, reached the German trenches, and held them for some hours, cut off from their own lines. So long as their grenades lasted, they were able to maintain their positions, but by midday they were sending out repeated messages : 'SOS Bombs'. From one o'clock onwards men came straggling back in small parties. By the evening there were only five British officers and seventy men remaining in the German

* Lt.-General Sir Thomas Snow, commander of the VII Corps.

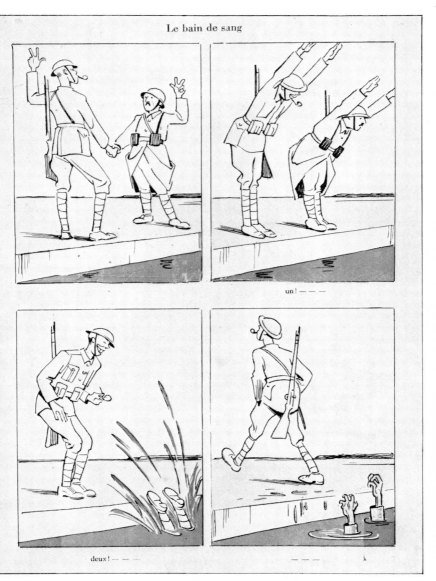

Launched to aid the French, the Arras offensive did
not ease their discontent. This leaflet was distributed
by malcontents in the French Army.

After a Church Parade, 21st of October, 1917. C-in-C
on the left.

Meinertzhagen and Lloyd (later Lord Lloyd) at Advanced
Intelligence H.Q. in the Sinai Desert, 1917.

...Ihnen den Charakter als General der Kaval-

...erie und gereicht es Mir zum besonderen

...von, Ihnen dieses hierdurch mitzuteilen. — Neu-

..., den 13. Januar 1914.

Generalleutnant z. D. Liman v. Sanders.

British Intelligence photograph of the Commission of Liman von Sanders, signed by the Kaiser.

The Hejaz Railway.

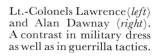

Lawrence and bodyguard.

Lt.-Colonels Lawrence(*left*) and Alan Dawnay (*right*). A contrast in military dress as well as in guerrilla tactics.

'El Aurens'.

Newcombe – the unsung hero of the Desert Campaign.

Joyce – front seat, near-side – in his Rolls.

Wavell as a Staff Officer, 1915.

line. At 9.30 p.m. their ammunition ran out, and they, too, returned. The 46th Division also completely failed in its attack, two battalions of the Sherwood Foresters suffering eighty per cent killed.

If an ostentatious attack is carried out as a diversion to a greater attack elsewhere, and to draw the enemy's reserves, then it is a better policy to select a weak position rather than one already immensely strong.

During the remainder of the Somme battle, the Third Army remained relatively inactive, and it took no further part in the main offensive; Allenby kept raiding parties (always encouraged by G.H.Q.) to a minimum, and his Army suffered less than half the average weekly casualties of the other two Armies (the First and Second) not involved in the offensive.

However, the Gommecourt disaster had done nothing to change the prevailing opinion of Allenby as a heartless and inept commander. One of his senior commanders, Maj.-General Sir John Keir, would not co-operate, and Allenby reported him to Haig. Keir spoke to Haig against Allenby most strongly, and there was an extraordinary scene, with Keir threatening to stir up trouble in London; but the C.-in-C. supported his Army commander and Keir was sent home. Although Allenby visited the forward trenches probably more than any other Army commander, he frequently spoilt the good impression this would have otherwise made by his violent outbursts of temper. He was particularly incensed by the sight of anyone not wearing a steel helmet; although his temper must have seemed an outrageous example of out-of-touch blimpishness to exhausted and shocked fighting troops, his attitude was more sensible than that of Maj.-General R. J. Pinney, who had earlier forbidden the use of helmets, believing that such modern contraptions would soften his troops (a man of strong teetotal convictions, he also stopped the issue of rum to his division).

During this comparatively quiet period, Allenby was better able to savour the life at his great château at Bryas (having moved out of two smaller châteaux). He by no means disliked the privileges of his position. The H.Q. mess was well known for its table, Allenby having personally secured a French cook from a co-operative French General. Allenby dominated his dinners; one apprehensive young staff officer, newly arrived, thought him more like a great emperor than a mere General. His wit continued to be caustic and dry, and his staff soon found that any careless remark was picked up and tossed back with devastating force and precision. He was very strict about the use of English. He would not tolerate abbreviations or split infinitives in official writings, even in hasty messages. At the same time, he abhorred flowery prose, and insisted on straightforward, simple writing (in which his own despatches were always couched). On one occasion at dinner, on hearing the word 'padre' used, he called down the table: 'Are you speaking Spanish down there?' He liked to be surrounded by intelligent men, and this he had now succeeded in doing. His two principal staff officers, one of whom, Bols, was to accompany him to Palestine, later achieved some eminence in life. One of his A.D.C.s was his nephew, Dick Andrew, from the Suffolk Regiment. Lord Dalmeny, witty, cultured and worldly, was now his Military Secretary. All were devoted to 'the Bull'.

Allenby took the greatest interest in the gardens of the château, writing from time to time about his latest discoveries to his mother. There were three little French village girls whom he practically adopted; with these he corresponded regularly, and helped in a number of ways, not least financial. His friendship with the Baroness de la Grange, who visited him from time to time, continued as before (his wife jokingly complained that if he was not more careful the 'affair' would get into the newspapers). This picture of Allenby dallying with children, sucking his beloved 'bull's eyes' sweets, dining and wining, and enjoying the company of a rich and cultured Frenchwoman, while his men languished in the incomparable squalor of attrition, is not, inevitably, an attractive one; the nature of high military command makes it impossible and unnecessary for a General to share the dangers and privations of his men, but the Generals in the Second World War contrived to be more tactful and less sybaritic.

Having passed out well at Woolwich, young Michael Allenby arrived in France as an officer in the Royal Horse Artillery at the beginning of 1916, three weeks after his eighteenth birthday. Allenby was delighted with him, but, knowing full well the terrible casualty rate among junior officers, was naturally apprehensive:

I am glad that Michael appreciates Bernard Shaw. He has, I think, a good taste in literature; which will be a great resource and advantage to him in life.

He is about 15 miles from here, living in a dug-out. I motored over, this morning, to see Michael. I found him, with another subaltern, deep in a weather-proof dug-out, dry and warm, with a fire. Outside a N.-E. blizzard was blowing, freezing snow and piling it in a big drift against the door leading down into his shelter; he is very well and cheerful.[6]

Michael took part in the Somme battle. On the 6th of September he was mentioned in despatches by his commanding officer for courageous work as a forward observation officer under heavy fire. On the 16th of September he took a party forward to register the fire on a trench that was causing serious trouble. In No-Man's Land they spotted a hand waving from a shell-hole; they crawled over and found an N.C.O. who had been badly wounded four nights previously. Under heavy fire, they carried him in. Michael was awarded the Military Cross. The citation said:

For conspicuous gallantry in action. . . . He displayed marked courage and determination throughout the operations.

For a time Michael's battery was in the Third Army, and whenever there was sharp fighting Allenby could be heard every evening striding down the corridor to the casualty-reports office; he would push the door open with his stick, burst in, look out of the window with his back

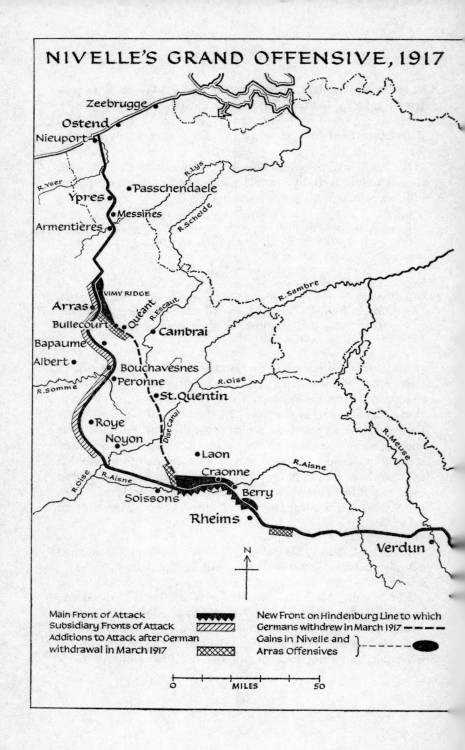

NIVELLE'S GRAND OFFENSIVE, 1917

Zeebrugge

Ostend

Nieuport

R. Yser

Passchendaele

R. Lys

Ypres

Messines

R. Schelde

Armentières

VIMY RIDGE

Arras

Quéant

R. Escaut

Bullecourt

Cambrai

Bapaume

Albert

Bouchavesnes

Péronne

R. Somme

R. Oise

St. Quentin

Roye

Oise Canal

Noyon

Laon

R. Aisne

Craonne

R. Oise

Soissons

R. Aisne

Berry

R. Meuse

Rheims

N

Verdun

Main Front of Attack

Subsidiary Fronts of Attack

Additions to Attack after German withdrawal in March 1917

New Front on Hindenburg Line to which Germans withdrew in March 1917

Gains in Nivelle and Arras Offensives

0   MILES   50

to the room, and inquire if there was any news of his son.

*   *   *

Just before Christmas of 1916 General Robert Nivelle succeeded Joffre in command of the French Armies. Nivelle was one of the most interesting personalities of the war. An artillery officer of good looks, pleasing presence and magnetic personality, he had been rapidly promoted since 1914; he first came to prominence at Verdun, where he succeeded Pétain, and had recovered there all the ground previously lost to the Germans (a useless strategic victory, but an important, if costly, moral one). He believed he could do the same thing for the entire Western Front, and return to France all the territory at that time in the hands of the invader. He was exactly the man for whom the nonplussed and frightened French politicians had been longing; he was, moreover, like Sir Henry Wilson, precisely the kind of soldier who appealed to the non-military directors of the war; charming, well spoken, and apparently cultured and intelligent; he was, at any rate, the inevitable contrast to 'Papa' Joffre. Lloyd George, recently appointed Prime Minister, was so taken by this dashing General, who spoke such exquisite English, that he tried, unsuccessfully, to get the British Armies under Nivelle's overall command. Lloyd George was already disillusioned with Haig, and was considering replacing him with General Lord Cavan.*

Joffre's plan for 1917 had been one of punching the German line in strength at several points, in which both Allies would co-operate; but by then everyone knew what happened when Joffre punched the German line. Nivelle's scheme was more grandiose, more exciting. There would be an enormous concentration of French infantry at the Aisne, and in a plan in which artillery fire and infantry advance were dovetailed with what appeared to be extraordinary

* According to Henry Wilson. A.P.

sophistication, the French would simply walk over the enemy defences and make a massive breach; after what had happened at Loos, Verdun and the Somme, it was necessary to have the faith of a fanatic to believe it would really succeed, and as the months went on the faith of most became very thin, though it had to be admitted that Nivelle himself was supreme in blissful confidence. The man, it was thought, may just be the saviour that is needed.

The British were now to take a secondary role. Haig was still adamant that the only place worth attacking was at his beloved Ypres (he was to get his way later, when no one could think of anything else), but he agreed that the Third Army should attack at Arras, in a largish offensive, in order to distract German reserves from Nivelle's operations farther south; these 'diversionary' attacks had been tried again and again, and had consistently failed. North of Allenby's Third Army was the British First Army, under General Sir Henry Horne, and the right wing of this, the Canadian Corps, was to co-operate with Allenby in attacking the redoubtable Vimy Ridge, which had resisted several previous attempts on it. Horne, a dour, silent man, was a friend and admirer of Allenby's, and was himself not lacking in all the qualities of generalship. Nivelle was against the Vimy plan, but Allenby and Haig insisted on it in order to protect the Third Army's left flank. Another, smaller, diversionary attack was to be conducted at Bullecourt by Gough's Fifth Army, just south of Allenby's sector.

The main attack, then, was to be Nivelle's huge push at the Aisne, with a smaller but nevertheless powerful British offensive around Arras, in which the Third Army had by far the major part.

Here, at last, was a chance for Allenby to show whether he could do better than his contemporaries in breaking through the German fortifications and opening up the war to a quick victory; or so he thought. But in the end, as Rawlinson at the Somme had found before him, he was fatally hindered by G.H.Q. whenever he wanted to make an original move.

Allenby's prime concern in his deliberations on the coming

battle was how to restore the element of surprise to the Western Front. He and his staff worked on their plan throughout the winter, and it was submitted to Haig and his Chief of Staff, that mathematical, clinical and most efficient mass-executioner, Lt.-General Sir Lancelot Kiggell. It was a meticulous and most impressive document, containing a number of original ideas, and many typical touches of Allenby common sense. Particular stress was laid on the importance of traffic control behind the lines during the course of the battle (although, in the event, there was a mighty traffic jam, due to the freakish weather); and also on the feeding of the men ('a satisfactory breakfast before attacking —care is to be taken that this meal is a good one'). Considerable use of mining was to be done, and this was, in fact, carried out with success, much of it by New Zealanders. Every artillery piece was to be brought up to the main point of attack to ensure a considerable preponderance over the enemy artillery; there were, in fact, 2,817 pieces (compared to the German 1,014). Considerable use, more than ever before, was to be made of aircraft;* 450 were put at Allenby's disposal, and he conducted the battle from a complete set of aerial photographs of the entire area. More use than before was also to be made of tanks, in which Allenby had always shown the greatest interest. Only forty, however, were available. Despite advice from the tanks' officers themselves, G.H.Q. decided that these should be used on a broad front, here and there, instead of in a concentrated attack.[7] Owing to the disastrous, premature showing of the tanks to the enemy at the Somme, the previous year, the Germans had now widened their trenches to trap tanks, and had also issued a great many armour-piercing guns. The officer commanding the Third Army tanks later wrote: "Allenby told me how confident he felt that the tanks would prove of great value, and assured me that he, personally, would give all the help he

---

* 'I realized very little escaped him. If Allenby thought a thing was "good" it was characteristic of him to use it to the utmost.'—Marshal of the R.A.F. Sir John Salmond, to the author.

could and would watch the activities of the new arm with the keenest interest. . . . Not only was he a born leader of men, with a most determined and resolute character, but he possessed an extremely imaginative and far-seeing mind and was not afraid to depart from the stereotyped methods of warfare.'[8]

None of these, however, were major points in the plan which Allenby submitted to G.H.Q. Its one really striking feature was the use of an intense, but revolutionary short artillery bombardment. Prior to this, it had been considered impossible to launch a large-scale attack with less than about one week's continuous bombardment from heavy artillery, in order to break the wire and flatten the enemy trenches. This policy had not been a great success; for one thing, there did not seem to be much difference in the effect of a barrage after about three days; a law of decreasing damage seemed to operate; for another, when the barrage began, the enemy knew when to expect the attack. Allenby's sole reason for a short barrage was to restore the element of surprise to warfare in the only way that seemed possible once the tanks had been so tragically revealed 'for the mere petty purpose of taking a few ruined villages', as Winston Churchill put it. The only other ways to obtain surprise were to attack in the dark, and the troops were not considered experienced enough for this (although, on Rawlinson's insistence, a night attack had met with success on the Somme), or to attack with no barrage at all. Allenby planned his barrage to last forty-eight hours; his artillery commander having first satisfied both of them that *rapid* fire could be kept up this length of time, if a strict rota system was used, by the gun teams, and that the guns would take the necessary strain. The British *Official History* says of Allenby's appreciation: 'Nothing of the sort had been projected by the British Armies since warfare on the Western Front had assumed its present complexion.'[9]

According to Wavell: 'G.H.Q. was profoundly shocked at these revolutionary ideas.' They replied that the Third Army plan was (*a*) impossible, (*b*) pointless, as other preparations and the short barrage would still reveal the attack to the

23255

enemy. Allenby replied that he had conducted experiments in rapid fire, and was completely satisfied as to the feasibility of his plan, for which, of course, he took full responsibility. He was aware that absolute surprise was probably impossible, but by cutting off the barrage about four days before the enemy would expect it to cease he could surprise them completely as to time of attack.

G.H.Q., however, were adamant; at one point it seemed as if Allenby might have to go; instead his artillery commander, who had staked his reputation and career on the scheme, was conveniently promoted and was replaced by an artillery commander of orthodox views. This placed Allenby in an impossible position, as he could not go against the advice of a specialist subordinate when it happened to coincide with the views of G.H.Q. A compromise was reached, and Allenby doubled his barrage to last four days.

The front of Allenby's offensive was to be some ten miles long, the ground being gentle, almost treeless downland. In the north, Vimy Ridge, a remarkable freak of nature, 475 feet above sea level, commanded a large area as it dropped abruptly to the valley of the Scarpe. The centrepiece of the battle area was the ancient town of Arras itself. Within range of the German guns, it lay little more than a mile from the front. Most of the old houses had capacious cellars, and some spacious caves and quarries were found just outside the town. These were linked here and there by tunnelling; they were ventilated and fitted with electric light. They could accommodate twenty-five thousand infantry, and shafts were dug from them right up to the front line; the troops would therefore reach the forward trenches confident and unshaken by enemy artillery fire.

During March the German forces, which had held the old line at the Somme, began their voluntary retreat on a fifty-mile front to the well-prepared and expertly placed Hindenburg Line. This manœuvre was unexpected; recently divisions had been decimated to take two hundred yards, and now Ludendorff, newly arrived on the scene, was giving up ten miles and more of his own accord. Allenby's right wing

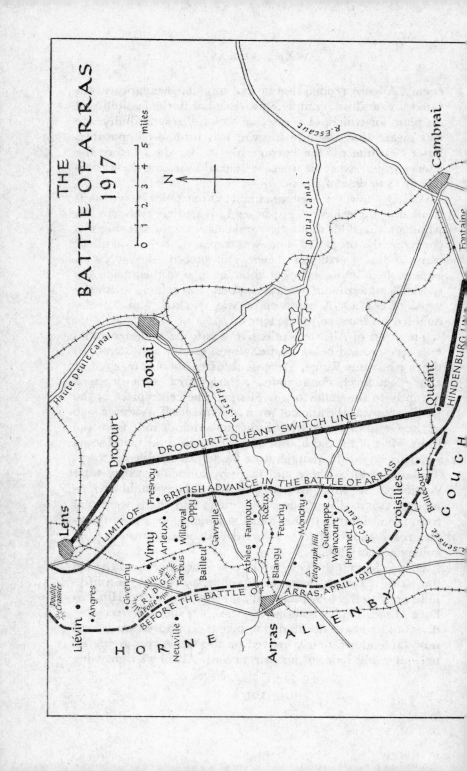

THE
BATTLE OF ARRAS
1917

0 1 2 3 4 5 miles

N

Cambrai

Fontaine

R. Escaut

Douai Canal

Douai

Haute Deule Canal

R. Scarpe

Drocourt

Quéant

HINDENBURG LINE

DROCOURT-QUÉANT SWITCH LINE

LIMIT OF

BRITISH ADVANCE IN THE BATTLE OF ARRAS

GOUGH

Lens

Fresnoy

Oppy

Gavrelle

Arleux

Willerval

Croisilles

Bullecourt

R. Sensée

Double
Crassier

Liévin

Angres

Givenchy

Vimy

Farbus

Bailleul

Athies

Fampoux

Roeux

Feuchy

Blangy

Monchy

Guémappe

Wancourt

Héninel

R. (or) I.

LA FOLIE
RIDGE

Neuville

BEFORE THE BATTLE OF

ARRAS, APRIL, 1917

Telegraph Hill

HORNE

Arras

ALLENBY

138

was thus moved forward several miles, and plans in that sector had to be hurriedly recast. The whole position was dramatically changed; whereas, before, the Third Army were attacking a German line already indented, they were now attacking a salient. Changing the place of attack, or calling it off, were not, however, seriously discussed.

The German defences consisted of three systems: the front alone, four miles from the second system, consisted of a network of three lines of trenches and well-placed strong points; beyond this again lay an emergency system, the so-called Drocourt-Quéant Switch. This latter had been constructed especially with the view to a forthcoming British attack at Arras, and was, in due course, inspected by Ludendorff. The German Chief of Staff expressed himself satisfied that, although the British might break the first line, they would be halted at the Drocourt-Quéant Line.

During the preparations, Allenby was twice taken sick, and spent some time in base hospital at Boulogne; this culminated in an operation for an abscess. Rumours spread that he was being put on the shelf because of the Gommecourt disaster. He did not appear on the sick list, and continued work from his room by constant use of the telephone; his car waited outside to take him to H.Q. whenever necessary. But he had always delegated responsibility freely, and the staff he had gathered around him were as competent as any in France; his sickness had no effect on the preparations for the coming battle. This delegating of responsibility pleased the strong men of character that Allenby liked with him, although it had not pleased Gough when he had served under Allenby in the Cavalry Division.

On the eve of the attack, Allenby was informed that the Commander-in-Chief still had no faith in his plan of attack, and that the Third Army commander must take full responsibility. It was made plain that if it was a failure, he would have to go.

The date fixed for the opening of the battle was Easter Sunday, the 8th of April, 1917; about a week before Nivelle's offensive was to begin. But at the last moment, after the barrage had begun, Nivelle, poised on the brink of his destiny, requested a postponement of twenty-four hours. Easter Monday broke with almost unprecedented spring storms of sleet and snow.

*　　*　　*

If ever a battle was dominated, from start to finish, by the vagaries of nature, it was the Battle of Arras. Snow in France at that time of year was unheard of; at first it came in squalls, with bright, sunny intervals between, and with the snow and sleet driven into the enemy's faces. It was a most fortunate aid to the attacking troops (many of them Scottish), who appeared out of the gloom and were soon pouring all over the first German trenches and taking hundreds of surprised defenders, sometimes with hardly a shot fired. At other places fighting was fierce, but by nightfall most of the triple-system of the first line of defence was in British hands. The offensive had got off to a brilliant start and it was evident from interrogation of prisoners that this was partly due to the shortness of the barrage (which had been more than twice as long as Allenby had wished) and the surprise of the Germans at the speed with which the British, using their tunnels and cellars, were able to bring up reserves. Allenby's meticulously planned 'creeping' barrage on the 9th of April, if not during the remainder of the battle, was one of the most successful of the war; a new gas shell, which helped to paralyse the German artillery, was also effective. That night it really seemed as if there was every prospect of a major breakthrough; Allenby, despite his previous doubts as to the use of horsemen in the war, hurriedly prepared his cavalry to exploit the opening. It had been the most successful single day's fighting by British troops since the start of the war.

The following morning, the 10th, was the time when the second system should have been completely over-run, but something seemed to have gone wrong, although at first it was not apparent precisely what it was. The weather, which had originally favoured the attackers, was now hindering them and working to the advantage of the defenders; slush and snow had turned to mud, and the bringing up of the guns, to lengthen the barrage, was seriously hampered; lines of communication became jammed; the movement of reserves was hindered by the large force of cavalry stumbling about over the torn wire, craters, devastation and mud in an effort to break through. In a hopeless ride, two brigades of the cavalry suffered severely; among the many killed was one of the Brigadier-Generals. Most important of all, perhaps, the tanks, from which much had been hoped, slithered about in the atrocious weather, often to little purpose; six of them, indeed, sank into a bog before they even reached the starting line. Individual tanks did good work in isolated incidents, such as the one which led the successful infantry attack on the vital strongpoint of Monchy-le-Preux (where the cavalry lost heavily).

During the day a little progress was made, but not what had been hoped for. The 11th was critical; once more progress was slow, and was now becoming extremely costly. The German reserves were arriving in strength and the chance of breaking the second line of defence had slipped away. A brilliant and major breakthrough, that might well have changed the whole course of the war, had nearly been won; but 'nearly' was not enough.

It had been shown that with careful planning, some surprise, and the right conditions, the German trenches could be taken—but only one system; the problem of maintaining momentum in order to go through the reserve defences as well, and make a complete breach, had still to be solved. The ability, at Arras, with which the Germans, having had many men taken prisoner, managed to recover and preserve their line by holding the rear systems was remarkable, especially as the German reserves had at first been held too far back.

Allenby himself had misjudged the situation. He had believed he was pursuing a beaten army; for this reason he had prepared the cavalry. His order was: 'All troops to understand that Third Army is now pursuing a defeated enemy and that risks must be freely taken.'* In fact, the enemy were not beaten; they were holding a strong defensive position, well placed and well prepared beforehand, and, far from being in retreat, were holding on in haphazard but desperate fashion in order to give their reserves time to reach the scene. It should be remembered, however, that there had been nothing like the opening day's success so far in the British experience of the war. Allenby's confidence may be judged from his letters to his wife, the most cheerful he had so far written in the war:

April 9: We have had a big battle today, gained a lot of ground, and taken a great many prisoners. I think that my losses are light. Fighting continues.

April 10: I had really a very big success yesterday. I won, all along the line; killed a host of Boche, and took over 7,000 prisoners. . . . Michael is safe and well. His battery was busy, but is now too far back to be much engaged today. Fighting has continued all today, and we are making continued progress. A Corps of the Army on my left also did a good attack; took the positions aimed at, and caught 3,000 or more prisoners. We have, at last, brought off what I have been working at all the winter. My staff have been splendid; and the operation—which required the most complicated and accurate calculations—worked like clock-work. Not a hitch anywhere. My artillery were brilliant; and the German guns were smothered from the start. The battle is not over, as we are still on the tail of the enemy, pressing and capturing their rearguards. For the moment my Headquarters are where they were.

April 11: The weather continues to be atrocious—snow squalls and cold wind. I'm afraid that poor Bunting will need a rabbit-skin, badly. Progress today is slower, but we have taken some more positions and more prisoners. . . . I have had many congratulations, including those of the Commander-in-Chief [Haig]. Our aeroplanes did good work. Yesterday and the day before they wrecked four railway trains, blocking the lines and preventing arrival of reinforcements. We have better machines than

* He was wrong, but this is an interesting example of one of Allenby's major tenets: the calculated risk of relentless pursuit.

the Germans, and more skilful and more daring flying men. . . .
I have just written and sent to the King a short account of
Monday's battle. He told me, last year, to send him anything
interesting of that sort.

April 12: My advance goes on, and we gain ground gradually.
Weather conditions are awful. Last night and this morning some
six inches of snow fell. . . . The cavalry nearly got a chance yesterday, but it did not quite come off. Wire and machine-guns
stopped them . . . they suffered somewhat severely. Some of the
tanks did good work. One youth took his tank into a village and
destroyed six machine-guns.

April 13: It has really been a big thing. I have taken 126 guns and
some 9,000 or 10,000 prisoners. . . . I attacked with twice the
number of troops that Wellington had at Waterloo. M. Clemenceau stayed with me last night. He, and the French generally, are
delighted.[10]

The letter of congratulations which pleased Allenby most
was one from French, now kicking his heels in London: 'I
always knew you only wanted the opportunity to score as
gloriously in command of an Army as you did in command of
the Cavalry. I think you know how much your success re-
joices me and all your old friends here. My warmest congratulations to you and your splendid troops. I am proud to
be your old Chief.'[11]

The Battle of Arras, however, had achieved only a limited
success, and it was by no means over. On the 14th of April
Haig, dissatisfied at the way things were going, ordered a
halt. He announced that the plan for the next stage would be
made at G.H.Q. This plan, a simple 'push', against the
German line, which had been reinforced and gained a second
wind, took place on the 23rd and 24th of April. It was a disastrous and bloody failure.* There was a further effort on the
3rd of May, a night attack on the insistence of General
Gough, whose Fifth Army also took part. This was another
costly disaster, with chaotic scenes as the inexperienced

---

* A letter from Kiggell, in the Allenby Papers, insists that 'these later
stages of the battle were forced on the C.-in-C. by Nivelle'.

reserves became involved in total confusion in the dark. The Battle of Arras, which had begun so confidently and which had for a moment quickened the pulse of all the Allied nations as nothing had for twelve months, thus petered out in inconclusive and hopeless fighting. British casualties at Arras were later stated to be 158,660, of which 87,226 were in the Third Army. Nineteen thousand German troops had been taken prisoner, a very satisfactory number, and about 250 pieces of artillery captured.

Late in the battle, when G.H.Q. had taken over, Allenby had received from three divisional commanders (one of whom was de Lisle) a 'formal resolution' expressing their views very strongly against isolated attacks, which frequently exposed the flanks of the attacking troops. Allenby, who would not countenance criticism of superiors in his presence, replied that he agreed with their views.

Meanwhile the attacks of the other two British Armies associated with the battle had met with varying fortunes; that of the Canadian Corps was a brilliant success, the Vimy Ridge, often thought impregnable, was courageously and successfully stormed in an engagement which is not entirely forgotten in Canada to this day. The troops of the unfortunate Gough, however, were at first repulsed in the attack on Bullecourt. Among many misfortunes, they did not receive adequate artillery support (due to no fault of Gough). Unfortunately Gough, impressed by the first hours of Allenby's success, had made a last-minute change of plan of attack, which upset some of his previous preparations; the result was a bloody chaos. Many of the attacking troops were Australians who had been in action, or in the front line, almost incessantly since the previous autumn, and one of their Generals (J. J. T. Hobbs) had protested strongly. Of this affair, the Australian *Official History* has this to say: 'Everyone was aware that the 4th Australian Division had been employed in an experiment of extreme rashness, persisted in by the Army commander after repeated warnings, and that the experiment had failed with shocking loss . . . [it has] indeed, never found a defender. . . . It was employed by British instructors afterwards as an example of how an attack should not be undertaken.'[12]

One of the Australian brigades lost 2,250 officers and men out of 3,000. When it was suggested to Haig that Gough's staff work was not all it might have been, he refused to listen. We are told by Wavell, however, that he was less unwilling to listen to criticisms of Allenby.

The Nivelle offensive had meanwhile opened and ended in utter fiasco. The great thrust that was to have won the war bent up like a cardboard knife attempting to cut a turkey. The protracted artillery bombardment had alerted the Germans in good time, and the French were once more asked to get up and walk towards the enemy machine-guns in their thousands, and into certain death; this they did, but it was to be for the last time. Nivelle had predicted a six-mile advance on the first day; he achieved six hundred yards. By the end of the following day he had lost over a hundred thousand men. Robert Nivelle had ended his brief moment as the saviour of France; he had promised too much, too loud, and too often; totally discredited, he was replaced by Pétain—a return to command by a 'serious' soldier who was both stubborn and aware that he no longer had a fighting army. With total disillusion at the direction of the war, and a feeling that they had been tricked by those who had promoted Nivelle, parts of the French Army shortly mutinied.

*   *   *

By spring, 1917, the conflict between 'Easterners' and 'Westerners' was well under way. Lloyd George, horrified by the enormous casualties of apparently fruitless battles on the Western Front, and apprehensive as to the political implications, was for ever promoting, as he said, 'My constant wish to strike the enemy where he was weakest.' He was particularly keen on knocking Turkey out of the war, in an effort to make contact with Russia and Rumania overland, and thus seriously expose the Central Powers to invasion from the rear, while the main German armies were held in France.

This policy of 'knocking away the props' Lloyd George considered essential to keeping Russia in the war and the Eastern Front active. It was beset by many difficulties, not least the fact that there were more Moslems in the British Empire than under any other rule. It was imaginative strategy, and in the past the most painless and shortest wars had been won through boldness and imagination. The Prime Minister, however, supported as he was by such 'Easterners' as Winston Churchill, had the greatest difficulty in getting the Army to co-operate. The 'Westerners', led by the C.I.G.S., Sir William Robertson, and kept up to the mark by Haig during his visits to London, were convinced that the war could only be won by defeating the German forces in a head-on clash on the battlefield in France and Flanders. It was then, and still is, a debate of much bitterness. The fact that, in the end, it was neither side which won the war, but a number of quite separate circumstances, prime among which were the effect of a naval blockade, and the entry of the United States into the war, leaves the conflict unresolved for ever.

Turkish aims in the war were to conquer Egypt and seize control of the Suez Canal; to dominate Persia and Trans-Caucasia, and set up pro-Turkish states in these areas; and to threaten India through Afghanistan.

When Lloyd George had become Prime Minister at the end of 1916, he had immediately endeavoured to try to instil some life into the affairs of the Egyptian Expeditionary Force, which for many months had been inactive against a considerably inferior foe. He wrote: 'In Palestine and Mesopotamia nothing and nobody could have saved the Turk from complete collapse in 1915 and 1916 except our General Staff.'[13] When the Commander-in-Chief in Egypt, General Sir Archibald Murray, who had been in Egypt for a year, having been replaced by Robertson as C.I.G.S., had at length been prevailed upon to move his forces into the advance, all had at first gone well; but when the Turks had decided to stand and fight, at Gaza, the British force had met with two severe repulses, which had inflamed the Prime Minister: he demanded more resolute leadership. The wretched Sir Archibald, hampered by a War Office which neither understood nor cared about his campaign, and who had endeavoured to conduct it with care and a proper appreciation of the importance of a strong supply line, was unceremoniously removed.

Lloyd George was anxious that the campaign should be taken over by General Jan Christian Smuts, of whom he was a great admirer. Smuts had been in London for the Imperial Conference, and had been asked to stay on so that the best use could be made of the vigour and extraordinary personality of this South African, who had become almost as British as the British themselves. He was known to have strong views about the importance of maintaining the links of Empire, especially the Suez Canal. Smuts had recently been in command of the East African campaign, where he had cleared the German colony there of German forces, but had not defeated the German force under von Lettow-Vorbeck; he had, to the satisfaction of von Lettow, chased this force with such ruthlessness that he had broken the health of his own army, a large proportion of which had died from exhaustion or disease, and most of the remainder of which had been sent home. Smuts had announced the campaign 'virtually over' and was received in London in some triumph; in the event, the campaign in East Africa lasted longer than that in Europe.

Smuts now considered Lloyd George's offer. He did not have a poor opinion of himself, and did not want to become involved in yet another 'side-show'. Despite the promises of Lloyd George, he came to the conclusion that a 'side-show' it was going to be; Robertson had indicated as much in private. The C.I.G.S. told him that the Army considered the whole plan a useless waste of manpower, and would humour the Prime Minister only as much as it was absolutely necessary from a constitutional point of view. Smuts later wrote: 'Sir William said to me, quite frankly, that if I were to accept the offer under the impression that something first-class could be done in Palestine, I would be making a great mistake, and he would dissuade me from accepting the command under such an impression. . . . Lloyd George often afterwards told me that I had made a great mistake, and it is a question whether he was not right. . . .'[14]

Smuts decided not to risk his reputation. He got out of the situation by saying that he could only accept if he could be allowed to land a large army on the coast behind the Turkish communications. Even Lloyd George could see that such a demand was exorbitant and impossible; such a plan had already been rejected in 1914 and in 1915, and this, no doubt, was known to Smuts. On the 31st of May, 1917, Smuts finally declined the Palestine Command in a letter to the Prime Minister: 'The most careful consideration has only strengthened my first impression that the Palestine Campaign will be a mistake unless at least the capture of Jerusalem is made a reasonable certainty.'[15]

Lloyd George then pressed Robertson to suggest a suitable replacement for Murray; he asked for someone both enterprising and forceful who could be relied upon to turn the campaign into an active rather than a passive one. Robertson looked about him. He knew that the relationship between Haig and Allenby had deteriorated, and that during Arras the former's doubts as to the latter's ability had increased. Moreover, Allenby, although not without his friends and admirers, was unpopular on the Western Front; his somewhat contemptuous handling of subordinates of pre-War days, such as Gough, and his reputation for 'bullishness' amongst the troops, had assured that. At the same time, Allenby, as a 'Westerner', was a little suspect.* He was certainly not an 'Easterner', but he was known to have odd views about the cavalry and about methods of frontal attack. He could not see eye to eye with G.H.Q. about artillery bombardments. He was also too closely associated with the uncomfortable memory of his mentor, Sir John French, who had been sent home for doing, only on a smaller scale, what Sir Douglas Haig was doing now. At the same time, if Lloyd

---

* After the war Allenby said : 'In undertaking their Eastern adventure, our statesmen showed strategical imagination and political foresight of a high order.'

George wanted someone forceful, there was no one more forceful in the British Army than 'the Bull'. Sir William Robertson must have been well pleased with his choice, and one can well imagine that it afforded him quiet pleasure; not only was he getting rid of Allenby, he was also giving Lloyd George the best man for the task. The choice was by no means untypical of the wily Sir William, who was, of course, a most confirmed 'Westerner'.

Lloyd George was well satisfied; he had got a good impression of Allenby's strong personality and obvious strength of character when he had met him in France. Moreover, he was aware of Allenby's reputation as a cavalry commander (a reputation which was better outside the Army than in it), and he was convinced that cavalry would play an important role in the campaign. The War Cabinet confirmed the appointment on the 5th of June, and a telegram was sent to Haig on the same day telling him to inform Allenby and to send him to London at once.

On hearing the news, Allenby was desolate. He was convinced he was being cast aside because of the limited success of the latter part of the Arras battle, over which he had enjoyed little control. His successor at the Third Army was to be General Sir Julian Byng,* who had commanded the Canadian Corps which had done so well at Vimy Ridge, and who was friendly with Allenby. To him Allenby spoke with some bitterness of what he believed was a disgrace and virtually the end of his active career; not so much against Douglas Haig, but against the General Staff, whom he believed were both incompetent and unfair. It looked like a victory for the Gough faction at G.H.Q. There was a dinner in his honour at G.H.Q. before his departure, and for this Allenby was somewhat ostentatiously late.

On arrival in London, however, Allenby began to realize that his appointment had possibilities after all. Lloyd George, enthusiastic and charming, sparked in the breast of 'the Bull',

* Later Field-Marshal Viscount Byng, Governor-General of Canada, 1921-26, and reorganizer of the Metropolitan Police.

always open to novel suggestions, some fire of the 'Easterner's' philosophy. He learnt that he was to have a great deal of freedom; and the policy in that entire theatre of war was not to be decided by the War Cabinet until Allenby had assumed control and had time to make an appreciation. Allenby was surprised, flattered and soothed. He was told by the Prime Minister, in the presence of Robertson,* that he was to ask for all the reinforcements and supplies that he needed.

'If you do not ask it will be your fault. If you do ask and do not get what you need, it will be ours,' said Lloyd George, ostensibly to Allenby, but in effect to Robertson. He added that he expected 'Jerusalem before Christmas'.

The Prime Minister then presented Allenby, with whom on this further acquaintance he had become more impressed, with *The Historical Geography of the Holy Land*, by Sir George Adam Smith, which included a detailed geographic survey of the area. 'I was convinced that this work was a better guide to a military leader whose task was to reach Jerusalem than any survey to be found in pigeon-holes of the War Office.' No gesture could have appealed more to Allenby, a lover of books. He had, however, already been given the book by McMahon. Lloyd George later wrote of Allenby: 'I was inspired with the deepest admiration for his character as a man and a soldier.' Allenby, in turn, had a high opinion of Lloyd George, and once said he had won the war ('though don't tell him so').

Allenby's appointment had received considerable notice in the Press, and he was delighted to see that nowhere was it considered a demotion; indeed, many of the pen-portraits of him that now appeared revealed that discerning correspondents, despite the veiled or open criticisms of the past, had a better idea of the real man than they had previously been prepared to admit: 'Sir Edmund Allenby is a man of almost giant strength and size, with a face whose grim determination, emphasized by the square jaw, is lit up by kindly eyes

---

* According to Lloyd George; Robertson denied being present.

and the occasional humorous expression.'*[16] Another opined:
'A man of his character has been badly wanted in Egypt for
some time past. Gaza ought to have been in our hands at the
end of last March, and would have been if the best use had
been made of the troops under General Murray's command.'[17]

In mid-June Allenby left for Italy, whence a cruiser took
him to Egypt. For the first time since he had commanded a
column in South Africa in what seemed a different age,
Allenby was completely on his own. He alone would make the
decisions that would affect the lives of thousands, that might
well determine the fate of large sections of the Middle East.
All thoughts of the trying and unpleasant competitiveness
and jealousies of France, and the frustrations of the Western
Front, were suddenly banished. Believing in his task, confident in his ability to do more than well, and well aware that
his moment of destiny and good chance had arrived—and
well prepared to follow the advice of his mother, whom he
had visited before departing, and grasp it—he was more
composed and content than he had been for many years;
suddenly the irascibility and unreasonableness gave way more
and more to the quiet good humour and full enjoyment of life
which in recent years had been increasingly swamped under
a hundred and one frustrations.

On the 28th of June, 1917, Edmund Allenby strode into
the polished halls of G.H.Q., Cairo, to take over command.

* Allenby was knighted in 1915.

CHAPTER 7

War: The Taking of Jerusalem

When a man knows he is trusted, he can do things.
ALLENBY

By all accounts, Allenby's arrival at Cairo was a remarkable occurrence; there have been many mentions of it in the past, and for those who were present it appears to have made a lasting impression. The general feeling in the campaign at that time was one of frustration, purposelessness and ennui. The Suez Canal seemed secure enough, but there appeared to be no hope of driving back the Turk*; moreover, no one in London seemed to take the slightest interest in the campaign. The Commander-in-Chief had been a somewhat colourless individual, who had some ideas but had himself been affected by the prevailing mood of depression and had made a fatal mistake in keeping his H.Q. in Cairo, at the Savoy Hotel, while his army sweated in the hot plains between Ismailia and Palestine. Desertion had become a serious problem; disillusioned soldiers, who had lost confidence in themselves and in their commanders, had been streaming back to Cairo and, at best, going absent without leave. Drunkenness and petty crime had been increasing rapidly. The E.E.F. was, in fact, approaching a very critical

---

* The only other activity concerned the extraordinary operations against the Senussi in the Libyan desert, mostly with the Duke of Westminster's Light Armoured Car Brigade.

condition; matters were not helped by an extraordinary crop of awards for gallant services being given to the large staff at Cairo, many of whom had never been to the front.

Allenby, freed from the bonds of France, was exploding with self-confidence, and the will to command on his own that had been bottled up since South Africa. He jolted G.H.Q. as a drifting boat which suddenly reaches the full stretch of the hawser. As Lawrence wrote: 'Allenby's coming had remade the English. His breadth of personality swept away the mist of private or departmental jealousies behind which Murray and his men had worked.'[1]

A senior intelligence officer at G.H.Q. was Colonel Richard Meinertzhagen, who had come from the East African campaign; an officer of original mould and a most untypical product of the pre-war regular Army. He wrote in his diary: 'Was introduced to Allenby, to whom I talked on Intelligence matters for a short while. My word, he is a different man to Murray. His face is strong and almost boyish. His manner is brusque, almost to rudeness, but I prefer it to the oil and butter of the society soldier. Allenby breathes success, and the greatest pessimist cannot fail to have confidence in him. . . . He looks the sort of man whose hopes rapidly crystallize into a determination which is bound to carry all before it. What is most satisfactory is that he means to become active at once and bring new life back into this Army. The Egyptian Expeditionary Force is already awakening from its lethargic sleep under Murray, and I am happy to say the G.H.Q. will shortly move into Palestine and be near troops instead of wallowing in the fleshpots of Cairo.'[2]

A number of staff officers who had been spending much time propping up the bar at Shepheard's Hotel soon found themselves on the boat home, as did a few elderly regimental Colonels and one divisional commander. The Chief of the General Staff, Maj.-General Sir Arthur Lynden-Bell, was among those who objected to the severity of Allenby's attitude, and he, too, was soon on the boat home ('medical reasons'). He was replaced by one who knew Allenby's methods of old, and who had always worked well with him, Maj.-General Louis Bols.

On his first morning at his desk, a Major-General of the staff brought Allenby a vast pile of routine papers. Allenby glanced at them, and then flung them on to the floor, saying that he should not be bothered with such details in future; these were, he said, the work of a junior staff officer. Allenby had brought some staff officers with him, including Dalmeny and Andrew, and on the same boat was Maj.-General John Shea, who had commanded a division under Allenby at Arras. The force was organized into three Corps: the XX under Lt.-General Sir Philip Chetwode, Allenby's old pre-war colleague and good friend; the XXI under Lt.-General E. S. Bulfin; and the Desert Mounted Corps (which included an entire brigade mounted on camels) under Lt.-General Sir H. Chauvel, an Australian. Chetwode was a good general, and Bulfin was a man of exceptional drive and energy.* The troops consisted of British, including survivors of Gallipoli and the famous 60th (London) Division, Australians, New Zealanders, French and Indians. Allenby had hardly been in Cairo a week before he disappeared across the Canal and went straight into the desert to inspect his Army, in a series of brief encounters with small and large groups of front-line troops (in much the same style as that employed by Montgomery when taking over command of the Eighth Army in the desert in the next war), and to make his appraisal on the spot; a move which astonished more than one staff officer. Meanwhile, G.H.Q. were told to prepare, in the C.-in-C.'s absence, to move themselves to the scene of operations. Shea said later: 'What was so typical of Allenby was that directly he arrived the first thing he did was to visit his troops, and as soon as possible bring his headquarters close to them, thereby establishing intimate personal contact, which continued

---

* F.-M. Lord Chetwode was C.-in-C., Indian Army, 1930–5. He died in 1950. Bulfin, an Irishman educated at Trinity College, Dublin, became a Colonial Governor and died in 1939. Chauvel was Chief of Staff in the Australian Army after the war until 1930.

throughout the campaign. The natural result of this intimacy was that he could push his soldiers very hard, for he was at times a very exacting taskmaster.'[3]

The front that Allenby visited had seen little action since the second repulse at Gaza. For some time past General Murray had quite sensibly been concentrating his efforts on a railway and a pipe-line, which brought the waters of the Nile into Palestine, across the hundred and twenty miles of desert that separated the front and the base area on the Canal. On leaving his command, Murray wrote in his despatch: 'The Palestine operations have been entirely dependent on the military railway which has been built across the sandy coastal tracts of the Sinai Peninsula from the Suez Canal. . . . the waterless nature of the country around Gaza prevented a most successful operation [the first attack] from being a complete disaster to the enemy. . . . A short period of development was to follow, during which the water supply, which was a continual source of anxiety, should be provided for. . . .'[4]

Murray, who has been somewhat unfairly treated by history as a result of Lloyd George's published strictures, having failed in an attack which he had advised against from the first, had a proper regard for the needs of supply. He went on in his despatch to show how there had been disagreement among his subordinate commanders during the Second Battle of Gaza.*

The force, at a halt before 'the Gaza line', now lay over two hundred miles from Cairo; its main strength before Gaza itself, but stretching on its right as far as Beersheba at the foot of the mountains. It was a wretched place in which to be asked to fight a war. There was little shade, and the temperature sometimes rose as high as 110 degrees; a hot wind from the desert brought with it choking dust-storms. The 'roads' were sandy tracks; supply difficulties were a

---

* On his return to England, Murray was given the comparatively humble war-time post of G.O.C.-in-C., Aldershot. He retired in 1922 and died in 1945.

continual nightmare, and the entire force depended for water on the few wells and the precarious pipe-line. Fever and septicaemia were widespread. Discipline was not good. Allenby wrote home:

I travelled in my own railway coach as far as the Canal—near Ismailia—then changed into a special train on this side. From railhead, which is quite close behind my front, we get about on horseback and in Ford cars. . . . Our railway uses a vast amount of the pipe-line water, and our thousands of horses, mules and camels drink a lot. The men are burnt as black as Arabs. One sees them sitting in the blazing sun, often, with practically nothing on but a helmet, and apparently enjoying it. The Australians, especially, enjoy being grilled. . . .

I have been motoring and riding round, looking at defence works and water supplies.[5]

The main picture that seems to have stayed in the minds of those who saw this tour is of the enormous General, with red-banded cap and cane across his knees, being driven around in an old Ford truck, a minute Australian driver in the cabin beside him dressed in vest and rolled-up shorts. Allenby had always been a stickler for correct dress and the observance of regimental regulations, but common sense, of which he had an abundance, dictated that in Palestine such procedure was impracticable, although one imagines that from time to time it cost 'the Bull' a great deal in self-control. One of his first acts on arrival in Cairo had been to revoke the order by which staff officers were required to wear breeches, riding-boots and spurs; trousers were obviously more suitable in the prevailing climate of the Middle East.

The Australian *Official History* writes of the tours of inspection: 'His tall and massive, but restlessly active, figure, his keen eyes and prominent hooked nose, his terse and forcible speech, and his imperious bearing, radiated an impression of tremendous resolution, quick decision and steely discipline. Troops who caught only one fleeting glimpse of him felt that here at last was a man with the natural qualities of a great driving commander. . . . At last they had a commander who would live among them and lead them. Within a week of his

arrival Allenby had stamped his personality on the mind of
every trooper of the horse and every infantryman in the
line.'[6]

The British *Official History* said: 'The influence of the
Commander-in-Chief in the moral sphere can never be too
much emphasized in considering this campaign. He was constantly up and down his line, so that there can have been few
commanders in modern warfare who were so well known to
their troops. . . . His Australian troops, for example, were
men of original and independent type, not nurtured in the
traditions of British military discipline and inclined to be impatient of them; yet their reliance on him was complete . . .
blessed with strength and endurance which made little
of very long drives in intense heat and on dusty, bone-
shaking tracks [he] was able to communicate . . . to subordinate officers and the rank and file themselves.'[7]

The reinforcements which Allenby demanded of London
on his return to Cairo were not immediately forthcoming,
although one division was on the way from Salonika. But the
increase in the size of the force involved further problems of
supply. With Robertson in control at the War Office, however, there was no question of Allenby's full demands being
readily met, despite Lloyd George's backing. There were
already seven divisions in Palestine, but now Allenby, taking
Lloyd George at his word, asked for two more entire divisions.
In a long memorandum to the War Cabinet on this subject,
Robertson wrote: 'The first rule in all wars is to concentrate
in the main theatre all forces that can be made available. Any
departure from this rule has invariably proved to be disastrous.'[8]

Allenby, in fact, received his two extra infantry divisions,
and a good deal of extra artillery and, especially, more units
of the Royal Flying Corps.* In the air the E.E.F. had been

---

* A few months later Allenby was asked by Robertson if he wanted any
more troops, and Allenby said he would like 13 divisions; even Lloyd
George was taken aback by this, and when Allenby later produced a
consummate victory with nine divisions, Lloyd George asked for an
explanation.

completely outnumbered by superior German planes of *Abteilung* 300, but soon the advantage was with the British. Eight tanks were also available, and Allenby, who had been impressed by their possibilities at Arras, despite their very limited success, intended to make much use of them in the forthcoming battle; in the event, they were too few and were asked to do far too much.

To keep an eye on what Allenby was up to, Robertson had posted a liaison officer to his staff. He had picked out for this special assignment a young officer of whom he had the highest opinion, Lt.-Colonel A. P. Wavell, whose career he had been watching since he was Commandant of the Staff College and Wavell his most brilliant pupil ('by far the ablest'). Wavell had headed the list of entrants to the Staff College at his first attempt. Thrice before the paths of Wavell and Allenby had almost crossed: in the column stage of the South African War, when Wavell had attended the cavalry manœuvres on the Berkshire Downs in 1910, and had been much impressed by Allenby's obvious qualities of leadership (if not entirely of his handling of the cavalry); and at Ypres. More recently Wavell had started the war as Intelligence Officer at French's G.H.Q. in France, had then become a junior staff officer in the 9th Brigade, had lost his left eye at Ypres, had served at G.H.Q. under Haig during the Somme battle, and had been sent as liaison officer to the Russian Army in the Caucasus (like Allenby, he had qualified as an Army interpreter—but in Russian*). Now these two great men had come together.

Wavell's first task was to return to London from Cairo and to put Allenby's case for reinforcements to Robertson. It should be stated at this point that Wavell was basically a 'Westerner', although he had a very poor opinion of the tactics and methods used in the Western theatre; but Wavell remained loyal to both the Generals between whom he had to shuttle to and fro. In Egypt and Palestine his duties at first

* In 1913 Wavell had published an English translation of a biography of the Czar.

were to act as onlooker, and this he did with such care that his account in *The Palestine Campaigns* will never be bettered. Quiet, popular, somewhat taciturn, well read and clearly a man of unusual capabilities, Wavell studied Allenby and the plan which was being prepared. His next visit to London was to take this plan for the approval of the C.I.G.S. and the War Cabinet; to their credit, they found it highly satisfactory. Lloyd George was well pleased. He later wrote: 'Allenby was not wedded to the fantastic obsession, which dominated the War Office and H.Q. in France, that the best place to attack the enemy was at his strongest point . . . in spite of the success of his plan, he has been severely blamed for this strategy in some military quarters, and the "Gaza school" have insisted that his proper course was to attack on that nearest and strongest point.'⁹

In fact, the plan to break the Gaza line and take Jerusalem, which Colonel Wavell took in his despatch-case to Whitehall, was well conceived.

There were three possibilities: to attack at the left, that is at Gaza, to attack in the centre, or to attack on the right, that is at Beersheba. The attack in the centre was discarded, there being practically no water in the area, and the Turks holding a defensive position in some strength. Of the other two, Gaza was the obvious place to attack. A coastal route was more favourable, as the left flank could be guarded by the Navy, which had control of the sea. It was nearer the main line of communication to Egypt. Existing communications and climate were better; it was, moreover, the most direct route. Beersheba, on the other hand, was also held in strength, but was not so well fortified as the Gaza area; an attack on it would entirely depend on whether the wells could be taken within a few hours of launching the offensive, as even with all the transport available to the whole force an advance could only be watered up to Beersheba; beyond Beersheba, the attacking troops would be dependent on what water they could find. The entire concept of the plan, indeed, had to be dictated by the need for water. Allenby had no wish, however, to launch another frontal attack on the trenches of

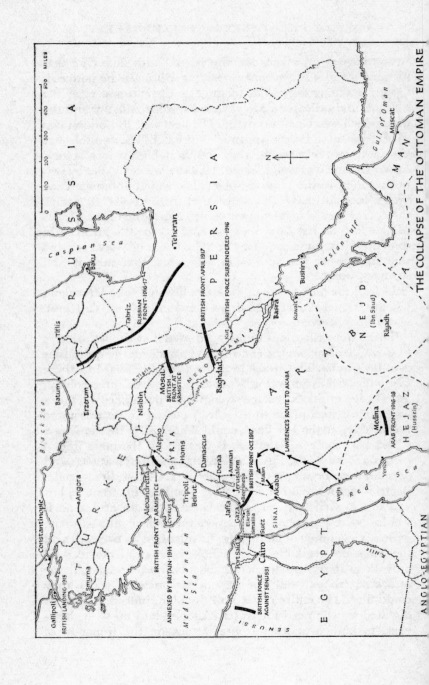

THE COLLAPSE OF THE OTTOMAN EMPIRE

Gaza, which the enemy were, no doubt, expecting. The plan which was presented to him suggested a thrust to the Beersheba wells, and then on to Jerusalem: its success would be largely dependent on the success of a feint at Gaza. It was essential that the Turks should be deceived. Once the Beersheba attack was under way and the enemy's reserves sent in that direction, Gaza could also be attacked. It was a daring plan full of risks and hazards; the kind of plan that many a General, thoughtful of his career and his reputation, would have turned down. Allenby realized immediately that it was the right one, and he accepted it with alacrity.

Allenby has often been credited with the plan of campaign for the taking of Jerusalem, but this is a mistaken view. The plan had been the brain-child of the staff of Chetwode's XX Corps, and primarily that of the principal staff officer, Brig.-General Guy Dawnay, a brilliant strategist and tactician.* Dawnay had been associated with the plans for the unsuccessful attacks at Suvla and on Gaza, and his reputation was low at this time. An intellectual, and a student of Greek history, he was one of the most outstanding of the extraordinary group of talented men then around Allenby; he was soon transferred from the XX Corps to work under Bols at G.H.Q.

G.H.Q. was now moved from Cairo to a hot and unpleasant, fly-plagued camp of huts and tents a few miles behind the line.

The German-Turkish force in Palestine and Mesopotamia, Group F (or *Jilderim*), was under the command of the German General von Falkenhayn, with a staff of sixty-nine German officers and nine Turks. Falkenhayn was one of the most senior German commanders; he had succeeded von Moltke as overall commander (i.e. Chief of the General Staff) in 1914, but had been replaced by Ludendorff after the

---

* Wavell claims that Allenby followed Roberts's plan for the relief of Kimberley. After the war, Dawnay became a most successful London business man. A slim volume of his poetry was published in 1919. He died in 1952.

failure of the attack on Verdun in 1916. He was hampered by acrimonious debate between the Turkish High Command and the Governor of Syria. His chief lieutenant was the experienced General Kress von Kressenstein, who commanded the force facing the British line at Gaza. An important German staff officer was Franz von Papen, who had formerly been military attaché at the German embassy in Washington, where he had dabbled in espionage. He had left America in somewhat sensational circumstances. In both Berlin and Constantinople the Palestine campaign had eventually been agreed to be of great importance; a determined effort to endanger, and perhaps gain control over, the Suez Canal was expected to have a vital effect on the war; the main link of the Empire would be broken, and many Allied divisions and resources from France would have to be sent into the Mediterranean area in an attempt to retrieve the situation.* Accordingly Falkenhayn had ordered von Kressenstein to remain on the defensive, and was now preparing an attack on Allenby's right wing; his plan, indeed, was almost exactly the same as the British plan in reverse. This was not entirely known to British Intelligence, and an intriguing period of guessing as to the enemy's intentions, bluff and double-bluff now ensued. Intelligence work played an important part in the campaign; more so than in any other campaign of the First World War.

The German-Turkish force was well equipped; there was one machine-gun to every 150 riflemen, a goodly proportion for that time. It remained to be seen whether machine-guns, hitherto invincible in the war, and an obvious threat to Allenby's cavalry, could outdo superior manœuvrability and Intelligence.

Allenby took a close interest in all problems connected with the coming offensive; in particular, he insisted, as always, that there should be meticulous and foolproof arrangements for supply. Over thirty thousand camels were

---

* In January, 1915, the Turks had reached the eastern bank of the Canal, and unsuccessfully attempted to cross it. They had been pushed back by a force under Allenby's friend Herbert Lawrence.

assembled to carry water to the troops attacking Beersheba. Roads were built in wild and arid country by many thousands of chanting, sweating Egyptians, hastily enrolled into a Labour Corps. New maps of the area beyond Gaza and Beersheba were prepared from flights of the R.F.C. The maps previously in use were some thirty years out of date; they had been made by Lord Kitchener, who had done a survey of the area when a Lieutenant in the Royal Engineers. In the corner of each was the imprint: "H. H. Kitchener, Lt." Allenby insisted on seeing for himself every aspect of all preparations; so much so that a signal was sent out from G.H.Q. every time he departed, in a cloud of dust, in one of the faithful staff cars. The signal was 'B.L.', which stood for 'Bull loose'.

The start of the offensive on Beersheba was fixed for the 31st of October; the latest possible date climatically, which risked discovery of British intentions, and forestallment by the enemy, but which allowed for the greatest possible time for the completion of Allenby's meticulous preparations. Allenby himself studied Palestine with the diligence of a student working for a doctorate, as much as of a General about to conquer the land. Papers which had appeared in the *Geographical Journal* were requested from his wife in London. Hogarth's *Ancient East*, J. L. Myres' *Dawn of History*, and Herodotus—all were studied. He made a careful study of the Crusades and discussed with his medical officers why the Crusades had failed. He learnt that Richard Cœur de Lion had failed to reach Jerusalem partly because his army had advanced at the worst time of year for malaria. He studied the disastrous epidemic of ophthalmia which had caused blindness among Napoleon's army in Egypt in 1798–1801. A doctor who knew him at the time wrote: 'His interest in everything appertaining to Egypt or Syria which might affect the troops or the progress of the campaign was insatiable. Whether it was a fly expert from the British Museum, a railway engineer, an expert on town planning or a naturalist who could tell him something about the flora or fauna of the country, he had them all up and sucked their brains of anything they could tell him.'[10]

Allenby's letters home record much of what he learnt every day about Palestine; they amount, in fact, to a fascinating travel book of the area at that time; antiquities, his observations of bird migration, detailed descriptions of villages and life therein, methods and economics of sea fishing, wild life, eating habits of the camel—he switched from one to the other, and many more, with the ease of a man with deep and intelligent curiosity. During preparations for the battle, a mosaic floor of great antiquity, 'probably Grecian of the 1st Century A.D.', was discovered. The only man at the front who knew how to excavate it and date it turned out to be the C.-in-C. Some weeks later Allenby asked for information about the ancient historical route across the Sinai desert, as described by Strabo, the Greek geographer of Christ's time. The relevant extracts from Strabo were eventually obtained in Cairo and sent on in the original Greek. The astonished staff officers watched as 'the Bull' translated them without difficulty.

Allenby took great care of his Intelligence arrangements for the coming battle. The Chiefs of Intelligence at this time were Colonel George Lloyd head of Advanced Intelligence, Wyndham Deedes in charge of Political Intelligence, Colonel Richard Meinertzhagen, head of Military Intelligence at G.H.Q., and Brig.-General Gilbert Clayton, Director of Intelligence in Egypt*; like so many of the leading figures who now almost miraculously appear around Allenby for the first time, they were extremely able and intelligent men. However, chief operator for the attack on Gaza was Colonel Meinertzhagen, a man ideally suited, both by temperament and experience, for the task; in East Africa, where he had been in charge of Intelligence, he had been engaged in a number of successful, original and daring deceptions.

Meinertzhagen installed a wireless-receiving station on the

---

* Later:—Lord Lloyd went on special missions to the Hejaz; Sir Wyndham Deedes, who worked with Allenby in Egypt after the war; Sir Gilbert Clayton, High Commissioner for Iraq. Meinertzhagen says that Lloyd was under him, but what his relationship was to Clayton is 'difficult to say'.

Great Pyramid in Egypt which intercepted and decoded enemy messages. The principal enemy Arab spy, operating from Beersheba, was 'eliminated' by sending him a letter of thanks for the information he had 'given' the British, together with payment in Turkish currency; the letter and reward were intercepted by the Turks, as arranged, and they executed their best agent (Meinertzhagen had also used this method in East Africa). Allenby vetoed another plan: for planes to drop, every evening, packets of cigarettes with propaganda leaflets, but on the night of the attack to drug the cigarettes with opium. (A typical Meinertzhagen thought, this.) Allenby thought it came too near the use of poison; but Meinertzhagen carried it out nevertheless 'on the principle that anything which saved casualties to our own men was justified'.* As for deception, it was spread about that Allenby would be away in Cairo from the 29th of October to the 4th of November (during which time it could naturally be assumed that no offensive would take place). But the main objective was to fool the Turks into believing that there was to be merely a feint at Beersheba, and that the major attack was to be at Gaza; to accomplish this a simple but effective ruse was organized.† Dalmeny, Bols and Dawnay were the only officers to know of it outside Allenby himself and the Intelligence section. A staff officer, ostensibly on reconnaissance, was to contrive to get himself chased by Turkish outposts, pretend to be wounded, and to drop a haversack, stained with fresh blood, containing papers, letters and maps, and money. These papers had been prepared with the greatest care and skill and, although most of them were innocent, here and there were clear indications that the attack at Beersheba was to be merely a subsidiary to another 'push' at Gaza. On the first occasion it was attempted, the

---

* Meinertzhagen tested the cigarettes himself: 'They were indeed strong. The effect was sublime, complete abandonment, all energy gone, lovely dreams and complete inability to act or think.'

† According to Lawrence in *Seven Pillars of Wisdom*, 'Meiner' was solely responsible for conception of this all-important ruse.

Turks did not perceive the haversack; on the second, they did not pursue. On the third try, Meinertzhagen himself went with the haversack. He wrote in his diary: 'I was well mounted, and near Girheir I found a Turkish patrol who at once gave chase. I galloped away for a mile or so and then they pulled up, so I stopped, dismounted and had a shot at them at about 600 yards. That was too much for them, and they at once resumed the chase, blazing away harmlessly all the time. Now was my chance, and in my effort to mount I loosened my haversack, field-glasses, water-bottle, dropped my rifle—previously stained with some fresh blood from my horse—and, in fact, did everything to make them believe I was hit and that my flight was disorderly. They had now approached close enough, and I made off, dropping the haversack which contained the notebook and various maps, my lunch, etc. I saw one of them stop and pick up the haversack and rifle, so I now went like the wind for home and soon gave them the slip, well satisfied with what I had done and that my deception had been successful. If only they act on the contents of the notebook, we shall do great things.'[11]

Thus was conducted one of the most famous and successful deceptions in the history of military Intelligence, to be written of many times, but not always accurately. The Turks were completely taken in and, indeed, so impressed were Head-quarters that an order was issued to all officers pointing out the dangers of being near the front line in possession of secret papers. Allenby wrote in Meinertzhagen's Army Confidential Report: 'This officer has been largely responsible for my success in Palestine.' Thus the work of a few days and the danger of a few minutes were to have a vital effect on an entire campaign. But Meinertzhagen himself, a most remarkable man, received no acclaim after the war, or, indeed, during it, despite the fame of his operation; a message was sent to Allenby, from the Desert Mounted Corps, mentioning the incident and complaining that Meinertzhagen had been guilty of negligence and stupidity.

It was at this time, before the Third Battle of Gaza, that

Allenby met another officer concerned with Intelligence: Captain T. E. Lawrence, who was concerned with the Arab rising, about which Allenby wrote home:

The Sherif of Mecca is in revolt against the Turks and is our ally. His followers are harrowing the Turks on the Aleppo–Medina railway, and are causing them a lot of trouble East of Palestine and the Gulf of Akaba.[12]

*   *   *

Lawrence, twenty-nine years old, had a face well beaten by the sun and creased by the torments of a highly intelligent introvert that gave him the appearance of being slightly older than his years. His short, thin body concealed an extremely strong and wiry frame; his most obvious features were deep-set eyes and a determined, purposeful-looking jaw. He was one of five illegitimate sons born to an Anglo-Irish baronet from Westmeath.* Before the war he had studied assiduously in two fields: military history and theory, and the medieval history of the Middle East. His readings in military history were impressive, and he had made a close study of the Napoleonic campaigns. A number of long and hardy visits to the Middle East and one book (*Crusader Castles*) had made him a lesser authority on the area. Lawrence had paid his way by odd jobs such as camel driving, harvesting and even coaling ships at Port Said; this had brought him much more into contact with Arab ways and thinking than other young graduates doing research in the area, and had made him remarkably tough physically. He had become particularly attached to Syria and its capital city of Damascus. Shortly before the outbreak of war, Lawrence and two others had undertaken an expedition across the little-known Sinai Peninsula, ostensibly for purely academic interests, but in fact to explore and draw up maps of the area for military use in the event of Britain and Turkey going to war. The rigours and

---

* Two of them were killed in action during the war.

the glamour of this expedition, especially the former, hinting as they did of challenge and danger, had much appealed to Lawrence. While he had as much dislike of extreme discomfort as any middle-class intellectual of his background, he had a greater obsession and need to prove his manliness than most men of action, and could seldom resist any challenge of that nature. He also, it would seem, had a rare talent for scrutinizing his own destiny. Altogether it was a very unusual young man who found himself, at the outbreak of war in 1914, still working on the maps of the Sinai Desert.

His work almost immediately came under military direction, and he found himself writing a guide of Sinai for the use of troops; within four months he was posted to Cairo to join the Intelligence staff of General Sir John Maxwell, Murray's predecessor. With him in Clayton's 'Arab Bureau' were D. G. Hogarth, Aubrey Herbert, Leonard Woolley and Philip Graves (brother of Robert, Lawrence's first biographer).* In Egypt, his task was to interrogate prisoners, draw up manuals on Arab affairs for officers posted to the area, and other fairly routine Intelligence tasks. He was not very good at the work and his superiors, who were probably better at it than he was, had a low opinion of his usefulness; he became more and more side-tracked into comparatively unimportant map-room tasks. He was not popular. Lawrence, unlike most of the rest of the staff in Cairo, had a good opinion of his own capabilities, and did not hesitate to make this plain—going as far, on occasion, as re-writing official reports. He was inclined to provoke, procrastinate and generally antagonize many people with whom he came in contact.

The Arab Revolt against the Turks began in Mecca on the 10th of June, 1916, as a result of protracted negotiations

---

* Herbert was the brother of the archaeologist Lord Carnarvon. Woolley was later Sir Leonard Woolley, archaeologist; he served in a similar capacity in the Second World War. Graves had been *The Times* correspondent in Constantinople, 1908–14, and was an expert on the Turkish Army; later he edited Abdullah's *Memoirs*. Hogarth became Director of the Bureau in 1916, and was followed by Cornwallis.

which had resulted chiefly from the initiative of Kitchener, and which had been completed by Sir Henry McMahon, Allenby's oldest friend, despite the opposition of the military establishment in Egypt. Hussein, Sherif of Mecca and leader of the Hejaz, was under the impression that his help against the Turks would be rewarded by Arab independence in the enemy-occupied areas of Palestine and Syria, but McMahon was adamant that he promised only part of Syria and Arabia. The correspondence, especially on the British side, was carefully ambiguous, and revealed that fatal hesitancy and indetermination which was to characterize British policy in the Middle East for the next forty years.*[13] Despite the advice of the British in the Persian Gulf and Mesopotamia, London preferred the intriguing Hussein to his more stolid rival Ibn Saud.

G.H.Q. was split as to the importance of the revolt. Many, including Murray, were convinced that it could be of little practical importance in the central campaign against the Turks. They insisted that the campaign would have to be fought on conventional lines between modern, organized armies; any support of the Arabs would amount to little more than the frittering away of valuable resources. Others, including Clayton and Lloyd, believed there were real possibilities in co-operating with the irregular forces of the Sherif of Mecca. The flag of independence had not long flown in Mecca before a British military and political mission went to the Hejaz to study the situation at first hand. The French were also very soon on the scene; they had post-war ambitions in the Levant and were determined to keep the closest watch on all events in the Middle East. After some initial success, however, the Sherif's army, under three of his sons—Ali, Feisal and Zeid—were repulsed by a Turkish force equipped with machine-guns. A static situation soon developed, with the Arabs frustrated and annoyed at the lack

---

* In a debate in the House of Commons on the 16th of June, 1964, it was stated that the secret background to this correspondence would be published 'in due course'.

of support from their co-belligerents. Ronald Storrs, a diplomat on the staff of the British Residency, was sent to Jiddah
to discuss the situation with Sherif Hussein's statesman son
Abdullah. Lawrence, who had already been on a mission to
Mesopotamia, asked to be allowed to go with him, and no
one at G.H.Q. was anxious to detain him.

British military aid and advice to the new Arab state had
recently come from the Sudan, with General Sir Reginald
Wingate, Commander of the Egyptian Army, in overall
charge of co-operation. McMahon was still, at this time, in
charge of the political aspect. Wingate himself believed that
there were military possibilities in the revolt; under him
worked a small but dedicated band of British soldiers helping
to train, organize and arm the Arabs. About 150 officers and
men of Armoured Car Units, the R.A.S.C., Royal Field
Artillery, and Staff were active in the Arabian desert, and
there were also a good number of British officers of the
Egyptian Army, Indian Army, Royal Engineers and
members of the Royal Flying Corps and Royal Marines
engaged in it, under the local command of Colonel C. E.
Wilson.* Of these, the most notable were Colonel S. F.
Newcombe,† a brilliant and daring demolition expert of the
Royal Engineers: Hubert Young,‡ who organized transport
and supplies: P. C. Joyce,§ who was to command British co-

---

* British Military and Political Representative in the Hejaz, 1916–19.
Died in 1938.

† An equally genuine but less influential hero than Lawrence. He had
served in the Egyptian Army 1900–11. Awarded the D.S.O. for his
services in the Hejaz. In civilian life after the war he became a world
authority on the unlikely subject of central heating. Died in 1956.

‡ Awarded D.S.O.; later Sir Hubert Young, adviser to Churchill on
the Middle East, and Governor of Nyasaland and Northern Rhodesia.

§ Lt.-Colonel P. C. Joyce; later military adviser to Feisal in Iraq.
Lawrence wrote: 'It was Joyce who ran the main lines of the Revolt,
while I was off on raids.'

operation with the Arabs in the northern desert; and W. F. Stirling,* who was Joyce's Chief of Staff.

During the desert war only one British serviceman was killed, and that was accidental. Professional soldiers, these men received no fame in later years, but their work had an important bearing on later events; to some of them the newly arrived Lawrence was an amateur soldier meddling in affairs he did not understand. Shortly their irritation was to be complemented by suspicion, for no sooner had he reached Feisal's headquarters than Lawrence seemed to be acting beyond his powers and beyond his somewhat nebulous assignment.

Lawrence was impressed by Feisal, and at this time, it seems, he began to see Feisal as leader of a future Arab state independent of Turkey and Europe, with its capital in his beloved Damascus. Feisal, slim, piercing-eyed and with natural dignity extraordinary even for an Emir, was an imposing person; his quiet, intelligent talk and easy air of command gave an impression of somewhat more shrewdness and determination than he probably possessed. Having sized up the military situation in Feisal's area with considerable professional flair and no illusions whatever, Lawrence went to Khartoum to report to Wingate. It was on this journey, partly on a British warship, that he first showed a reluctance to discard the Arab dress which he had taken to wearing while at Feisal's camp. He advised that money, weapons and a few British officers should be despatched to Feisal at once. This did not impress Wingate, who believed a large British contingent should be sent into the Hejaz, in addition to the ancillary services and instructors who were already there. Lawrence was aghast at the prospect; believing that such a British force would be followed by a French one, and

---

* The remarkable Lt.-Colonel Stirling; later adviser to Feisal in Damascus, Freeman of the City of London, Administrator of Sinai and Jaffa, Adviser to the Albanian Government, 1923–31. On 'special service' in the Middle East throughout the Second World War, lived in Syria and Egypt until expelled in 1951. Died in Tangier, 1958.

that what was a pure and romantic uprising for political independence would be smothered under the ambitions of the European Allies. He also believed that the Arabs, sensitive and proud, would fight better on their own than when co-operating with European-trained troops, who would inevitably consider them second-class soldiers.

Ironically, it was Wingate's suggestion, thoroughly alarming Cairo as it did, which probably set Lawrence on the road to his destiny. For on his return to G.H.Q. in Cairo he found himself in some favour. Murray and his senior staff officers, anxious to retain all their troops in Egypt and Palestine, had not expected to find a supporter of the Arab rising agreeing with them. Lawrence, indeed, had an interview with the Commander-in-Chief; and Lynden-Bell agreed to send out further supplies and instructors to Feisal. G.H.Q. had already become partly won over to the Arab venture, and had written to the War Office commending it. McMahon, meanwhile, had become hopelessly involved in the intricacies existing between the two factions in Cairo, and was replaced, in due course, by Wingate as High Commissioner; a victory of the growing pro-Arab faction, but one which was greeted with mixed feelings by Lawrence.*

Sometime on this return to Cairo, Lawrence got word of the Sykes-Picot Agreement; this was a secret Anglo-French arrangement concerned with the break-up of part of the Ottoman Empire after the war. By it, both countries and Russia were to have well-defined spheres of influence: Britain in Palestine, Mesopotamia and around the Jordan; France in Syria and the Levant; and Russia in the Caucasus. To ensure recognition of their claims, the French had sent a brigade of five battalions, a squadron of Spahis and supporting artillery to serve on the Palestine Front with the E.E.F. (The Italians, also, were represented by a token contingent.) As far as Syria was concerned, especially, it was evident that this agreement ran counter to the agreement which McMahon had made with Sherif Hussein on behalf of the British

* McMahon is remembered for his demarcation of the Indian-Tibetan boundary, to which he has given his name. He died in 1949.

Government, although at this time word of the Sykes-Picot agreement had not yet reached Mecca. On hearing of the agreement, Lawrence was dispirited and depressed, although he had long suspected such a situation; indeed, as a man of common sense who had thought deeply about the Middle East, he could hardly have avoided doing so.

Lawrence was soon sent back to the Hejaz, where he found the revolt at a low ebb. An attempt to take Medina had been thrust back with heavy loss, there was dissension between the Sherif's sons, and the Arab forces were deserting. The small group of British officers, of whom Lawrence was an awkward member, attempted to resolve the situation by organizing a joint land-sea operation; six warships with Arab infantry and Royal Marines would advance up the coast and land at Wejh, while Feisal attacked the port from inland. With the loss of Wejh, the Turkish position at Medina and in the Hejaz generally would become extremely difficult; only one other port of note, Akaba, would remain, and the Turkish force would be forced to rely increasingly on the valuable and remarkable Hejaz Railway which snaked across the desert for a thousand miles from Damascus to Medina.

It was, in the circumstances, an ambitious plan, and depended on both land and sea parties arriving at the same time. Lawrence and Newcombe accompanied Feisal on the long and difficult inland march across uninhabited and little-known territory. After three weeks, they arrived three days late; Wejh had been taken by the combined British-Arab force. In Cairo, Khartoum and Jiddah, this seemed to most people a victory for the professionals and a defeat for the amateurs. But after a short period of depression and tantrums, Lawrence got on with the task of improving Feisal's army. Gradually, the tribesmen were wedded into a co-operative body with common pride. In these endeavours, Lawrence made much use of the gold with which he had been liberally provided.

The Arab campaign, under the advice of the British officers, now centred on breaking the Turks' hold of the railway, and thus cutting off the Medina force from aid. An attack on Akaba was considered impracticable, two naval expeditions there having already failed to hold the town against Turkish counter-attacks. Lawrence and Feisal, however, believed that Akaba could be taken from the land, although many believed the march from Wejh to Akaba was impossible. With a tiny force Lawrence left Wejh on the 9th of May. After sundry adventures, he entered Akaba on the 6th of July, with a force he had recruited on the way, and took the surrender of the Turkish garrison. It was a remarkable feat of endurance even for the Arabs, accustomed to many days in the desert; it was also a sensible and practical military manœuvre. He had covered about eight hundred miles to attack a place which had been only two hundred and fifty miles away, and had thus caught the defenders, facing the wrong way, totally unprepared to ward off a determined attack. It had been a brilliant operation, both in courageous conception and in ruthless execution, and Lawrence had been totally responsible for both. Newcombe said Akaba was 'entirely conceived by Lawrence, who was its real leader and animating spirit.'[14] His success meant not only a superbly placed base for future operations—Feisal's force was now transported to Akaba by the Royal Navy—but also the end of a serious threat of German submarines operating from the Red Sea.

The capture of Akaba made Lawrence's name more widely known among those interested in the Arab campaign; it also subtly further removed him from his official function, which was a G.H.Q. liaison officer with the Arab army; he had become an active leader in the revolt.

Having helped to establish the defence of Akaba against counter-attack, Lawrence made the cross-desert ride from the newly won port to the eastern bank of the Suez Canal, a matter of a hundred miles, in forty-nine hours; his excitement and desire to break the news at G.H.Q., where he had always felt underrated, was understandable.

He received a splendid welcome, although in some quarters there was still a grudge against the amateur who insisted on dressing up like a 'damned Arab', even at G.H.Q.

By now Allenby had taken over command, and the first meeting between the two men took place. Lawrence had his prejudices about Allenby, as he had about all Generals; he had already seen the new C.-in-C. walking the platform at Ismailia station: 'a very large and superior General', and he had wondered 'if this heavy, rubicund man was like ordinary Generals, and if we should have trouble for six months teaching him.'[15]

Lawrence, announced by Andrew, strode into 'the Bull's' extremely orderly office in Arab dress, his sandals slip-slopping on the well-polished floor. It was, as Lawrence himself afterwards agreed, a somewhat comic affair. Allenby was extremely large and, to all appearances, more than conventional: Lawrence was rather small, and could hardly have appeared more unconventional. Allenby, who had been given a good report of Lawrence by Clayton, glared at him balefully. Lawrence did most of the talking, about his policy of spreading the revolt northwards to Damascus, and sapping the Turkish strength by making them guard every mile of the railway, instead of mounting conventional operations at Medina and elsewhere, and Allenby said practically nothing. After Lawrence had made a long string of requests, Allenby merely said: 'Well, I will do for you what I can.' Lawrence was overwhelmed. He gained a high opinion of Allenby at this time, but Allenby had mixed feelings about Lawrence. He was much impressed by the Akaba operation, and realized that Lawrence could be of use to him; for he had a greater opinion of the importance of the Arab revolt than had Murray. For the time being he decided to back him and give him what he asked; a common-sense decision, typical of Allenby. It is not often appreciated that most Generals of the period would not have countenanced Lawrence's conceit in appearing, a serving officer on duty, before their desks in Arab costume; neither would they have listened long to his grandiloquent promises; nor borne his new-found self-confidence, which at this time was a little overbearing. Whereas most other people at G.H.Q. believed that Lawrence was a show-off, Allenby found him fairly 'unassuming'. In subsequent meetings a gentle, but mutually enjoyable, mental battle developed between the two; Allenby, as was his wont, testing and probing Lawrence with unexpected questions, and Lawrence occasionally retaliating with some unexpected answers. Allenby, in the public's mind the most conventional and reactionary General in the British Army, agreed to promote Lawrence to a Major and recommended him for the Order of the Bath.

Personally, Allenby could not make up his mind about Lawrence's character, but such doubts did not greatly concern him. The only interest in Lawrence that Allenby ever permitted himself to have, was contained in the question: Will he help me to beat the Turks, or will he not? By promoting him and making him responsible in future to the C.-in-C. himself, he had, however, made Lawrence one of the most important men in the Arab campaign, and freed him from the control of his superior British officers in the Hejaz. All Lawrence's major views and requests were accepted by Allenby: Akaba was to become an important base, supplying the Arab advance northwards into Syria; arms and ammunition were to be poured into it; more gold was to be given him; Feisal's force was to advance on Allenby's right wing; and an airstrip was to be built at Akaba and biplane bombers supplied to break up Turkish concentrations. Most important of all, however, was the decision, prompted by Lawrence, to bring Feisal's force under the control of Allenby and G.H.Q. rather than of Hussein in Mecca and Wingate in Cairo. When agreeing to this apparently practical suggestion, Allenby did not appreciate the political complications it was certain to involve when the liberating Arab force entered the longed-for promised land of Syria. The two men did not discuss the Sykes-Picot agreement, but the knowledge of it continued to trouble Lawrence. His illegitimacy, and non-public-school background, no doubt made him feel something of an outsider, and he was more and more tempted to associate his loyalties with the Arab cause rather than the British whenever he believed them to conflict. In his actions, on the other hand, he dutifully carried out such orders as he received. Allenby

The Mayor of Jerusalem offering the surrender of the
Holy City to Sergeant Sedgewick (*left*) and Sergeant
Hurcombe, just before 9.0 a.m. on the 9th of December,
1917.

Allenby just prior to his official entry into Jerusalem; photograph taken by Lt.-Colonel Davis, the U.S. Military Attaché.

Allenby listening to his Proclamation, ending four centuries of Turkish control of Jerusalem, from the steps below the Tower of David, the 11th of December, 1917. Lawrence and Wavell are among the officers present.

Holding the line, before the final offensive of 1918.
A Lewis Gun section of the 2nd Leicestershire Regiment.

The bridge over the Yarmuk valley which Lawrence
never succeeded in destroying.

Lowell Thomas (back to the camera) meets Feisal.
Lawrence stands between them.

Part of Capt. Pisani's French Contingent, under
Allenby's command, on the march.

Allenby arrives in Damascus on the 3rd of October, 1918.

Arrival at Alexandria as Special High Commissioner, the 10th of November, 1919.

At the Residency, Cairo. The stork and his friend 'the Bull'.

later said that Lawrence accorded him 'the utmost loyalty'. Lawrence's position was an impossible one for a sensitive and thoughtful man, and in the end it nearly resulted in breakdown.

Allenby, on his part, had no doubt heard of the agreement in London before leaving for Cairo; or, if not, he would certainly have heard of it in due course in Egypt. It is equally certain that he would not have concerned himself with it. His job was to beat the Turks. In a letter home, he wrote:

Photographs of the Sherif of Mecca and the proclamation by him is one of the means we have of inducing the Arabs to desert the Turks. We drop these papers—and packets of cigarettes— over the Turkish lines, from aeroplanes. The proclamation is an appeal from the Sherif to the Arabs to leave the Turks and join in the war against them for the freedom and independence of Arabia. A good many come in as a result of our propaganda.[16]

Back in Akaba, 'El Aurens', now a great hero of the Arab force, helped in preparations for the coming offensive and raided the railway.* At the same time, other British officers were also raiding and sabotaging the railway. Lawrence's first description of this work, in public print, published a few days after the end of the war, was perhaps his best:

'We reached the line, and wandered up and down it, by day and night, keeping hidden, till we found a place that pleased us, and there we laid an electric mine. The line crossed a valley on a high bank 500 yards long, pierced by three small bridges about 200 yards from each other. We laid the mine over the southernmost, connected it electrically with the firing mechanism under the middle one, and arranged for two Lewis guns to take position under the northernmost

---

* His new standing in the force, directly under Allenby, placed him in an unusual position. Normally, he would have come under Colonel Joyce, senior British officer with Feisal. Joyce has written to the author: 'Always a lone bird, he enjoyed much freedom, which I, who had many responsibilities of my own, did not interfere with. When he left Army H.Q. and returned to the desert, he was just Lawrence of Arabia and his movements unpredictable.'

one. From this northern bridge ran up a long transverse gully westward. It was about two feet deep, and sprinkled with broom brushes, behind which the men (on foot) and the Lewis guns hid till wanted.

'On the first day no train came; on the second a water train and a line patrol together. On the third, about 8.0 a.m., a train of twelve wagons came down from Maan and passed slowly over the embankment. The Beduin were all lying behind their bushes, the Lewis gunners were under their arch, and the firing party under theirs, dancing a wild war dance as the train rumbled over their heads. One man was left right out in the open to give the signal to the firing party when to fire the mine; he looked a harmless enough Arab, and the officers in the train amused themselves by firing at him with their pistols. As soon, however, as the locomotive was over the mine he jumped up and waved his cloak, and instantly there was a shattering roar, a huge cloud of smoke and dust, the clanking of iron and the crushing of woodwork, and the whirring noise of the fragments of steel from the explosion sailing through the air.

'Till the smoke cleared there was dead silence, and then the two Lewis guns which had come out to right and left at the edges of their abutments raked the troops as they leaped out of the derailed trucks. The Beduins opened a rapid fire also, and in six minutes the affair was over, as the Arabs charged home on the wreck. We found that we had more prisoners than we wanted, some seventy tons of foodstuffs, and many little things like carpets and military stores. The Beduin plundered at lightning speed, while we signed the duplicate way-bills and returned one copy to the wounded guard, whom we meant to leave at the place. Then we fired the trucks and drove off our now overladen camels before the relief parties of Turks, who were hurrying up from north and south, could cut us off.'[17]

After some weeks Lawrence was summoned back to G.H.Q., for further discussions with Allenby about the part Feisal's force was to play in the Gaza–Beersheba offensive. This meeting between the two men did not go as well as their first. Allenby had given Lawrence everything he had asked for, but the Hejaz Railway was still in operation. He wanted to know why. Lawrence, who was, as before, in Arab dress for the interview, was startled and taken aback; he explained that he wanted to keep the railway open so that the troops at Medina could just survive. This caused the Turks considerable effort in resources, and was less cost to the Allies than if the Medina garrison were in prison camps in Egypt. It was part of Lawrence's basic military theory, and part of his quest to find out if 'a war might be won without fighting battles'.[17] This answer did not satisfy Allenby, and he now ordered that the railway should be closed, and that a general Arab uprising should take place behind the Turkish lines to coordinate with the Gaza-Beersheba offensive. Lawrence's appreciation was sounder than Allenby's. Liman von Sanders wrote in his memoirs that he frequently asked to abandon the railway and Medina, both of which were severe strategic handicaps, but the Turks refused to do so for reasons of prestige, religion and politics; a large force, which could ill be spared, was thus devoted to guarding the track and bridges from the Arab-British raids.[18] Moreover, Lawrence did not think a general uprising was practical; he also believed that it would not fit into his plans for Feisal to be the leader of an Arab state based on Damascus; from his point of view it was obviously best if all risings in the area were led by Feisal himself. These latter points, of course, Lawrence did not mention to Allenby. He suggested, instead, an attempt to destroy the rail link between the Palestine front and the north, by attacking it at its most vulnerable point—the bridge over the Yarmuk River. Allenby agreed. Lawrence decided to lead this spectacular raid himself, while Feisal and the Arab army in the north, supplied from Akaba, moved forward to protect Allenby's right flank and threaten the enemy's rear.

With supplies pouring into Akaba, the Arab army was becoming transformed. Now it was to take a responsible part in the campaign; as an integral part of the British force, rather than as a guerrilla operation. Lawrence wrote: 'We now formed part of the army of General Allenby. Akaba was on his extreme right, and the Arab army formed his right wing. Our plans were only part of his plans, instead of being joyous ventures of our own. The Arab army, however unorthodox its elements, tried its best to fulfil the wishes of the Commander-in-Chief and to contribute its uttermost to his plans. In return he gave it the materials, the advice, the advisers, and the help it needed, and enabled Feisal to transform what had been a mob of Beduin into a small but well-made force of all arms.'[17]

The raid on the bridge was an extremely daring and difficult operation, involving a march of four hundred miles, most of it behind the Turkish lines. If the bridge could be blown, it would have a great effect on the coming offensive; spanning a deep gorge, it could not be repaired in less than several weeks. Allenby was emphatic that it should be destroyed immediately after the offensive had opened.

The expedition consisted of Lawrence, an officer of the Royal Engineers named Wood, a machine-gun unit of the Indian Army, and some tribesmen. From the start everything went wrong. Wood had never undertaken such a mission before; he had arrived recently from France, where he had received a head wound. The Indians had difficulty with their camels; Lawrence began to suspect that one of the Arabs in the party was a traitor. Then, when they had been on the trek for over a week, the caravan of raiders, bowed on their stalking camels, snaking forward under the hot sun, heard faintly but clearly from the far distance the 'quiet, steady thudding of the heavy guns preparing assault in Palestine'. Lawrence made excitedly back down the column, urging everyone on for one last effort. It was essential to reach the Yarmuk River bridge in time. After three years, the smouldering Palestine campaign had at last reached its climax.

*　　*　　*

During the final preparations for the battle, and throughout its full course, Allenby had been going about his work with deadened heart. Fate had so arranged affairs that, at the brink of his greatest moment—the entry into Jerusalem—he should suffer the greatest, indeed the only, personal tragedy in his life.

Michael, the only child, upon whom he had lavished affection and the highest hopes, was killed in action near Nieuport on the 29th of July. His commanding officer wrote to Lady Allenby: 'I am terribly grieved to have to tell you that Michael died of wounds this afternoon. He was hit by a stray shell, when coming back to the battery from a detached gun, which we have got half a mile away. This was about 11.0 a.m., and a piece went through his shell helmet. That was his only wound, and he never regained consciousness. I cannot tell you how much I sympathize with you. He was such a charming boy, so full of life and spirits, beloved by officers and men, a splendid soldier and the bravest of the brave. . . . He had just been recommended for promotion to Captain. I have never had a subaltern whom I have grieved so much to lose.'[19] The splinter had gone completely through the steel helmet, but Michael Allenby had lived for five hours before dying. He was buried with many others at Coxyde, close to the Belgian coast, just one among most of the rest of his generation who died on the inconceivably murderous Western Front. All the men from his section were present, and ten officers from Brigade G.H.Q. dutifully attended the military funeral of the General's son. The Corps Commander could not go himself, but sent his A.D.C.

Like so many, practically all Michael's adult life had been crowded into one year; Royal Military College, commissioned in the Royal Horse Artillery, awarded the Military Cross, killed. But in that short time he had made a mark on those who knew him as being an exceptional and interesting young man. A few days later his C.O. wrote an appreciation of Michael to Douglas Haig: 'He was the finest practical gunner of his rank that I have ever seen in France. The men all loved him and would do anything for him. In the mess he amused us greatly by his Socialistic views and his defence of Conscientious Objectors. He read the *Labour Leader*, *The Nation* and the *Manchester Guardian*, but although I really think he was serious, we never took him seriously. . . .'[20]

Haig immediately sent this to Allenby, and a letter of condolence in his own hand: 'My dear Allenby: One line to tell you how terribly sorry I was to hear of your boy's death, and to say how truly I sympathize with you in your great loss. His death is also a very great loss to the Army: he was bound to have gone a long way had he lived, for he had all the qualities of a first-rate commander of troops. I enclose a few notes on the poor boy which I got from his Battery Commander. As they were given to me quite independently, you may certainly conclude that they represent the truth. I heartily congratulate you on having had such a splendid son. With heartfelt sympathy and all good wishes to you in your difficult task. Believe me, Yours very sincerely, D. Haig.'[21]

This generous letter ended the bad feeling that had existed between Allenby and Haig at the time of the Somme and Arras battles. Allenby immediately sent a copy of it to his wife:

I enclose a copy of a letter I had from Douglas Haig. I keep the original till I can give it to you safely. I am proud of his congratulations, and so will you be. . . . Everyone who has known you or me, or our glorious boy, writes; and my experience is just yours—all their sympathy is real.* . . . You are the mother of a hero. Your son could have been no other. One letter he wrote to you is a mirror in which the whole character is shown. Devotion to his work. Humour, dry but never cynical. Joy in all aspects of life. Wide interests in literature, sport, politics. All unaffected and honest.[22]

A brother officer, who was himself killed shortly afterwards, wrote home to his wife about Michael's death, and she thoughtfully sent the letter on to Lady Allenby. 'It has upset the Battery dreadfully, for everybody loved him very dearly. He was always so cheerful and hard-working and plucky,

* Allenby had letters from Lord French, Lord Derby, the Army Council, and the Sherif of Mecca.

afraid of nothing whatever, and always keen to have the dangerous jobs. Such a child, too—he was barely 20, and out here before he was 20.'[23]

Allenby's letters at this time of extreme stress are of interest, as they reveal better than any others the great depths of character, strength of will and noble ideals which he possessed in full measure:

Michael was always the same; keen on his work, thoughtful beyond his years, but cheerful and brave. I have never known a boy of his age who had so mastered his self. His self-control was complete; and though his quick perception was always awake to the dangers which he faced daily, his well-balanced mind never dwelt on them. This, and his real interest in his work, made his life a happy one, even in the days of terrible stress which he has had to face for so many months. Whenever he came to stay with me, he was always the same; a friend on real terms; and yet, unaffectedly, he always kissed me when we met and parted—as he did when a child.

Michael achieved, early, what every great man in the world's history has made it his life's ambition to attain—to die honoured, loved and successful, in full vigour of body and mind.[24]

At G.H.Q. Allenby gave little indication of the suffering he had been undergoing, although one who knew him well described him as 'a broken man'. Shortly after hearing the news, alone with Wavell, he repeated Rupert Brooke's poem, 'The Dead', from memory. Lady Allenby wrote to her mother-in-law: 'I had a letter from Lord Dalmeny this morning, written after Edmund had the news of Michael's death. He said Edmund was wonderful, and did his work as usual. I also saw a Colonel Wavell* yesterday who had just returned from Cairo. He had been with Edmund inspecting his Front, and he said Edmund walked him off his legs and never turned a hair. This is a man, I should say, of 39 or so.'[25]

Allenby was drawn to his mother more than he had been

---

* This is the first mention of Wavell in the Allenbys' correspondence. Allenby first mentions him in a letter on the 27th of August, 1917.

for some years; a grandmother many times over, she took the closest interest in all the descendants of herself and Hynman Allenby, was still active, and still dominated the family. He had been writing frequently to her about Michael's death, and it is fitting to close this section with a short extract from a letter to her that is the best expressed that Allenby, a practised and careful letter-writer, ever wrote. The staff officers, impressed with the apparent toughness with which 'the Bull' had taken his blow, would naturally have known nothing of the tear-smudged letter that is today the most eloquent relic of a love between a father and a son.

War takes the best. He was all that one could desire as a son; and I am proud to have been his father. He never gave Mabel or me one moment of trouble or anxiety. We shall remember him only with love, pride and gratitude. There is not a day of his life I could wish to be otherwise than as he lived it. In simplicity, gentleness, cheerfulness and honour, he walked; from his birth until his death. I rejoice in every remembrance of him.[26]

* * *

Allenby now delved deep into his work and concentrated every moment of his day on the business at hand. The wound was thrust down, deep into his soul. He seldom discussed Michael from this time, but as a man who loved children and youth, and who had for years considered himself primarily a family man, despite the separations demanded by his career, he was never able to overcome his great disappointment, although he rode the actual grief and strain with courage.

The battle opened, in the last week of October, with an artillery barrage on Gaza, almost comparable to those of the Western Front, which was complemented by a naval bombardment from British and French warships. The Gaza–Beersheba line had been fortified, under German guidance, with the latest techniques; wire entanglements of great depth, and an intricate system of trenches, linked with reserve systems by communicating trenches.

The offensive consisted of a number of blows alternating at each end of the line. They kept the defenders in a constant state of doubt as to Allenby's intentions, and prevented them from making adequate arrangements for defence. The effect was like that of a system of 'combination punches' as used by a clever, quick-witted boxer.

The heavy bombardment on Gaza fixed the enemy's attention on his right. Von Kressenstein was now expecting a landing behind Gaza; with British command of the coastal waters, it was an obvious move. The 'haversack ruse' had convinced him that the attack would be directed on Gaza, and so, when the offensive on Beersheba was launched four days later, he was not unduly perturbed, believing this to be the British feint. Orders had been issued to the Turkish divisions, and they were fully prepared for an offensive, but not for a bewildering succession of blows. 'Everything points to the enemy's intending to make a real offensive. The enemy's commander, General Allenby, was on the Western Front this year. It is understood that he is wont to attack after a violent but short artillery bombardment. . . . [we are] in a position morally and materially to defeat the enemy. The victory is with God.'27

Meanwhile, Chetwode's XX Corps had marched to its jumping-off point after one of the biggest and certainly the best-conducted night marches of the war; it had 'frightened' Chetwode himself. Tents and dummies had been left at the deserted camps near Gaza to deceive the enemy further. As usual with an Allenby attack, every conceivable hitch had been considered before, staff work had been imaginative and meticulous, and all went as clockwork.

As the *muezzin* sounded the new day from the minarets of Beersheba, the infantry stormed the defences to the town. While the hopelessly outnumbered garrison were thus desperately attempting to hold the line, and while all their attentions were fixed to the front, the Desert Mounted Corps, who had ridden through the night, appeared on their left flank in striking distance of the town and the all-important wells. The 4th Brigade Australian Light Horse charged, in a cloud of dust, full tilt for Beersheba. With tremendous momentum, they swept over the astonished and terrified defenders, shooting and stabbing, pierced two defence systems, and forced their way through the disorganized Turkish infantry into the streets of Beersheba. The wells were taken intact, just as they were being prepared for demolition.

Two days later an attack on Gaza, where the enemy no longer knew whether to expect an attack or not, was successful. After a brief burst of fighting, the town was abandoned and was soon in British hands, and von Kressenstein, by now thoroughly alarmed, wondered from where the next blow would come: right or left?

Of the Gaza attack, Meinertzhagen wrote in his diary: 'The enemy's resistance was feeble and he was taken completely by surprise. A captured document shows that the enemy believed our camouflage, and the dummy notebook was a great success, for the enemy had all his reserves in the wrong place. . . . So far so good, and we enter on this the Seventh Crusade, once and for all to evict the Turk from the sacred places of Christianity.'[28]

Soon von Kressenstein's uncertainty was put to unhappy rest; the XX Corps followed up the snatching of Beersheba with a tremendous push beyond the town. The 10th, 60th and 74th Divisions rolled back the Turkish front, and the entire left wing of the enemy line was in rapid retreat. Meanwhile a small force of seventy men on camels, under the command of Newcombe, had delved far into the desert east of Beersheba, and had appeared behind the enemy line on the Jerusalem–Beersheba road. They cut all communications, set up a road block, and prevented the movement of reinforcements. They were surrounded, and captured after their ammunition ran out. This raiding party had caused much confusion, as for a time it was thought to be part of a large flanking movement. Newcombe, a most resourceful and courageous officer, had been one of Lawrence's companions on the survey of the Sinai Desert before the war. The raid had been his own suggestion, had been organized by himself, and played a large part in the success of Allenby's operations beyond Beersheba.* In the *Seven Pillars of Wisdom*, Lawrence himself was quick to admit that others 'could tell a like tale', and this was certainly true of Newcombe, who later escaped as a prisoner-of-war from Turkey and married the girl who helped him escape. As Lowell Thomas said, 'the Newcombe story has just about everything.' Indeed, Lowell Thomas tried, unsuccessfully, to get Newcombe to let him write his story. After his escape, Newcombe continued in clandestine operations against the Turk.[29]

Allenby, outwardly austere and calm, but still desolated by the death of his son, had a hard time during the early part of the battle. His experience at Arras, where a brilliant and exciting beginning had only led to frustration and disappointment, was still fresh in his mind. He conducted the timing of his blows with care, and did not agree readily when the XX Corps asked for two days' grace in order to restore their creaking supply line. He now unleashed the next blow: a follow-up at Gaza, and soon Bulfin's XXI Corps were proceeding up the coast road into Palestine.

By now the Yarmuk River bridge should have been blown by Lawrence's party, thus throwing the whole Turkish military system in Palestine into confusion. Allenby waited to hear news of its destruction. But he waited in vain.

Lawrence had found that keeping his small force together had been a desperate struggle; the whole affair had become a somewhat humiliating nightmare. After courting disaster on a number of occasions, but blessed by luck whenever they needed it most, the caravan reached the bridge on time. While Lawrence and the Arabs placed the explosives under the bridge, Wood and the Indian machine-gunners covered them from the gorge. It was a moonless night, and the rushing torrent drowned their noise as the demolition party slid

---

* Lawrence told Liddell Hart that Allenby had asked him to conduct this operation, but he had turned it down because it went against his wish to keep a clear space between Arab and British forces. Lawrence spoke highly of Newcombe's performance.

and slithered down the rocks, while a sentry paced up and down above; but one of the Arabs dropped his rifle, thus setting off the alarm, and after some bursts of fire from the covering party and the guard, Lawrence and his men hastened away with the explosives undetonated.

After blowing up a train farther down the line, Lawrence went into hiding in one of his beloved ruined Crusader castles with his friend Emir Ali.

Allenby, to whom all this was unknown, soon realized that silence from the desert meant the plan had failed. Nevertheless, both his advances were going well, and he was now able to write home with some satisfaction:

The Turks are having an awful hammering. A few pockets of Turks, in isolated trench systems, are holding out east of Gaza. They will be starved out, in time, so I am only shelling them, and not wasting men in attacking them. Cavalry are pushing north of Gaza, in pursuit, and I am moving infantry in support of them. Here and there rearguards are making a stand and showing fight, but I think that Kress von Kressenstein's army has lost its fighting value—for some time at any rate. I have just written a narrative for the King—my first letter to him since I came out.[30]

My pursuing troops are ten miles beyond Gaza and travelling fast. A lot of Turks are cut off just N.-E. of Gaza. I don't know if they will be caught; but there is no time to waste in catching them. My army is all over the place now, on a front of 35 miles. I am at the centre of telegraph and telephone lines. . . . all my staff wear happy expressions of countenance. Would you go to Norton, the chemist, and get me some bicarbonate of soda. Also I want a roll of gummed paper ribbon; for sticking torn maps together.*[31]

I went to Gaza this afternoon. There is an old and a new town, but I had not time to explore either. . . . I have two Press representatives at my Headquarters; Reuter's man and another from

* Lady Allenby, as a result of representations to Robertson by Wavell, had been allowed to go to Cairo.

the London Press. I let them have all the information that I can without giving away secrets.[32]

The presence of these reporters ensured that news of the breaking of the Gaza–Beersheba line, which had appeared invulnerable for so long, was soon being flashed around the civilized world. Was it possible, the newspapers asked, that Allenby would succeed where so many had failed for so long, and bring Christian dominion to Jerusalem? Allenby now directed himself to answering the question. Throughout the attack he had made daily consultations of the experiences of the Crusaders in the geographic history given him by Lloyd George, and of the military passages of the Old Testament.

He insisted on the pursuit being followed up with the utmost ruthlessness on the enemy, and with no excuses from his own troops. Some of the staff officers and commanders who had helped present Allenby with the masterly plan for assault now found themselves in a situation they had not foreseen. On more than one occasion Allenby was approached personally and asked to rest troops; each time he declined to do so. Although the supply lines were stretched to their limits, and in some cases horses were being watered only once in seventy-two hours, he ordered the advance to continue. He was adamant the enemy must not be allowed time to prepare a line of defence; that, in the end, would cause more hardship. During the pursuit, the Dorsetshire Yeomanry covered sixty miles in fifty-four hours without water for their horses; the record for the advance was held by the Lincolnshire Yeomanry, the horses of which lasted eighty-four hours without being watered. Not surprisingly, the animal casualties were high.

Falkenhayn now endeavoured to control the situation himself from Jerusalem. Turkish defence stiffened, and the advance was slowed. Despite a charge by the Worcestershire and Warwickshire Yeomanry at Huj, the Mounted Corps were unable to make a complete breakthrough. Five days later there was another cavalry charge, this time by countrymen from Buckinghamshire and Dorset; leading the Royal Bucks Hussars, Major E. de Rothschild was killed,* as was his cousin Neil Primrose, younger son of Lord Rosebery and Dalmeny's brother. Individual Turkish units fought with unexpected courage and even fanaticism. Falkenhayn and the German Staff, misjudging the overall state of their forces, prepared and ordered a counter-attack. The orders for this were intercepted by British Intelligence. Meinertzhagen wrote in his diary: 'Last night we got Falkenhayn's order for a counter-attack. It was sent out in cipher by wireless from Jerusalem. Von Kress received it, but had to have it repeated as he said it was mutilated. We deciphered the first message, and by this means our troops got the enemy's orders and were able to act on them before the enemy commander himself knew what was expected of him.'[33] Wavell records that on hearing of the counter-attack Allenby did little more than cast a contemptuous glance, over his shoulder at the G.H.Q. map, judged the situation and took no further interest in it. The Turkish attack, made near the traditional place where the Crusaders were held up in their approach on Jerusalem, was duly launched. At first it seemed to be more dangerous than G.H.Q. had expected, but it was held—the Australian cavalry again playing a notable part—and soon petered out.

Allenby's lines of communication, with his two great thrusts deep into Palestine, were now stretched to the limit; many of his commanders believed beyond it. On the 11th of November a telegram arrived from the War Office urging him to exercise caution before advancing farther. Ignoring all pleas, Allenby asked his dusty, ill-fed, thirsty and exhausted army, which had just made an advance of about forty miles, to launch an attack immediately on Jerusalem's defences and take the Holy City itself. As it turned out, his decision was the right one, but it took courage and self-confidence out of the ordinary to make it. If the attempt to take

* His brother, Major James de Rothschild, was in charge of enlistment of Jewish volunteers in Egypt and Palestine.

the city had been repulsed, the weary British troops might well have been forced back to their starting point, and Allenby, no doubt, would have found himself back in London with some difficult explaining to be done.

One who had witnessed the advance wrote: 'Many facts were overlooked by certain writers who emphasized the enormous numerical superiority of the British troops. Allenby made the supreme moves for the capture of Jerusalem in a continuous offensive with two divisions suffering like the Turks from casualties, fatigue and sickness, and mounted forces from which on successive days brigades had to be retired because of the thirst and exhaustion of the horses, for water remained an intolerable problem. He successively defeated and separated the combined armies, which comprised nine infantry and one cavalry divisions, based on excellent defensive positions adjoining the railroad, and retiring on well-organized communications, by forces which had raced some sixty miles from their base. Each move in the game was strategically masterful, daring in conception, and tactically perfect.'[34]

On the 16th of November, Jaffa, the seaport of Jerusalem, was taken by advance troops of the British left-wing thrust up the plains; with its capture, the advance on the British left came to a halt on the banks of the River Auja. Leaving one mounted division and one infantry division on that flank, Allenby assembled the remainder of his force in the foothills of Judea, preparatory to the push on Jerusalem. The Judean hills had always, from time immemorial, proved an almost impregnable defensive position for the defenders of Jerusalem. To make matters worse, the weather, as expected, had finally broken; mists and downpours made the task of advance and supply increasingly difficult. Camels, on which the force was reliant for supplies, found the slippery pathways and rocky hillsides difficult to negotiate. The worst handicap of all was that Allenby was determined to avoid fighting in the vicinity of Jerusalem itself; a difficult encircling movement was, therefore, planned, to force the evacuation of the city. Allenby, as usual, passed the plan, which was a good one on paper but quite unsuited to the conditions. The infantry struggled on across the hills, in cold and worsening weather, and meeting fierce and determined opposition. To men who had only a few days before been fighting in the parched heat of the plains, the conditions were particularly sapping of strength, and miserable. At length the commanding height of Nebi Samwil, overlooking the city, was reached; bitter and costly fighting took place as Turkish counter-attacks attempted to retake the position from the 75th Division, consisting of men from the English Western counties and Indians. Fighting took place all around, and in, the buildings, which were a place of pilgrimage to Moslems, Christians and Jews; this was perhaps the only sacred place in the Holy Land which was badly damaged by fighting throughout the campaign. According to von Papen, it was evacuated by Falkenhayn in order to preserve it from further damage. It was the spot on which Richard Cœur de Lion was said to have refused to look upon Jerusalem, the city he could not take.

The advance became bogged down in heavy fighting. Meanwhile, the mounted troops had been progressing along a goat track, and had been forced to retire after heavy counter-attack. Up till now the attack had been pressed by Bulfin's XXI Corps, which were now relieved by Chetwode's better-staffed XX Corps; this change-over was itself a most hazardous move. Falkenhayn wisely chose the moment for his most powerful counter-attack to date, but once again the operation became dissipated somewhere between German Staff and Turkish infantry. Allenby wrote:

It must be very cold and wet where my advanced troops are fighting; up in the mountains, N.W. and N. of Jerusalem. They find the country very difficult; but they are making progress, though news comes in very slowly. Tomorrow I shift my head-quarters forward, some 30 miles, and I shall live in a tent.[35]

At Ludd [Lydda] I went into the Greek Church of St. George. He was born there. The Church is partly old-5th century, partly new; with florid ornamentation within. In a vault—with old painting on the walls—is a sarcophagus or tomb. But St. George is not inside it. They preserve one or two of his bones in a casket of silver. The bones are old and polished, and may be his. I hear that my old opponent, Kress von Kressenstein, has been removed from the command of the 8th Army, which has been given to a Turk. I fancy that there is little love lost now between Turk and Boche. Will you send me two more bottles of bicarbonate of soda?[36]

I hope my roads will dry today; as things are in an awful state, and it is difficult to get food and ammunition up to my men in the mountains. All is going well there, but the difficulties of the ground and the weather make our movements slow. Consequently, we can't pursue with full effect; and events do not march with the rapidity which my impatience would desire.[37]

Wingate, now High Commissioner in Cairo, and friendly with Allenby, visited G.H.Q. and wrote back an enthusiastic letter to Lady Allenby: 'I cannot tell you how intensely interested I have been in seeing the magnificent results of [Allenby's] splendidly successful campaign. I can only express unbounded admiration of Sir Edmund and his work—when one sees the immensely strong positions of the enemy, the country, and the difficulties which have been so successfully overcome by him and his army. I am confident this campaign will go down to history as one of the finest military achievements on record.'[38]

On taking over the front, Chetwode decided on a less ambitious plan than that which had met with so much difficulty hitherto. There was only one good road to Jerusalem and, although it was the obvious route, Chetwode decided to straddle his attack across it so that artillery support, which so far had been lacking, could be provided. This attack met with success, and the 60th (London) Division pushed on down the road and broke the Turkish defences west of the city at dawn on the 8th of December. Rain and mist continued throughout the day, and the division hovered outside the city uncertain as to the defensive strength of the Turks. There was no question of fighting in the city itself, but

Chetwode's plan, unlike Bulfin's, had not demanded a Turkish evacuation. No one was quite certain what to do next.

At advance G.H.Q. Allenby paced in his tent, during a heavy rain-storm, wondering what was happening at the front, and waiting for news. He was thus not particularly interested to hear from Major T. E. Lawrence of the failure on the Yarmuk River bridge. Lawrence had been flown up from Akaba with orders to report, but in the prevailing atmosphere talk of past failures was not of great interest. Lawrence merely told the C.-in-C. that he had failed to blow the bridge and, much to his relief, Allenby asked for no details. While Lawrence was still in the tent, a staff officer entered to inform Allenby that Jerusalem had been evacuated. Allenby told Lawrence, who might well have expected recrimination or a posting back to his former humdrum duties, to stay with G.H.Q. Clayton generously suggested that Lawrence should be among those present at the official taking of the city—he had not forgotten the taking of Akaba—and Allenby assented.

Jerusalem had been evacuated by the Turks, civilians and military alike some hours before. Falkenhayn had previously departed for Aleppo. The last wireless message to Damascus had been sent: 'The enemy is in front of us, only half an hour from here. . . . Adieu from Jerusalem.' The Turkish Governor had then personally smashed the telegraph equipment with a hammer. He was the last civilian to leave the city, doing so in a cart which he commandeered from an American resident. With the gunfire dying away, the caves, cellars and houses of the city began to discharge a throng of excited townsfolk, who had been sheltering in considerable alarm.

The last fighting took place on the Mount of Olives, where there was a sharp rearguard action. Up the Jaffa road, the 60th Division waited. The Mayor came out with a white flag, making the most of the situation, with the keys of the city and a letter of surrender, which he proposed formally handing over to the British.

The first British soldiers he met were Sergeants Hurcombe and Sedgewick, of the 2/29th London Regiment. They declined to accept the keys of Jerusalem and the letter of surrender. A few minutes later the Mayor came upon two British officers of the Royal Artillery: Major F. R. Barry and Major W. Beck. After a short parley, they all went off and met Lt.-Colonel H. Bailey and Major M. D. H. Cooke. The former refused to accept the surrender of the Holy City. By this time the Mayor, it seems, was in a state of some exasperation. Brig.-General C. F. Watson, commanding the 180th Brigade, then appeared, and he succeeded in calming the Mayor; he also, however, declined to accept the surrender. With due modesty and sense of history, no one felt that he was quite the man for such an historic event. The message of surrender was sent to Maj.-General J. S. M. Shea, commanding the 60th Division. Maj.-General Shea thereupon consulted Lt.-General Sir Philip Chetwode. Chetwode told Shea to accept the surrender forthwith, and this he did, in the name of Allenby, at 11.0 a.m. on the 9th of December, 1917. It was forty days since the opening of the offensive at Beersheba, and four centuries and one year since Turkish rule of the city had begun. General Watson, arriving at the Jaffa gate, was the first British soldier to enter, his brigade having been appointed to take over the city and maintain order.

Two days later, in a simple but impressive ceremony, Allenby made his official entry into Jerusalem. French and Italian representatives walked on either side of him. They were followed by Chetwode and twenty officers. Next to Colonel Wavell, just behind Allenby, was Major Lawrence; he wore an assorted uniform, which had been collected together for him by Allenby's staff out of their spare clothing: the red tabs were those of Dalmeny. Wavell and Lawrence thus began a friendship which was to last till Lawrence's death.

A Guard of Honour, picked from all the countries represented in the campaign, wos drawn up at the gate. Allenby walked under the gate, betraying no sign of emotion whatever; aloof, apparently unmoved, and without dawdling.

Thus did the Christian nations return to Jerusalem after 730 years. It was noted that when the Kaiser had visited the city, he had entered the place on horseback. A semi-official account of the Allied entry recorded: 'Many wept for joy, and priests were seen to embrace one another, but there were no theatricalities. . . . The General entered the city on foot, and left it on foot, and throughout the ceremony no Allied flag was flown.'[39]

Far away in London, Bonar Law, Chancellor of the Exchequer, made a formal announcement to the House of Commons, in which he stated: 'The capture of Jerusalem has been in some degree delayed in consequence of the great care which has been taken to avoid damage to sacred places in and around the city.' The great bell of Westminster Cathedral rang for the first time for three years. The bells of every church in Rome rang for an hour. In Paris there was a special service in Notre Dame. Wireless messages flashed round the world. Every newspaper in the English language was full of the capture of Jerusalem. It was, after years of wretchedness and misery, an event which captured and held the imagination of the world. Allenby's name was on everyone's lips, as no other General's had been during the war. Among the congratulations which descended in an avalanche on him was a cable, followed by a letter, from French, both couched in extraordinarily generous terms: 'I regard the capture of Jerusalem and Bethlehem as the finest feat in the war. . . . Your success is so gratifying to me personally because I can never forget the deep debt of gratitude I owe you for all the splendid, loyal help and support you gave me in France.'[40] A telegram from the War Cabinet, obviously inspired by Lloyd George's enthusiasm and tempered by Robertson's phlegm, read: 'War Cabinet wishes to congratulate you on the capture of Jerusalem, which is an event of historic and world-wide significance and has given the greatest pleasure to the British and other Allied peoples. Your victorious campaign for the conquest of Palestine in the face of very great transport and other difficulties constitutes a notable military performance, and the War Cabinet views your continued progress and success with the greatest interest and confidence.'[41] The reference to the transport difficulties, and rather obvious lack of reference to the Turkish opposition, would not have been lost on Allenby. In fact, the approximate official strengths during the fighting for Jerusalem were: British 18,000 infantry, 8,000 cavalry and 172 guns; Turkish 15,000 infantry, 800 cavalry and 120 guns.[42]

In Palestine itself, Allenby was hailed by a considerable section of the population as a prophet, *Nebi*, who by tradition was to enter Jerusalem on foot and make it a city of great prosperity and power. They called from the streets: '*Allah Nebi*'.

Meinertzhagen, who was watching all these events closely, wrote in his diary: 'It would be a short but awkward step in this superstitious country to translate Allenby into a Messiah, but he is much too worldly, genuine and free of all such pretensions to willingly assume such a cloak.'[43]

The subject of all this attention wrote to his wife:

Today I entered Jerusalem, on foot, with the French and Italian commanders—Lt.-Colonel Piépape and Major Apostino— of the detachments in my Army; and the Attachés, and a few Staff Officers. We entered at the Jaffa Gate; and, from the steps of the Citadel, hard by, issued a proclamation in many languages to the assembled multitude. Great enthusiasm—real or feigned— was shown. Then I received the notables and heads of all the Churches, of which there are many, including Abyssinian. After this, we reformed our procession and returned to our horses, which we had left outside the walls.[44]

Allenby's proclamation was as follows:

Lest any of you be alarmed by reason of your experience at the hands of the enemy who has retired, I hereby inform you that it is my desire that every person should pursue his lawful business without fear of interruption. Furthermore, since your city is regarded with affection by the adherents of three of the great religions of mankind, and its soil has been consecrated by the prayers of pilgrimages of multitudes of devout people of these three religions for many centuries, therefore I make it known to you that every sacred building, monument, holy spot, shrine, traditional site, endowment, pious bequest or customary place of prayer of whatsoever form of the three religions will be maintained and protected according to the existing customs and beliefs of those to whose faiths they are sacred.

While inside the city, Allenby had received a message from George V. 'I sent a suitable reply from the Holy City.' Back at Shea's H.Q., the party were given the best lunch that could be prepared, it being felt that something special was in order for a special occasion: salad, chicken mayonnaise, and *foie gras* sandwiches, as Lawrence recorded. At this lunch the French Attaché, Picot, who already had caused Lawrence trouble in the Hejaz, suggested that he would set up a civil government in the town the following day. There was a long silence. Lawrence wrote: ' . . . we turned to Allenby and gaped. Even he seemed for the moment at a loss. We began to fear that the idol might betray a frailty. But his face grew red: he swallowed, his chin coming forward (in the way we loved), whilst he said, grimly: "In the military zone the only authority is that of the Commander-in-Chief. Myself." '45

The holy places of the Jerusalem area were quickly occupied by British troops. Bethlehem had already been taken, although its capture had presented problems, as there was no question of artillery fire being used in the area. Columns of tired, battle-worn marching troops went through the winding valleys of Jerusalem to take up positions at the re-aligned front some ten miles beyond; counter-attacks to take the city, ordered by Falkenhayn, having been thrust aside. Military notices appeared. Red-tabbed staff officers went to and fro. And, the most familiar sight of all, the Commander-in-Chief motored here and there, sitting bolt upright in the back of his open car, the flag on the bonnet streaming in the breeze. Everyone felt excited about the land they had come to. The *Official History* says: 'The testimony of officers of all grades of seniority leaves no doubt that the spiritual and historical traditions of the country in which they had fought had an influence upon the troops.'

After the crossing of the Auja River was achieved, the entire front subsided into inaction in heavy downpours of rain. All advance was halted by a violent rainstorm on Christmas Day. Allenby wrote to his wife:

Today we occupied Bethany. It was a brilliant day; hoar frost here, in the early morning, and then iced sunshine; with no wind. We could see, from the top of the house where I met Chetwode, the mountains of Moab, deep blue and huge.

The rocky and mountainous country they fought over is indescribable. Guns could give little support; and the Turks were driven out [of the district] by rifle- and machine-gun fire, followed by the bayonet.[46]

Bols and I went to Bethlehem. There we met the dignitaries of the Church of the Nativity. We went quite quietly; but, directly I was recognized, they roused the town. The Church bells rang, and all the populace turned out. In the Church, they showed us the Grotto of the Manger, and the place where the Magi worshipped. When we came out, speeches were made. All the inhabitants were in the streets, and women seized my hand and kissed it. It was interesting. . . . When we came out of the Grotto, into the Church, the organ played 'God Save the King', and did it very well. . . . I walked through Jerusalem later. I don't allow people in the old town, yet; and I wanted to see if all was in order. Everything was quiet. I'll tell you all about it some day.[47]

I am glad you feel the fascination of the Nile and the desert at sunset. It appeals to me, very strongly. I always feel carried far beyond this world to something or some place I can't understand.[48]

I picked some bright scarlet anemones today. I enclose [?], of which a few are already in flower; and clematis, which is flowering freely. It is a smaller plant than the European, and clings to the low bushes. . . .[49]

The capture of Jerusalem was immediately followed by a personal occasion for Allenby, which, despite the tremendous notoriety he had now achieved, went unnoticed in the Press and elsewhere:

Twenty-one years ago we were married. Since then, I have had twenty-one years of perfect happiness. That happiness has been marred by one great sorrow; but the remembrance of Michael will always be with us, and will be nothing but a joy. The sorrow not to have known him would be far greater than the grief of losing him for a while. For all this happiness, I thank you.[50]

CHAPTER 8

War: Armageddon

Allenby was the image we worshipped.
LAWRENCE

Allenby now faced the problems of continuing the campaign, taking all of Palestine, and advancing into Syria. His last instructions from Robertson had been to establish a line from Jaffa to Jerusalem, and this he had now done; although he had no doubt that he would be requested to move on in due course, he was startled to get a fairly peremptory command from the War Cabinet to do so forthwith. Lloyd George was enjoying the taste of victory in the Middle East (as much over the 'Westerners' as the Turks, one feels), and he wanted more. Allenby's armies were quite unable to do so, and Allenby made this clear; the Prime Minister did not appreciate the dangers in attacking immediately, in the rains, before the elongated lines of communications had been reorganized. He always felt that if Allenby had pushed on from Jerusalem immediately, Turkey would have been knocked out of the war early in 1918, within 'two or three weeks'. The controversy has seemed somewhat ironic to those who served under Allenby in Palestine, and who had every reason to know that Allenby in pursuit of an enemy was no sluggard. Further advance was not possible with the resources at Allenby's disposal. Allenby told Robertson that with his existing force he could clear Palestine by the following summer, but if an advance to Aleppo was required, he might need sixteen infantry divisions. There was only one place such reinforcements could come from, and Robertson considered Allenby's suggestion outrageous. Wavell was despatched to London to soothe frayed tempers and patiently explain Allenby's needs.

The Supreme War Council at Versailles, which had recently been constituted in a belated attempt to bring about some co-operation between the Allies and to provide unified direction of the war, was about to discuss the greatest and most open tussle between 'Easterners' and 'Westerners' of the war. Wavell, who was now coming to be trusted by both sides as being one of them, was promptly sent off to Versailles. One of the leading figures at the Council was General Sir Henry Wilson, who had a great desire to be different from the other British Generals without being a confirmed 'Westerner' or 'Easterner'. He believed that Western Front strategy since 1916 had been 'puerile, useless and costly'. Wilson, although an Ulsterman, was associated with the anti-Gough faction, did not get on with Haig, and was a former protégé of French; he had, therefore, some common ground with Allenby, and the two men had always had a good understanding, despite the fact that Wilson had served under Allenby on the Western Front and Allenby had nearly asked G.H.Q. to send him home, so unsatisfactory had he found him. Although he went against the declared opinion of G.H.Q., Wilson recommended that Allenby should have all the support he needed to follow up his offensive, subject to the security of the Western Front. He was not supported in this by Allenby's emissary Wavell, but at a historic victory for the 'Easterners' the Supreme War Council adopted Wilson's suggestion, in principle, on the 18th of January, 1918. But Robertson remained unmoved. He pointed out that the Council had made the proviso that the security of the Western Front took priority over all else and, with some justification, that Russia was virtually out of the war, and that much of the object of the Eastern theatre was therefore removed. Nevertheless, a mission was sent out under Smuts, who had not had a great deal to do since arriving from East

Africa, to examine the situation, and to report back to the War Office how the Council's directive could best be carried out.

This was a rather galling experience for Allenby. Smuts had a great reputation as a General, but less practice; he had turned down the command of the Palestine theatre, and was now coming out as an expert. The whole affair, however, went off cordially, and Allenby accepted the situation without rancour and with goodwill, which is more than can be said for some of his staff.

Within a month, Smuts visited the Palestine front and cabled home his assessment; this agreed with practically everything he had been told by Allenby. Its major point was that, with the resources available, it would be impossible to continue the offensives in both Palestine and Mesopotamia; one would have to be sacrificed, and Smuts recommended that it should be Mesopotamia. After reinforcements, Allenby should attack first across the Jordan River. After this there would be an advance up the coast, isolating Damascus. The timing would depend on the rapidity of railway construction behind the line. 'The destruction of the Hejaz Railway so as to isolate the Turkish Medina force' was also urged. To this the War Office replied (on the 7th of March): 'We attach importance to cutting the Hejaz Railway as already planned.' When the Medina link was at length destroyed, however, the importance of this was hardly evident. Smuts informed the War Cabinet that he agreed with all this, and then went home.

Three divisions and a cavalry brigade were sent to Palestine from Mesopotamia, and an Indian cavalry division from France; the latter had proved unsuited to conditions on the Western Front, and neither Haig nor Robertson felt its loss to them would be severe. Allenby had already moved up his G.H.Q. to a position between Jerusalem and Jaffa, and while his staff were preparing details of the plan, and while supplies were being organized, he found himself increasingly involved in political problems. As Commander-in-Chief of an occupied territory, he automatically became the supreme power over civilian affairs. Fortunately among his well-picked and talented staff were experts on the area and its problems, such as Clayton, who were able to advise him. Clayton relinquished his post as Director of Intelligence and became Chief Political Officer. At this time, however, Allenby lost two valuable assistants: Meinertzhagen and Guy Dawnay. The former was posted to the War Office. Dawnay, having proved his great qualities at last, was sent off to the Western Front. His brother, Lt.-Colonel Alan Dawnay, was concerned with the Arab revolt, and soon he was to prove almost as useful as his brother. On departure, Meinertzhagen entered in his diary: 'It had indeed been a very great pleasure to work under [Allenby], and I trust it will not be the last time, for he is a splendid soldier. If any one man has by his personality and influence won a campaign, it is Allenby. The spirit of the whole force is his, and I regard him as the greatest soldier we have in these troublous times.'[1] Brig.-General Wavell, however, returned from Versailles and was given the post of Chief of Staff to Chetwode in place of Brig.-General W. Bartholomew, who replaced Dawnay under Bols.

The various creeds in Jerusalem were continually causing trouble with their ancient frictions; the question of which flags were entitled to fly there was solved in typical Allenby fashion when he decreed that the only flag which would be flown in Palestine during the military occupation was his own Union Jack.

On the 9th of November, at the time of the Third Battle of Gaza, the important and controversial Balfour Declaration had been made, in the form of a letter to Lord Rothschild. It said that the British Government favoured 'the establishment in Palestine of a national home for the Jewish people'. (Although Balfour wanted the United States to assume responsibility for Palestine after the war.[2]) Allenby, continually concerned about public order, had immediately forbidden its publication in Palestine.

Water was still the greatest problem of military supply. Even in Jerusalem itself it was quite inadequate for the needs of the Army. The Roman aqueduct, constructed by Pilate during Herod's reign, was restored, and a reservoir—described as 'practically liquid filth'—was restored.

Arrangements were made to co-operate more closely than hitherto with Feisal. Much to Lawrence's relief, Allenby had not been disillusioned by the Yarmuk River fiasco; indeed, he intended to make greater use of the Arabs than ever before. But he now insisted that the Arabs should co-operate even more as an integral part of his force; the coming offensive over Jordan would attempt to link the British and Arab troops. For this purpose more supplies, instructors, machine-gunners and armoured cars were sent into Akaba and forward to the Arab army. Soon there were an armoured car battery and a flight of planes at Akaba; the French had four machine-gun detachments there and two light artillery pieces. Feisal's army was officially designated the Arab Army of the North. Meanwhile, the remaining Arab forces continued in the less glamorous occupation of holding the unfortunate Turkish garrison at Medina.

All this was very much against the views of Lawrence, who believed that the Arabs were only useful as guerrillas. He believed that joining the British and Arab forces, as Bols, Wingate and others advised, would be 'like mixing oil and water'. Allenby's idea was the same as that of Sir Reginald Wingate before him, and Wingate had recently visited Allenby at the front; it was also the view of most of the British officers concerned with the rising. They were convinced that, if left to themselves, the Arab forces would prove so unreliable as to be worthless.

One of those who drilled and trained Feisal's three thousand men at this time, in an attempt to make them a modern military force, was Nuri-as-Said, who had been an officer in the Turkish Army, and who became Prime Minister of Iraq till he was murdered in the revolution of 1958. Lawrence himself returned to Akaba, in a fairly indefinite capacity, and raced across the desert and mud flats in armoured cars, contemplating on the application of speed and armour to war. When he heard that the Turks had put a

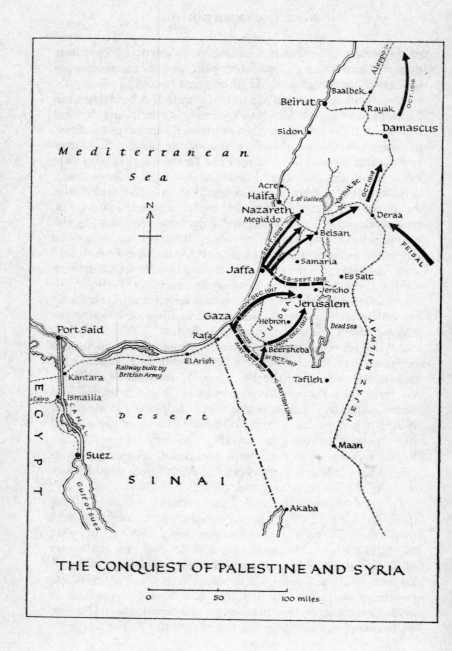

THE CONQUEST OF PALESTINE AND SYRIA

0   50   100 miles

generous ransome on him, alive or dead, he formed a personal bodyguard of some ninety cut-throats armed with weapons 'borrowed' from British supplies at Akaba. At Tafileh, he was involved in a bitter fight, and did well when virtually in command of defence against a strong counter-attack. As a result of this action nearly a whole Turkish Army Corps, and a German battalion, were thrown into action against the Arab army at Tafileh; this force eventually retook the town, partly due to the 'German Lawrence'[3], Niedermayer. Lawrence followed this set-back with a daring and successful raid on a port of the Dead Sea; but this did not, as he later suggested, entirely stop the Turkish Dead Sea traffic. Apart from Akaba, his greatest and most unquestioned success, some of Lawrence's daring activities had either met with failure or were not of decisive value to the Allies. His best activity still concerned the railway.

Smuts had no sooner left the scene than Allenby set off the preliminary operation to his plan—the crossing of the Jordan. The 60th Division, with desert-toughened Londoners, advanced from Jerusalem to Jericho, and the Anzac Mounted Division moved from Bethlehem towards the Dead Sea. In both cases the difficulties of the ground were worse than those provided by the Turks. This was followed by a general advance by the whole XX Corps up the Jordan valley, thus setting the stage for an advance into the Moab Hills and a crossing of the Jordan. Allenby hoped to reach the Hejaz Railway in the region of Amman; he would thus not only cut off the Turks opposing the Arab armies, but would also concentrate the attention and reinforcements of the enemy on their left flank, while Allenby prepared to strike on their right. It was, however, a terrible place in which to ask men to fight; Allenby knew this, and had discarded the area as one for his main thrust partly for that reason. The heat was stifling in the river valley, well below sea level. There was little cover or vegetation on the dusty plain beyond the river, which stretched like a hot, brown carpet for nearly ten miles to Amman; below, the narrow stream, called the River Jordan, cut through it like a cool, green ribbon.

The advance to Amman began in the third week of July, 1918. The river was successfully crossed, but from then almost everything went wrong. Struggling up the hills the other side, the attacking troops found it impossible to take the well-defended heights; they were handicapped particularly by lack of artillery. It was an ill-considered offensive; the topography was better suited to defence than attack. Within two weeks the force, apart from a small bridgehead, was back again across the Jordan River. It was a humiliating experience for Allenby, his staff and the army, which greatly outnumbered the defenders.

A month later, having been promised help from rebel Arabs, independent of Feisal, behind the Turkish lines, Allenby ordered another attempt to take Amman. The Arab help never materialized—a fact which did not surprise or displease Lawrence—and once more the British force trudged back across the Jordan after advancing six miles beyond the far bank; Allenby himself gave orders for withdrawal on the spot.

These two reverses seemed to put Allenby in a very bad position, but from then onwards the Turkish command were increasingly sensitive of their left flank and kept about a third of their forces east of the Jordan. The operations had thus had some strategic success, but this was off-set by the tactical victories of the enemy and the bad effect on morale of the British troops. Allenby must take his share of responsibility for the over-confident attempts to reach the Hejaz Railway. The railway's farthest tentacle, its full extension to Medina, had already been effectively cut (to the relief of the German staff) by Alan Dawnay and a party of Arabs in a brilliant raid which destroyed an enormous length of track in one day; so effectively, indeed, that the break has not yet been restored and the Medina rail link has been unused since that day.*

* Despite this, Medina, living on local produce, held out till after the Armistice. After the war, Alan Dawnay wrote a history of the Coldstream Guards. He died in 1938, when Director of Public Relations at the War Office. The Hejaz Railway is to be rebuilt by a British firm.

It was at this time that Allenby became aware that he was faced by a new adversary. The fall of Jerusalem had been received very badly in Berlin, and Falkenhayn had been replaced by General Liman von Sanders. Von Sanders, like Allenby a cavalry man, had a very good knowledge of the Turkish forces, having been attached to them since 1913, when he had been sent to Constantinople as head of a military mission to regenerate the Turkish army. At that time he had met and become friendly with Feisal. Since then he had achieved great fame as a defensive commander for his tenacity at Gallipoli. On relieving Falkenhayn on the 1st of March, 1918, almost his first action was to replace most of the German staff by Turkish officers. One who stayed was von Papen, who found Sanders 'a corpulent and charming gentleman who maintained excellent relations with a great many Arab sheiks, including Emir Feisal'.[4] Even Falkenhayn's Chief of Staff, von Dommes, was replaced by a Turk. Von Sanders's first offensive action on the Jordan was a failure, as the Turkish troops did not support the German battalions which were used to launch the attack; the Australian defenders refused to give ground, and the result was a costly failure for the German–Turkish force. Von Sanders then concentrated on defence. Although he had much less command of open movement than had Falkenhayn, von Sanders was one of the best defensive Generals of the day and, what was even more important, he understood Turkish methods and appreciated the strengths and weaknesses of the Turkish troops, which Falkenhayn had never done.

By now news had come of the great German successes in France, where at last the stalemate had been broken, and the Western Front, like some hitherto dormant snake feeding on a thousand corpses a day, had suddenly unleashed itself and curled out in a great arc towards Paris; it was the last chance for Germany, taken in the gap between the collapse of Russia and the build-up of American forces in the West, and had met with extraordinary success, despite the bloody battles of the Somme and Passchendaele which, when they had failed to break the line at two of its strongest points, had been continued in attempts to 'wear down' the enemy. In fact, having been on the defensive for so long, the German forces in France were now in a better condition than the weary and battered British, and the totally disillusioned French. It seemed as if Robertson's prognostications had been right, and now reinforcements were urgently demanded from Palestine. One source suggests that Allenby himself was considered for Europe, to replace Haig as C.-in-C.[5] Within a few weeks two complete divisions, the 52nd and the 74th, were sent back to Europe, and the other divisions were denuded of British battalions, twenty-four more going before the end of May; in addition, nine Yeomanry regiments, five and a half heavy batteries and five machine-gun companies were sent to the Western Front; about sixty thousand front-line troops altogether. It was clear that the general offensive, agreed upon with Smuts, would have to be abandoned, although, including the ancillary and base troops, there were still over a quarter of a million British servicemen in Egypt and Palestine in September, 1918, more than twice the number of Indians. The two divisions were replaced by the two on their way from Mesopotamia, but the twenty-four British infantry battalions were replaced very gradually, and then by unseasoned and ill-equipped troops from India. More R.A.F. and Australian Flying Corps units, including Handley-Page bombers, were flown out to combat renewed German air strength, and fast motor launches were brought up to operate on the Dead Sea; the flag-ship, the *Miranda*, had once been well known on the Riviera, where it had won many prizes for the Duke of Westminster.

Reorganization took up most of the summer, and this time was also well used by von Sanders. The Indian cavalry regiments were all armed with sword or lance, and thus Allenby's cavalry became so in the true sense of the word, and not mounted riflemen as before; this caused the greatest pleasure to old cavalrymen, but considerable alarm to others. The Anzac Mounted Division, consisting of Australians and New Zealanders, however, insisted on retaining their rifles, although the Australian Mounted Division added the sword to their equipment and had some training in its use. As may be imagined, Allenby, who had so recently been totally disillusioned as to the worth of his own arm in modern war, found all this much to his liking.

The Indian infantry was of poor quality. Battalions were arriving in Egypt with companies which had never fired a rifle; one battalion was not even equipped with the modern service rifle. There were few trained signallers, machine-gunners or drivers. Wavell was told by a training officer of the XX Corps that it normally took two years to train an Indian signaller; he replied that now it would have to be done in two months. The junior British officers knew little more than their troops, and, what was perhaps worse, hardly any of them spoke Hindustani. In one battalion only two British officers could understand their men, and there was only one Indian officer who spoke English. Many of the regiments, such as the Jodhpore Lancers, had been raised by and belonged to Indian princes, and had reputations mainly founded on colourful ceremonial duties. The great tradition of the Indian Army, which had long been a by-word in Britain if not elsewhere in the world, had already received a rude shock in East Africa and Europe, where some of its regiments had turned out to be of little value. The Indians were now put into divisions with the remaining British troops: the 10th Division consisted of Irish and Indian battalions; the 53rd of Welsh and Indian; the 3rd of English, Irish and Indian; the 7th of Scottish, English and Indian; the 54th of East Anglian battalions and Indian; the 60th of Londoners and Indians; the 75th of West-country battalions and Indian. The force thus organized, still as the Desert Mounted Corps (Chauvel), the XX Corps (Chetwode) and XXI Corps (Bulfin), contained such famous units as the 1st Leinsters, the Connaught Rangers, the Bengal Lancers, 1st Manchesters, 1st Seaforth Highlanders, Auckland Mounted Regiment and 1st Australian Light Horse. Commanding one of the re-formed divisions was

Maj.-General A. R. Hoskins, who had recently been Commander-in-Chief in the East African theatre, but who had
been somewhat ignominiously removed when he failed to
end that campaign within a few weeks; on handing over
to Hoskins, Smuts had publicly declared that the campaign
was as good as over and could be finished off 'in a few weeks';
Hoskins had to pay the penalty for Smuts' ill-considered
optimism.

Thus, when his army was finally reorganized, Allenby
had troops from many countries and territories under his
command: Britain, Australia, New Zealand, India, Hong
Kong, Singapore, France, Italy, South Africa (artillery and
one battalion), the West Indies and Egypt. There was even
a detachment of Rarotongan islanders, from the Pacific, who
manned the surf boats which brought in supplies to the
harbourless sections of the coast. There were suggestions
of sending Canadian, Japanese and Chinese troops to the
campaign. Three battalions of Jews, the 38th, 39th and 40th
Royal Fusiliers, were sent to Allenby as the first practical
result of the Balfour Declaration. Serving in them was
David Ben Gurion, destined to become Prime Minister of
Israel.[6]

The army continued to languish, during the long, hot
months of summer, beyond the Auja, and in the Jordan
valley. The retention of a large force in the latter increasingly
became a medical problem; while insisting that the men
should stay there, against medical advice, in atrocious conditions, Allenby gave every help he could, as Commander-
in-Chief, to the medical services. He gave priority to anti-
malarial measures, such as the draining of marshes, above all
other work. One of the Australian medical officers wrote: 'I
found I was dealing with a man of scientific instincts. He
supported the Army Medical Service thoroughly. . . . He
was, as far as I know, the first Commander in that malarial
region in which many armies have perished to understand the
risk and to take measures accordingly.'[7]

In personality, Allenby was still as formidable as ever, and
high command had not mellowed him. He was still capable

of great outbursts of rage, but now he recovered his equani-
mity more quickly, often very suddenly, to the surprise of his
victim. It is probable that there was still an element of simulation in these explosions; however, they were, by all accounts,
as alarming as ever. This unpleasant trait was the flaw in
Allenby's character, but it is certain that he did not realize
the horrifying aspect he could present on these occasions;
he never fully understood the strength of his own personality. One Colonel of the Royal Engineers was sick on the
floor outside Allenby's office after an interview; another
officer had to be actually carried out of Allenby's room,
having collapsed on the floor before his desk. A staff officer,
who had written for *The Times*, was delegated to write a
report for London. When completed, author and report
were brought before Allenby, who was a stickler for simple
but correct prose. The Commander-in-Chief read the document, exploding several times with 'damned rot'. Before he
could make his complaints more specific, the staff officer had
fainted in Bols's arms; when he came to, he was sick. On such
occasions Allenby would invariably express his bewilderment to a member of his staff, and would later go out of his
way to make some pleasantry to the officer concerned. A
junior member of his staff wrote: 'To meet him for the first
time, under conditions of military discipline at any rate, is to
undergo a somewhat trying ordeal. His keen grey-blue eyes,
under heavy brows, search the face while he probes the mind
with sharp, almost *staccato*, questions about everything under
the sun except that which is expected. He cannot suffer fools
gladly, and demands an unequivocal affirmative or negative
to every query he makes. He has a habit of asking questions
on the most abstruse subjects, and an unpleasant knack of
catching out anyone who gives an evasive answer for the sake
of politeness.'[8] Wavell wrote: 'His manner was often gruff
and abrupt; his questions were straight and sharp; and he
demanded an immediate, direct reply. Any attempt at
prevarication, and indefiniteness, even hesitation, might
provoke a sudden explosion of anger that could shake the
hardiest.'[9] For inefficiency in military matters, Allenby was

invariably severe. He demanded perfection, as he had always believed that mistakes in preparation, or carelessness in training and orders, could prove disastrous in battle. He made no allowances for the wretched conditions in the Jordan valley, and the Australians there, particularly, resented this. Nevertheless, the nickname of 'the Bull', which had itself replaced 'Apple-pie', was coming more and more to be superseded by yet another: 'the Chief'.

*   *   *

Unlike the Gaza–Beersheba operation, Allenby's next offensive was his own in conception, although in some respects it did follow closely on Napoleon's plan for the conquest of Syria. Lawrence wrote that the victory was 'the logical fruit solely of his genius and Bartholomew's pains'. After a morning ride, Allenby strode into the office of his Operations Staff and announced it in outline. At first it was met with misgivings, for it would be an effort not only to break the line, but to destroy the enemy forces and force Turkey out of the war in one blow. It was known that the Turks had difficulties of their own, and that their army was in a poor condition; but to some Allenby's plan seemed over-confident. It was not forgotten that the new C.I.G.S. himself, General Wilson, with whom Lloyd George had replaced Robertson in an abortive effort to get rid of Haig, had advised a defensive role until such time as reinforcements could be sent from France.* Allenby, even though his force had been greatly diminished in quality and experience, thought such a policy excessively timid. Having stated his plan in outline, he left it to his staff to prepare in detail;

---

* Later Field-Marshal Sir Henry Wilson, he remained C.I.G.S. until 1922, in which year he was assassinated by Irish gunmen in London. Few telegraphs between Wilson and Allenby have survived, as Wilson used a personal code for them and, strangely, copies were not filed at the War Office.

this was in the tradition of the great commanders of the past rather than of the modern trend, which was that staff teams should conceive of strategy with regard to resources and expert knowledge of conditions and present it to the Commander-in-Chief for approval. Few people, even on his staff, knew of Allenby's plan during the troops' long wait in the hot season in the Jordan valley.

It was to be the Gaza–Beersheba movement in reverse. Allenby and Smuts had already decided to attack the Turkish right, on the coastal plain. Allenby now decided that, after an infantry assault, the Cavalry Corps would ride through the breach, across the Plain of Sharon, and then turn eastwards, across a range of hills, some forty miles behind the enemy line, cut the Turkish lines of communication, and forcing a capitulation, move on to Damascus. It was a simple but extraordinarily bold conception, involving the largest mass of cavalry attacking an unbroken enemy in modern history; it could only have originated in the mind of a commander of supreme self-confidence. The initial infantry assault was to be undertaken by Bulfin's XXI Corps, while the XX Corps would be drastically depleted but would launch a mock offensive on the enemy's left. The force on the far left of the enemy, in the Jordan valley, would co-operate with Lawrence and the Arab Army of the North to take Deraa, a vital rail junction. A great concentration of British troops now began near the Mediterranean; once again it was essential that the enemy should misconstrue Allenby's intentions. Despite his preponderance in strength over the Turks, Allenby insisted on the greatest lengths being taken to deceive the enemy, and his instructions were most intelligently carried out. New camps were made in the Jordan valley, with fifteen thousand dummy horses made of canvas; bridges were constructed across the river; every day West Indian battalions, like extras in a film, marched towards the left of the Turkish line, and every night they secretly returned again in trucks; they were not, of course, admitted to the high and secret counsels of G.H.Q., and what officers and men must have thought of the General

Staff when, wearily, they arose every morning, only to be told that they had once more to march back again, can be barely imagined. A dummy G.H.Q. was constructed in the eastern area, even to the laying down of telephone lines, and Lawrence's men spread faulty information about the activities on the Turkish left; sand sleds were drawn back and forth across the ground, to raise clouds of dust, to give an impression of great activity; signallers made much use of their wireless sets. Meanwhile the movement was, in fact, going the other way, and troops poured into the camps near the coast, which, like the camps on the other flank, with the kind of foresight that reveals outstanding staff work, had been purposefully built to double the size necessary even before Allenby announced his plan; thus battalions, which had previously occupied two camps both of which were battalion size, now moved into one camp. No extra tents were erected; no unnecessary movement and transporting of troops was allowed by day. The deception met with total success. Bartholomew, succeeding Dawnay, was a man of equal intellect, and in some respects of even greater ability. Much of the credit for the details of the plan must go to him and to Bols, still Chief of Staff.

The Turkish armies opposite were meanwhile bombarded from the air with propaganda leaflets telling them to desert the German command and give themselves up to the British; these had great effect. There were swarms of Turkish deserters in Syria, and before the attack Turkish troops were crossing the line on an average of seven a day. They provided useful information for British Intelligence. The enemy were deployed in three armies, two between Jericho and the coast, and one covering Amman and the Jordan. Allenby's intention was to round up the two armies facing the main part of the line. The total forces opposed to the British offensive would be about 26,000 infantry, 3,000 cavalry and 370 guns; another 6,000 were engaged in duties on the Hejax Railway.[10] Allenby's force, on the front line, consisted of 57,000 infantry, 12,000 cavalry and 540 guns. When this overwhelming superiority became obvious to the staff officers, a good deal more enthusiasm for Allenby's plan was felt. The Turkish troops, moreover, were ill-fed and badly supplied; the inefficiency of their lines of communication was notorious, but at the same time it was known that Turkish infantry could be courageous and tenacious fighters when ill-supported or cornered. A new commander of one of the Turkish armies was known to be a General of quality. He was General Kemal Pasha, who later became better known as Kemal Ataturk and who restored the Turkish nation after the war. Kemal was appalled by the state of affairs he had found on his arrival. The only encouraging thing that could be said from the Turkish point of view was that they still had great strength in machine-guns.

The German troops were in good morale, but were affected by disease. Berlin had lost interest in the Palestine campaign during the summer inactivity, and wished to withdraw German troops from the theatre; this measure had been cancelled when von Sanders threatened to resign if it were carried out. The crack Asia Corps of German troops (the predecessor of the Afrika Corps of the next war, although much smaller) had exceptional machine-gun strength, each battalion being able to call on thirty guns. There were also German artillery, anti-aircraft guns, trench mortar units, and transport; it was only through the dedicated work of German medical teams that disease did not run riot throughout the entire force. As the main attack was expected in the east, there were no German troops beside the coast; as von Sanders acknowledged, they were not entirely advantageous to him, as their supply requirements were much greater than those of Turkish troops.

On the 9th of September, 1918, Allenby issued his order. It began with the sentence: 'The Commander-in-Chief intends to take the offensive.'[11] It was typical of Allenby's masterful mood. All who were present at his final conferences were almost hypnotized by his determination. Wavell wrote: 'Those who attended them will not easily forget his almost presumptuous confidence about the issue of the operations, the clearness and incisiveness of his instructions, and his occasional abrupt impatience at some objection or difficulty.'[12]

His letters to his wife, however, reveal that Allenby was not expecting the tremendous and almost instantaneous success which he, in fact, achieved; he expressed himself 'aghast' at it. It was always his policy to appear supremely confident before a battle, and at such acting he was expert. He had, nevertheless, every reason to be genuinely confident. At the point of attack, he had successfully continued to assemble 35,000 infantry, 9,000 cavalry and 385 guns opposite a totally unsuspecting and ill-equipped enemy of 8,000 infantry and 120 guns. Edmund Allenby was not the man to be intimidated either by the fruits that destiny now held before him or by unnerving thoughts of the shame of failure against such small odds. The barrage, which, as usual, Allenby had insisted on being as short as possible, was fixed to open at 4.30 a.m. on the 19th of September. The stage was therefore set for what was to be probably the most crushing attack that has been delivered in modern war.

* * *

The offensive was to be in three phases: the encirclement of the two enemy armies, the taking of Damascus, and the destruction of the remnants of the enemy forces in the chase to the Turkish border. It was won before it began. After the original conception, Allenby's part was twofold; the urging on of his forces in pursuit, and making the difficult political decisions regarding the occupation of Damascus.

Chetwode's XX Corps duly launched its mock offensive, almost simultaneously with the cutting of the railway at three places on all sides of Deraa, and with the bombing of vital points on the enemy's lines of communication. Lawrence, who had been at G.H.Q. for some of the planning of the operation, had a hand in all three cuttings of the line, together with other British officers, members of the Camel Corps and Feisal's demolitionists; but once again he failed to destroy the bridge at the Yarmuk River. These rail breaks put the enemy lines of communication into chaos. The bombardment near the coast was due to begin just over twenty-four hours later.

On the evening of the 18th of September Allenby strolled through the vineyards which surrounded his house and discussed the flora of the district with a junior staff officer. He then went to bed early, and ordered breakfast for four o'clock the following morning: the first indication of the timing of the attack that even many of his staff had received.

At 4.30 a.m. the following morning he stood outside, with about twelve officers, silently watching and waiting. Allenby, looking at his watch, suddenly boomed out 'Zero!' in his most stentorian tone, and at that moment the sky went alight, to be followed a few seconds later by the crash of explosives.[13]

With the barrage creeping before them, the infantry began their advance at the same moment, and aircraft took off to bomb the Turkish H.Q. at Nazareth and to patrol the enemy airfields in order to keep German and Turkish planes on the ground. The most important targets for the bombers were the telegraph communications out of Nazareth; this was brilliantly accomplished, every line being destroyed or damaged, and enemy H.Q. thus remained ignorant of the state of affairs throughout the first stage of the battle. The concentration of the barrage was one gun to every fifty yards assaulted. (As compared to one gun to twenty yards at the Battle of the Somme in 1916.) Two destroyers shelled the coast road.

Within a few hours the infantry had broken the enemy line from where Richard Cœur de Lion had outmanœuvred Saladin on the 7th of September, 1191; teams of wire-cutters followed at their heels, and within minutes of the breach being made a passage was cleared, and through it thundered nine thousand horsemen, the majority of them armed with swords or lances; in ten minutes the van was well behind the Turkish line and leading the way up the coast. By 10 a.m. two divisions had ridden through; for once static defence had been broken by the use of surprise. After about ten miles the majority veered off to the right and rode eastwards across the plain towards Jenin and Megiddo, the remainder disappearing up the coast in a great cloud of dust towards Caesarea. Megiddo was the place which is, in the Hebrew tongue, called Armageddon, which, as described in *Revelation* xvi: 16, was once before the scene of mighty catastrophe.

A ridge of hills that bordered the plain was successfully navigated, and on the 20th of September the cavalry, fanned out, were racing towards Megiddo, Nazareth and the Jordan. Liman von Sanders, aware that a great offensive had opened, still had no idea of the speed at which events were moving. The two Turkish armies were now being pushed back by Bulfin and Chetwode, and were suddenly aware of the danger in their rear. They were trapped.

On the night of the 19th of September, Allenby wrote to his wife:

Now my cavalry is many miles North of Arsuf; making for the Turks' communications in the valley of Esdraelon. His infantry and artillery are falling back, hunted by my airmen, with machine-gun fire and bombs. So far many guns and 2,500 prisoners have been caught, but there will be many more. My losses are light. I bombed the Headquarters of Liman von Sanders and his two Army Commanders last night. On the East of Jordan, the Arabs are up, and they have cut the Hejaz railway, North, South and West of Deraa. So Liman von Sanders has lost his only railway communication with the outside world. I really don't know what he can do; and I am beginning to think that we may have a very great success. The weather is perfect; not too hot, and very clear; just right for my artillery and aeroplanes in pursuit. My horses are . . . in sufficient strength to be irresistible.

And on the 20th of September:

My cavalry are now in rear of the Turkish Army; and their lines of retreat are cut. One of my Cavalry Divisions surrounded

Liman von Sanders's Headquarters at Nazareth at 3.0 a.m. today;
but Liman had made a bolt at 7.0 p.m. yesterday.* . . . I went along
the Nablus road. It is strewn with broken lorries, wagons, dead
Turks, horses and oxen; mostly killed and smashed by our bombing aeroplanes. The same bombing of fugitives, on crowded
roads, continued today. I think I ought to capture all the Turks'
guns and the bulk of his Army. . . . My losses are not heavy in proportion to the results gained. The Cavalry H.Q. are at Armageddon at the present moment. It is called a different name on the
map. European news is good, too.

On the 21st, Allenby wrote:

I think that the Turkish Army is practically destroyed. We
have taken well over 20,000 prisoners. . . . I met and passed
through thousands of them today, many of them Germans. Most
of them dog tired. All my troops have marched and fought
grandly; some of the infantry have done twenty miles across the
mountains today.

Two days later:

Prisoners still roll in, and the roads and defiles of the mountains
are encumbered with guns, wagons, motor-lorries and all sorts of
stores. It will take weeks to collect them. I've been going round
hospitals today. . . . I've told them that they've done the biggest
thing in the war—having totally destroyed two armies in thirty-
six hours. The VII and VIII Armies, now non-existent, were the
best troops in the Turkish Empire, and were strongly backed by
Germans and Austrians. . . . I have just heard that my cavalry
have taken Haifa and Acre today. They had a bit of a fight at

* Mercifully for those responsible, Allenby was misinformed. Von
Sanders was in bed when British cavalry, having been outside the town
for some hours, arrived in the streets of Nazareth at 5.30 a.m.; he was
woken by 'shouts and cries of alarm'. The British immediately occupied
the Germania Hotel, but the German G.H.Q. was in a house 200 yards
away. To his surprise, von Sanders learned that the British had omitted
to block one road out—that to Tiberias. With British troops taking over
the town, the German C.-in-C. and his staff left H.Q. at 8.30 a.m., but
did not ride out of the town, on the still-open Tiberias Road, until 1.15
a.m., nearly eight hours after the British entry. It is doubtful if Allenby
was ever told of this.

Haifa.* . . . Aeroplanes are pulverizing the retreating Turk in the Jordan locality.[14]

I have been out, all day, visiting hospitals and the French Detachment. The French fought well and had some 150 killed and wounded. . . . I, myself, am almost aghast at the extent of the victory.[15]

By the 1st of October he was able to write:

I have just cabled the War Office that I have taken Damascus. My mounted troops and the Arabs had surrounded the town yesterday, and it was entered this morning. I have, as yet, no details. I shall probably start, myself, for Damascus tomorrow. I do not propose to remain there, and shall probably be back here on the 4th.

The cavalry casualties, from the opening of the offensive, had been little more than five hundred; four times as many were to die from disease shortly afterwards.

Among the few who had escaped the capitulation of the two Turkish armies, writhing in the mesh of their own jammed transport, were most of the German infantry and General Kemal with a small party. Allenby, as usual, had insisted on no delay after the collapse of the two enemy armies, and ordered the cavalry on to Damascus;† not so much for political or purely military reasons, but medical: he told his medical staff that history showed him that after fourteen days of the opening of the offensive, malaria would be the worst enemy of the army. When Chetwode's troops had taken Nablus, Chetwode himself was hard on their heels into the town. He was surprised to meet there the Com-

* The Jodhpore Lancers had charged into the city centre, lancing Turks in the streets, after having first charged full pelt into quicksands outside the town, in which they lost their leading horses and men.

† Before the offensive, Allenby had told XX Corps staff that the capture of Damascus was an objective of the offensive. In this respect the *Official History* (Egypt & Palestine, II, Vol. 2, p. 560) hardly does Allenby justice.

mander-in-Chief, just arrived in the staff car in which each day of the offensive he motored some 150 miles. Allenby's first remark to Chetwode was a query as to why the exhausted infantry were lying by the roadside. Not long afterwards the infantry were up and marching a further ten miles. When Allenby, at the apex of the military hierarchy, let off steam, the escaping energy was strong enough for it to be neatly channelled down as far as the company commander level. He always believed that the more severe the orders the farther they would go.

The remaining Turkish army, east of the Jordan, had been retreating rapidly before the small British force left in that area, mainly Australians and New Zealanders, and before the Arabs, the former spending much of their efforts keeping the Arabs from massacring the Turkish prisoners. After the fall of Amman, it was a race for Damascus between Feisal's force in the east and the British cavalry in the west. Lawrence, aware of the proximity of an Arab dream and feeling himself on the brink of a supreme moment of his life, but uncertain of his own single-mindedness and ability to grasp and use events, was anxious to get there first. He reached Deraa, with his personal force, before Feisal's regular troops and, according to British officers who met him there, had little control over the excesses of his force. When the three British cavalry divisions arrived on the outskirts of Damascus on the 30th of September, units of Arab irregulars had already entered the city, Turkish administration had ceased, and the Arab flag hoisted. (When this news reached London, there was some dismay and irritation, but Lord Robert Cecil stated, for the Government, that Allenby had been authorized on the 1st of October to allow the Arab flag to be hoisted in Damascus.) Lawrence wandered about a camp set up by the Australians dressed, as usual, in Arab clothing, and casually accepted as an Arab; he felt deeply the awful duality of his position.

Next morning, the 1st of October, Lawrence, with the Arab army, rode into Damascus, to be greeted by representatives of the local pro-Feisal group and to be cheered by a great throng, as the legendary 'Aurens', in the streets. But on arrival at the Town Hall they came into immediate conflict with a rival group, which had formed a Syrian government of liberation, ostensibly owing allegiance to the Sherif of Mecca. Chaotic scenes followed, with excited chiefs and politicians, so near to their ambitions, but so far from agreement, coming to blows. Lawrence, appalled and bitter, tried to save the situation for Feisal. In the confusion, he seems himself to have been the only man to have wielded much power.

During the day the Australian Light Horse had also entered the city, but were in no mood to concern themselves with the anarchy which had replaced Turkish evacuation. They passed quickly through the city, in chase of the retreating Turks, retiring north. Meanwhile, the commander of the city's defences, a General of the Turkish Army, but Arab by birth, tired of waiting for the British to take over, had galloped out to the cavalry lines, no doubt thinking that a safer place of captivity than the tumultuous city. In good spirits over his escape from the Arabs, he was so helpless with laughter at breakfast in the British mess next morning that, as the *Official History* records, he fell over the table 'and upset the scrambled eggs and cocoa'.

Lawrence continued his efforts, the following day, to launch Feisal as 'King of the Arabs', on a sea of confusion. He had obtained little sleep since leaving Deraa, and was in a state of physical and mental exhaustion. By midday, Australians were taking over military control of the town, and there was no formal Arab government to confront them. Lawrence's feverish political activity did not seem to tie-up with his theoretically modest and impartial position as Allenby's representative with the North Arab Army; this assumption of authority particularly puzzled and displeased Chauvel, the cavalry commander, who now came on the scene. By the evening of the 2nd of October, Lawrence had succeeded in getting the electricity supply going again (it had been out of action for some weeks), and the trams were also working three days later. He had also done something for the fire

The Prince of Wales and the High Commissioner in Cairo, June, 1922.

services, public sanitation and relief work. The Australians, however, complained bitterly about the ghastly state of the Turkish hospital, and demanded that Lawrence should do something about it. Rapidly overwhelmed by events, Lawrence now spent much valuable time attempting to do this, only to be struck across the mouth by a British Major for his pains.

As he left the hospital, he recognized Allenby's Rolls-Royce outside the leading hotel. With considerable relief, he ran inside and met Allenby within a few seconds, filthy, dishevelled and on the point of collapse. Allenby, as always, gave priority to his interview with Lawrence, thus astonishing Chauvel and others not acquainted with the unconventional relationship, respect and understanding existing between General and Major. Allenby listened to all he had to say; he then confirmed the orders that Lawrence had already attempted to lay down. Effective martial law in the city was now under the control of the British High Command, but Allenby was prepared to accept Feisal's occupation, the anti-Feisal opposition having been put down fairly ruthlessly, and conveniently for Allenby, by Lawrence and his lieutenant, Kirkbride.* Lawrence wrote of how Allenby 'smoothed out all difficulties. . . . I let my limbs relax in this dreamlike confidence and decision and kindness which were Allenby.'[16]

Allenby's duty was clear: first to restore law and order, and then to follow the lines of the Sykes–Picot agreement. He sent for Feisal, and told Lawrence to be present as interpreter. Allenby wrote home of this famous meeting:

On arrival, I went to the Victoria Hotel. Later, the Sherif Feisal arrived, and came to see me there. He was mounted on a big Arab, with a large escort of Arabs, all mounted. He is a fine, slim, sharp-featured man of about 35. Lawrence was there, too and interpreted.† I had a long and satisfactory talk with Feisal.

* Later Sir A. Kirkbride, Minister to Jordan.

† Feisal spoke English, and Lawrence spoke bad Arabic.

He will take over the administration of Damascus; or, rather, will put in a Military Administration. His flag now flies. The town is quiet now, but there was a little pillaging and shooting the day before yesterday, quickly repressed by Lawrence. My cavalry had some sharpish fighting outside the town, and a good many dead Turks are still lying about; but my losses were very slight. The number of prisoners is appalling; over 20,000 taken in this business, brings the total—as far as I can guess—to 80,000 or 90,000. I've only reported 71,000 officially. Barrow [commanding 4th Cavalry Division] had to leave 2,000 behind as they could not keep up. He put them in villages and told the inhabitants to take care of them. Very likely their throats are cut by now. Lawrence tells me that his Arabs found one village where 40 women and 20 or 30 children had been bayoneted by the Turks, in pure wantonness. After that very few, if any, prisoners were taken by them.*[17]

Allenby pointed out that, in control of the city, Feisal would be responsible to him, and that in deference to French claims a French liaison officer would be appointed. Feisal objected very strongly. He said that he knew nothing of France in the matter, but that he was prepared to have British assistance. He said he had understood from Lawrence that the Arabs were to have the whole of Syria including the Lebanon but excluding Palestine; a country without a port was no good to him. At first, he declined to have a French liaison officer or to recognize French guidance in any way. Allenby thereupon turned to Lawrence and asked him if he had not told Feisal that the French were to have a Protectorate over Syria. Lawrence according to one who was there, said: 'No, sir, I know nothing about it.' Allenby then claimed that he must have known that Feisal was to have 'nothing to do with the Lebanon'. Lawrence said: 'No, sir, I did not.' After some further argument, Allenby told Feisal

* This letter to his wife reveals how well Allenby trusted Lawrence and the special relationship he had with him—mentioning him, as he does, in the same breath as one of his Generals. It also corroborates Lawrence's own claim to have been in control of the city during the Damascus revolt. The village was Tafas (*Seven Pillars of Wisdom*, pp. 630-1).

that he was Commander-in-Chief and that Feisal was at that moment a Lieutenant-General under his command and that he would have to obey orders. He would have to accept the situation until the matter was thrashed out after the war. Feisal accepted the decision, and left with his two companions, one of whom was Nuri-as-Said, by then his Chief of Staff. Also present at the meeting had been Chauvel and his Chief of Staff (Godwin), Bols (who had accompanied Allenby to Damascus); Joyce, Stirling, and Young of the Hejaz Mission; and Cornwallis of the Arab Bureau. Lawrence then protested to Allenby that he could not work with a French liaison officer and that he was due for leave. He would like to return to England. Allenby promptly said, 'Yes, I think you had!' Lawrence left the room. It is clear that both Allenby and Feisal believed he had let them down in his liaison duties. But no sooner was Lawrence out of the room, than Allenby ordered that the suggestion should be made to London that Lawrence should have an audience with the King. He also said that he would write to the Foreign Office, suggesting that Lawrence should be interviewed there so that he could explain the Arab point of view.[18]

Lawrence left Damascus the following day, in Chauvel's car, having handed over his duties to Cornwallis, a young man of whom Allenby had a high opinion.*

Allenby cabled to the War Office: 'Feisal is being warned that if he attempts to control the Blue area, the settlement of which must await the Peace Conference, he will prejudice his case. He is also being told that the Lebanon's status is a peculiar one.' Before leaving Damascus, Allenby dined with Feisal:

He gave me an excellent dinner; Arab dishes, but all good, served in the ordinary way of civilization. Water to drink. This morning Feisal sent me a big sideboard, or hall table, of the best

---

* Later Sir Kinahan Cornwallis, he helped Feisal establish himself in Iraq. Ambassador to Baghdad, 1941-5.

Damascus inlaid work. I believe it took over three years to manufacture. I'm having it sent to Beirut, and thence to Cairo by sea.* In return I propose to give him one of my photographs in your silver frame. I can't run to giving him a present of equal value to that which he gave me. I have had long talks with him on politics. He is nervous about the peace settlement, but I tell him he must trust the Entente powers to treat him fairly. You would like Feisal. . . . He has beautiful hands, like a woman's, and his fingers are always moving nervously when he talks. But he is strong in will, and straight in principle.[19]

*   *   *

Among congratulations which Allenby received on the taking of Damascus were one from King George V ('a great exploit in the history of the British Empire'); the War Cabinet ('intense admiration of the vision and resource in planning, and the energy and determination in execution, which you have displayed throughout the present operations . . . brilliant and decisive victory, which is not only an un-rivalled feat of arms, but will have a profound effect on the situation in the Near and Middle East'); the Sherif of Mecca, now styled 'King Hussein' ('I ask Almighty God to enable me to kiss you between your eyes') ; and from Generals Foch, French, Haig, Pershing and, most generous of all, from the discredited but still gallant Nivelle. A little later the American Consul-General in Cairo passed on to Allenby an extraordinarily glowing message from the U.S. Secretary of State : ' . . . May I not express the belief that along with the record of your feats of arms that have filled the world with admiration there will be recounted as equally great your acts as a sagacious and humane executive. The evidence of your work of preservation and reconstruction are found in every part of the Holy Land, and it will never be forgotten that you administered the law and justice well.'[20]

Less than 17,000 troops of the remaining Turkish force had

* It is now in the library at Haileybury College.

escaped from Damascus, and they were in poor condition. The main difficulties in pursuing and defeating them were the length of supply lines and the sudden increase in malaria, which, as Allenby had predicted, was now taking a grip on his force; to this latter was added Spanish influenza, which was now sweeping the world, undernourished and tired by a long and wretched war. Nevertheless, the War Cabinet urged Allenby to go from Damascus and take Aleppo. Tyre, Sidon and Beirut had already been occupied by the apparently indefatigable infantry of the XXI Corps. In the case of Beirut, the French Navy and Feisal's Arabs had got there first, to stake their respective claims. The Arabs were removed, with some difficulty. Indian infantry moved on up the coast, and the 5th Cavalry Division moved out of Damascus to storm Aleppo, two hundred miles away. The division was commanded by Maj.-General H. J. M. Macandrew, the man who, three and a half years before, had reported Allenby to Haig as not being 'cavalry minded'. This was a most ironic twist of fate, for now Macandrew was to direct the last great cavalry action of history.

Although considerably reduced by sickness, Macandrew pushed on in hot, turgid weather. Allenby was apprehensive as to the outcome of this venture, as there was a strong German contingent in the area, but Macandrew cabled him that he was confident of success. Kemal and von Sanders had organized the defence of the city, and were in superior strength, but the British cavalry were supported by a column of Feisal's Arabs. Despite an order from Chauvel to halt, Macandrew went on; Aleppo was actually taken by Feisal's troops, but the weakened cavalry charged the main Turkish force eight miles from the town. It was Allenby himself who first realized that this engagement had occurred only a few miles from the place where one of the first organized cavalry actions, by Alexander the Great in 333 B.C., had been fought. Outnumbered by about six to one, the British were forced to withdraw and await reinforcements. Before they arrived, Turkey, her main army battered beyond repair by Allenby's two great offensives, and also hard-pressed in the Salonika campaign, sued for peace on the 31st of October; it was three years since she had entered the war. Liman von Sanders had handed over command of the remaining Turkish forces to Mustapha Kemal on the preceding day.

Thus ended the Ottoman Empire.

During the offensive over 70,000 Turks had been taken prisoner, together with 3,700 Germans and Austrians. British casualties since the 19th of September had been 5,666, of which the cavalry suffered only 650. As Liddell Hart has said: 'Making all allowances for the British superiority in strength, it must rank as one of the masterpieces of military history, as perfect in execution as in design.'

The British front had been moved forward 350 miles in exactly six weeks. To judge this achievement, which was made without much mechanization or the technique of parachute drops, another statistic may be measured and, with reservations, compared: the farthest stretch of the German *Blitzkrieg* in the Battle for France in 1940 was some 225 miles, accomplished, between the 16th of May and 22nd of May, in seven days.* Lloyd George, without whose enthusiasm the campaign would not have taken place, should be permitted the final words: 'Had this offensive been undertaken at an early stage in the war, and properly supported from home, the Turkish collapse would have come sooner, and the repercussions in Europe would have been shattering.'[21]

* Von Kluck's advance on the German right wing in 1914 was 180 miles in four weeks. Both these advances encountered much stronger opposition than did Allenby's.

CHAPTER 9

Allenby the General

I have always tried to keep my mind from stagnation.
ALLENBY

Allenby's tenets as a commander were simple—and sound.
A note for a talk after the war survives. It is brief, but
illuminating:

Thorough preparation.
Deception. Concentration of strength; with *strong* feints.
Beersheba and Gaza: coastal plain and Transjordan raids.
Reinforce where winning; and accept losses, when winning;
but cut losses when losing. *Live*, to fight another day.
Make sure that you have men under you whom you can trust,
and don't worry them by interference; but see that your orders
are carried out.
Trust your luck; but you can hedge a bit. Example good luck:
thunderstorm before Beersheba. Bad luck: weather in Amman
raid.[1]

There in a nutshell is Allenby's military philosophy. To it
one only needs to add: be confident, be relentless in pursuit,
and do not fear the unconventional. Above all else: surprise
and mobility.
Allenby's use of Lawrence has achieved fame; his early
use of air power is less well known. Lawrence described how
Allenby's belief in the importance of air power was an essential
part of his campaign. He saw to it that Brig.-General

W. G. G. Salmond, commanding the R.F.C. in the
Middle East, had control of the skies before the second
offensive; this turned out to be one of the crucial factors. Air
power, as Lawrence said, was an 'indispensable part in
Allenby's scheme: the perfection of this man who could use
infantry and cavalry, artillery and Air Force, Navy and
armoured cars, deceptions and irregulars, each in its best
fashion! . . . The co-operation of the air with his unfolding
scheme had been so ready and elastic, the liaison so complete
and informed and quick. It was the R.A.F., which had con-
verted the Turkish retreat into rout, which had abolished
their telephone and telegraph connections, had blocked their
lorry columns, scattered their infantry units.'² One of
Allenby's air staff officers recalled: 'He was quick to realize
how usefully aeroplanes might be employed in Palestine and
how vital was the command of the air. One of his first acts on
reaching the advanced headquarters before Gaza was to
make a personal investigation of the equipment and organization of the units of Royal Flying Corps under his command.
Before any advance was attempted, he secured the mastery of
the air by equipping us with Bristol fighters and made, for
the first time, arrangements for the adequate use of air intelligence. Throughout the spring and early summer of 1918,
Allenby steadily pursued his policy of increasing his air
forces, and of encouraging their personnel by his own constant interest.'³ In his last despatch of the war, Allenby
wrote:

Brilliant work has been done by the Royal Air Force and the
Australian Flying Corps, not only during the actual operations,
but in the preceding months. The process of wearing down the
enemy's strength in the air had been continuous throughout the
summer. Our ascendancy in the air became so marked towards
the end of August that only a few of the enemy's aeroplanes were
able to fly, with the result that my troops were immune from air
attacks during the operations, and the whole strength of the Air
Forces could be concentrated on the enemy in his retreat. Besides
taking an active part in the fighting, the Air Forces provided me
with full and accurate information as to the enemy's movements.

In the same despatch, Allenby, who used every ploy in his last campaign with a symmetrical perfection that will always delight the historian and the arm-chair strategist, also acknowledged the part played by the Arabs of Feisal and Lawrence:

The Arab Army has rendered valuable assistance, both in cutting the enemy's communications before and during the operations, and in co-operating with my cavalry during the advance on Damascus. By throwing itself across the enemy's line of retreat north of Deraa it prevented the escape of portions of the IVth Turkish Army, and inflicted heavy casualties on the enemy. [4]

Allenby's insistence on careful and thorough individual training before an offensive, to instil in the troops confidence in themselves as much as to develop their skills—a policy sometimes disastrously lacking on the Western Front in Europe, and the forerunner of Wavell's theory of the 'individual infantryman'—played an important part in his success:

After taking Jerusalem, a large part of my Army was taken away and replaced by troops from India, many of them only partly trained. The way these men prepared themselves for the work they had before them was excellent, and deserving of the highest praise. I was told it would take seven months to train them, but we trained them in ten weeks. . . . What carried these troops to victory was the fact that during the summer they had been training mind and body with one object in view—that was to beat the enemy. [5]

After the war, Allenby seldom expressed himself on military affairs, but on the very rare occasions he did so, he wrote with his customary sense:

Unnecessary fighting can be averted if the statesmen are strategists and the strategists statesmen. These two bodies must work together and keep in touch. For strategy is war policy, and policy is peace strategy. . . . Obviously future wars will be fought by airplanes, and certainly will begin in the air. But we need every sort of arms in war. The best Generals are those who combine their arms with the greatest effect. Aviation has given war a third dimension. Hitherto we used to war flat, by land and sea. Wellington always wondered what was on the other side of the hill. He often waited weeks and months to find out. Now a plane flies over, and within an hour you know exactly what is going on there. Aviation will become more and more important in military tactics. . . . There was no outstanding error in the last war, but many small ones. The main thing we found we did wrong was not having compulsory service sooner. In another big war we shall have learned to organize better. Many of our best brains went out to the front and got killed. They could have contributed much more by remaining behind. Organize your reserves, instead of wasting them. That is the great lesson this war taught us. In a future war not only the men will be mobilized, but the wealth of the nation as well.[6]

In South Africa, Allenby had proved himself a thoughtful and vigorous commander, not afraid of responsibility or unconventional ideas. In the manœuvres before the First World War he had been both brilliantly good and thoroughly bad. As commander of the cavalry in France and Flanders, he had been totally overcome by circumstances, but kept his head, if not his troops. In the stalemate of the Western Front he showed a desire, and some ability, to do something better than hurl men at immensely strong fortifications; a cavalryman himself, he was able to see that his own arm of the service was, in the circumstances, no longer of much practical use; he endeavoured to restore an element of surprise to the proceedings. In Palestine, he found practically everything in his favour, and with consummate care traced out for himself a battle of a General's dreams.

It is, of course, true that Allenby relied greatly on his staff. He saw himself as an over-all commander, outlining the general strategy, co-ordinating the air, naval and military arms with the tactical schemes of a brilliant staff. This has sometimes been held against him; it is difficult to see why. Allenby surrounded himself by good staff men; on his arrival in Egypt and Palestine those who did not come up to the highest standards were sent home. This caused considerable bitterness, but not among those whose lives were saved as a result of well-planned and successful battles. In his role as overlord, Allenby was the first of the modern Supreme Commanders. It is also held against Allenby that he had a numerical strength over the enemy. This was, in fact, what was most right about his campaign. As with Montgomery's crossing of the Rhine in 1945, delayed until Montgomery was convinced of his own overwhelming strength, the troops engaged have never been known to complain.* Moreover, Allenby's basic principles, as enumerated above, were his own, gained from hard, commonsense thinking and long experience, particularly under conservative commanders in the South African War; any staff which worked under Allenby knew the plan it submitted would have to follow the principles of 'the Chief'.

---

* Perversely enough, Wavell, the apostle of mobility, concentration and pursuit, believed Montgomery's desire to strike at Berlin in a single thrust was wrong, and that the Eisenhower plan of a broader front with several thrusts, which was in the event employed, was the best one. He was one of the few British Generals to hold this view.

CHAPTER 10

Allenby and Lawrence

I'm a funny card, really.
T. E. LAWRENCE

Allenby was never quite able to accept Lawrence as the great war hero which he was shortly to be proclaimed, nor, as he has been described, as 'the only man of genius that the war produced'. The streak of theatricality in Lawrence was not the sort of thing towards which he was likely to be sympathetic. Lawrence's addiction to Arab dress during the Peace Conference, for instance, and his 'Prince of Mecca' entry in *Who's Who*, would not have endeared him to Allenby. Nevertheless, he had the highest regard for him as an unconventional soldier, and was interested in his complicated character.

He realized, at their very first meeting, that Lawrence's enthusiasm for the Arab revolt, if harnessed to his own ends, might make a substantial contribution to the campaign. Meinertzhagen, who, as Chief of Military Intelligence, saw a good deal of Lawrence when the latter was at G.H.Q., wrote in 1921 : 'Lawrence owes everything he has ever had to Allenby. He was created by Allenby, rewarded by Allenby, and his reputation, such as it is, is of Allenby's creation.'[1] According to Lord Rosebery (previously Dalmeny), in an article in the *Daily Telegraph*, Allenby wished at one time to recommend Lawrence for the Victoria Cross. (Rosebery also pointed out that Allenby's advance could not have continued if Feisal's Arabs on his right flank had turned hostile.) According to Lawrence himself, Wingate wanted to recommend him for the V.C. after Akaba, and it was Allenby who suggested a knighthood;[2] and the latter is quite possible. Allenby told his A.D.C. in Cairo that he resented Lawrence's refusal of honours, but that the Lord Chamberlain, who got a 'wigging', should have foreseen it.

To Lawrence's surprise, it did not take him weeks, or even months, to win over Allenby: merely about twenty minutes at their first meeting. Lawrence was so astonished by this that he was inclined to hero-worship Allenby ever after. Moreover, after the failure at the Yarmuk bridge, many commanders would have been frightened off, especially as there was still bad feeling against Lawrence at G.H.Q., some of it from men whom Allenby trusted. He used Lawrence most cleverly, realizing that here was a man who had to be given full scope and plenty of rein if he were to be of any use at all. He bullied him and flattered him by turn, but never ignored or insulted him, nor even treated him as a General might a very junior Major, and later a Lt.-Colonel; nor did he expect Lawrence to treat him with the conventional niceties of military rank. Lawrence, in his brashest moods, spoke to Allenby in a way that probably no other General of the war would have stood for. A good, working relationship developed between the two men. For much of the time Allenby was, in effect, the only man from whom Lawrence took orders, and to whom he reported: a unique privilege among the British officers in the desert. The collision of these two strong, but totally different, personalities is one of the most fascinating in military history. That this brilliant amateur and great professional worked so well together is very much to the credit of both of them. But there is no question that Allenby was not the dominating personality. As Wavell, who admired both men, has said: 'Lawrence had great courage, versatility and quickness of mind, but Allenby was unquestionably the stronger and greater character of the two outstanding figures in this campaign.'[3]

There were few in Palestine who were not susceptible to Allenby's personality, and Lawrence was particularly vulnerable in this respect. He had previously formed a very bad opinion of all Generals, like many students of military matters who find themselves in humble positions in armies; he referred to them as 'reds', a reference to their traditional complexions, and equivalent to 'blimps'. When he first saw the new Commander-in-Chief at Ismailia Station, he must have formed a very bad impression of him, for 'the Bull', who looked as if he had been born and moulded for the express purpose of being a General, was very red indeed, being fresh to the Egyptian sun. But, as he soon discovered, here was a General who could quote Milton's *Comus* at length, and who would break off a discussion about strategy to discuss roses, French literature, the habits of birds and, incredibly, Crusader castles; and, what was more, a man who clearly preferred such discussion and only returned to the military subject on hand with evident reluctance. Lawrence never really got over his surprise at discovering that the Commander-in-Chief relished the war very much less than he did himself. He wrote later of Allenby's 'self-standing quality of greatness', and referred to the two of them as 'lion and mouse'. Nevertheless, if he thought it suited him, he could speak against him. At a private luncheon party given by Winston Churchill in London on the 24th of December, 1921, Lawrence was highly critical of his former commander. At the time Lawrence was courting Churchill, the Colonial Secretary, in order to get Arab kingdoms for Feisal and his brother Abdullah, and he said what he thought Churchill wanted to hear.[4]

Lawrence's other surprise about Allenby was the extent to which Allenby relied on his staff, and this appears to have been his one major reservation about Allenby as a commander. It surprised a number of other astute observers, including Meinertzhagen. But Allenby, who certainly had no inclination for or liking of some of the irksome tasks of a commander, was a delegator supreme. It has already been

noted how his harshest critic, Gough, considered this his
weakest point. He knew his own limitations, and was glad to
lean on men like Dawnay. Allenby did not have a quick,
agile brain. As Lawrence said: 'His mind is like the prow of
the *Mauretania*. There is so much weight behind it that it
does not need to be sharp like a razor.' He saw his job as the
leader, as the man who had to make the critical decisions
without fear, and as the man whose duty it was to make sure
that, the decisions having been made, they were given the
best possible chance of success—especially in the matter
of preparations before an offensive. Oddly enough, one
of the occasions that Allenby did not rely on the staff was
in his dealings with Lawrence, and the latter benefited,
perhaps, more than anyone from Allenby's willingness to
delegate. Lawrence wrote: 'Allenby never questioned our
fulfilling what was ordered. Power lay in his calm assumption that he would receive as perfect obedience as he gave
trust.'[5]

Both Allenby and Lawrence were progressives. But Lawrence had thought more about warfare than Allenby had
done, and the latter, despite his experiences in South Africa,
was never fully inclined to accept Lawrence's pleas that the
Arabs should be used as guerrillas instead of as an organized
right wing to the British force. Lawrence wrote: 'Our
tactics were always tip and run, not pushes, but strokes; we
never tried to maintain or improve an advantage, but to
move off and strike again somewhere else. We used the
smallest force, in the quickest time, at the farthest place.'[6]
There was, however, plenty of justification for Allenby's
belief that, unless organized, the Arab support would dissi-
pate itself somewhere in the desert in private squabbles. In
the matter of the Hejaz Railway raids, however, Lawrence
was right. Despite von Sanders's own incontrovertible admis-
sion that the railway attacks were his greatest bane, critics
have continued to suggest that Lawrence was employed on
spectacular but unimportant sorties; in fact, he and the other
British demolitionists were seriously undermining the whole
Turkish force by piercing the wounded and useless limb that

it refused to amputate, and which it dragged behind it.* However, disregarding Lawrence's failures, Allenby supported some guerrilla activities, including the vital breachings of the railway around Deraa. Eventually, he was quite as enthusiastic about the armoured car—although its possibilities in the desert were limited at that time—as was Lawrence himself, which is saying a great deal. His ideas on the use of the aeroplane, under Salmond, were quite as advanced as those of Lawrence.† He used these techniques not because, like Lawrence, he had studied their application to war, but because he was prepared to try anything that might help him to beat the Turks. And yet, as will be seen in a later chapter, Allenby's confidence in Lawrence had the greatest effect on Wavell, an observant and thoughtful spectator to all these affairs, and it thus had a direct influence on the Second World War.

*   *   *

Allenby has been credited with saying to Lawrence, still only thirty at the end of the war: 'In fifty years your name will be a household word; to find out about Allenby they will have to go to the War Museum.' Lawrence's fame has often been laid at the door of the American reporter Lowell Thomas. Thomas, and a photographer named Harry Chase, had been sent to Europe to find a dramatic and heroic war story to help get America into the war; unable to find anything suitable on the Western Front, they appealed to John Buchan, then with the Ministry of Information. Buchan arranged for their transfer to Allenby's Headquarters, where he thought they might find what they sought. Thomas,

* The idea that the Hejaz Railway was too well defended to be totally destroyed by attacks from Arab tribesmen had been predicted by one of Wingate's Intelligence officers, who had travelled its entire length, as early as 1907.[7]

† Brig.-General Geoffrey Salmond (Air Commodore, 1918), commanding the R.F.C. in Palestine; brother of Maj.-Gen. John Salmond, commanding the R.F.C. in France.

Lord Allenby, Lord Balfour and Sir Herbert Samuel
in Jerusalem, March, 1925.

Reviewing French Dragoons at Reims after the war.

with excellent news sense, realized that in Lawrence he had found the story of a lifetime, and Chase found Lawrence the most willing subject among the various British officers based at Akaba. After the war they did a two-man lecture-and-slides show, first at the Century Theatre, New York, in March, 1919, and then at Madison Square Garden. Thomas, who had a great opinion of Allenby, called the show 'With Allenby in Palestine and Lawrence in Arabia'. He apparently felt that he could hardly get away with the Lawrence material unless he harnessed it to the unquestionable authenticity of Allenby, who had become a well-known name in America at the time of the entry into Jerusalem. Allenby, indeed, was the best-known British General in the United States. But to Thomas's surprise, the audiences, starved of excitement and glamour in the war, were clamouring to hear more of Lawrence; soon Thomas dropped some of the Allenby side of the show, making it more and more a colourful account of Lawrence's adventures, some of it supplied by Lawrence himself. Thus Lawrence became a legend in America when he was still practically unknown in his own country.

The English impresario, Percy Burton, who had managed Henry Irving and Sarah Bernhardt, saw the performance at Madison Square Garden and asked Thomas and Chase to bring the show to London. He had never before heard of Lawrence. He enlisted the help of Sir Evelyn Wrench and the English-Speaking Union. In London, in September, 1919, the performance, entitled 'With Allenby in Palestine', was given at the Royal Opera House, Covent Garden, at the Queen's Hall, and at the Albert Hall. It was a tremendous success.* The critic of the somewhat caustic and left-wing *Nation* wrote: 'I am not greatly in love with war films, but I make a well-merited exception in favour of Mr Lowell Thomas's pictures of Allenby's Eastern Campaign. Somehow,

---

* It was not, however, the first in London. In April, 1919, an illustrated lecture—'Allenby & His Crusaders in Palestine'—had been given by Miss Frances Newton; it had not mentioned Lawrence.

overdone with soldiering, popular fancy has all but missed its two romantic figures, Allenby and Lawrence. Allenby's capture of Jerusalem, his gift of organization, his wonderful strategy in Northern Palestine, and his way with Orientals, exhibit him as perhaps the one soldier-statesman of the war. But Lawrence has remained almost unknown.'[8] Lawrence himself, who had been made a Research Fellow at All Souls, Oxford, in order to give him time to write up his experiences, went to London and heard it several times. Allenby also went to it. He wrote to his mother:

We went to a Covent Garden entertainment yesterday. Lowell Thomas had asked us to accept a box. I had a very enthusiastic reception, and was often vociferously cheered by the whole house.[9]

Soon over a million people had seen the performance. A three-year tour of the English-speaking world followed, and Lawrence's immortality was assured. Lawrence was hardly the man to denounce publicly some of the exaggerations of the 'Sheik of Araby' type that some have said were in the show. Naturally this fame displeased a number of people; every generation finds it difficult to accept its own legends. The idea of Lawrence floating about in the desert, his robes flowing behind him, was difficult to accept for some like Richard Aldington in his critical biography *Lawrence of Arabia*, Aldington was an ardent Francophile, who had fought and suffered in the holocaust in France and Flanders. Some who had known him as an obscure staff officer in Cairo mistook the vision which he had, and which they lacked, for ambitious push. Most of those who have bitterly attacked Lawrence's achievements have been French, Zionist or members of the Mesopotamia group, who resented Lawrence's efforts on behalf of the Hashemite sons of Hussein. (The next generation of Wingates, Orde Wingate and Sir Ronald Wingate, Sir Reginald's son and Political Officer in Mesopotamia during the war, were associated with the last two attitudes respectively.) The two most balanced critiques of

Lawrence, however, are by French and Swedish authors.[10] Some critics found Lawrence's later life melodramatic and distasteful. There were rumours that he was illegitimate, that he was homosexual. But the iconoclasts were unable to destroy the pure nugget of solid achievement in Lawrence's career. His book, *Seven Pillars of Wisdom*, provided them with ammunition, for it was not only written and presented in a self-conscious and flamboyant style, strongly flavoured with its 1920s period and with Lawrence's hero C. M. Doughty, but it also contained minor contradictions and errors. But the book had been seen by Allenby, Storrs, Alan Dawnay (a good friend of Lawrence) and others, and passed by them. Only one of those who served with Lawrence in the Hejaz ever spoke up and questioned his reputation, and he had not been in the campaign long, and was associated with the Mesopotamia and pro-Ibn Saud attitude. The only other who even offered mild criticism, along lines of it not being 'the whole truth', was Wavell; and yet Wavell, a man of the highest principles, would not have become a friend of Lawrence's right up till the latter's death, if he had suspected him of being a charlatan. The basic facts of Lawrence's career were true, and not even Aldington could deny them. Lawrence's sorties were not invariably successful, or even important, but the taking of Akaba was as heroic a deed as most in the war; the trips to the Yarmuk River were hazardous in the extreme. The worst faults of the *Seven Pillars of Wisdom*, if read as military history, are its omissions. The work of other British units, and particularly of the French, whose ambitions in the Middle East Lawrence abominated, are given little space. But Lawrence wrote a personal history, based on his own experiences; these he embellished here and there,* and wherever they probably are so embellished, as in the flogging episode, it is to accentuate Lawrence's toughness and manliness. As military history, the book is particularly invaluable for its finely observed and carefully drawn

---

* Lawrence frankly admitted this to Meinertzhagen on a number of occasions.

pen-portraits of the leading Arab and British figures of the campaign. Being primarily a personal history, there was no reason why Lawrence should write at length about others, and anyone approaching the book as a history of the campaign would get a one-sided impression; however, when Lawrence did mention the work of others, it was frequently with generosity, as, for instance, in the case of Alan Dawnay ('Allenby's greatest gift to us'). Lawrence was frank about the important part that gold played in his successes (about £500,000, of which Lawrence had spent all but £10,000 by Damascus). According to Storrs, the cost of the desert war to Britain was £11 million; for a time Hussein received £125,000 a month from Storrs.

Despite Thomas's efforts, to say nothing of those of Ronald Storrs and Robert Graves, the Lawrence legend would have been inevitable and irresistible: attending the Peace Conference dressed in his Emir's robes; his work under Churchill at the Colonial Office; his prominent part in the setting up of Iraq, under Feisal, and Jordan, under Abdullah, Feisal's brother; his translation of the Odyssey of Homer; his 100-m.p.h. motorbike, and his work on speed boats (Lawrence was never loath to prove his manliness); his literary friendships with Shaw and others. If a man can be judged by his friends, then Lawrence had little to fear. Among the seven friends who got together to make a public appeal for a memorial to Lawrence in St. Paul's Cathedral were Allenby, Winston Churchill and George Bernard Shaw. Above all, the legend could hardly have failed when Lawrence, scholar, ex-colonel and king-maker, opted for obscurity or, as some say, 'backed into the limelight', despite Churchill's offer of 'Governorships and great commands',[11] and spent nearly thirteen years in the ranks. The hardness of service life at that time was as hateful to Lawrence as had been some of the rigours in the desert, but he seemed to welcome their challenge to his will and his body. Perhaps, even on the 13th of May, 1935, as he drove at breakneck speed through the winding Dorset lanes, T. E. Lawrence, aged forty-six, had still not satisfied himself as to his own

ALLENBY AND LAWRENCE

fibre; but the hard, wiry little frame, although broken, its system smashed beyond repair, took seven days to die. At his burial Storrs and Newcombe helped to carry the coffin.

The debate on Lawrence continues, though his book is rightly accepted as a unique masterpiece. Who was right about Lawrence: the critics of later years who did not know the man, and were thus both ignorant and unencumbered with the bonds of personal relationship; or those, like Allenby, Wavell, Storrs, Newcombe, Stirling, Liddell Hart and Graves, who had known him? Stirling wrote: 'Lawrence took the limelight from those of us professional soldiers who were fortunate enough to serve with him, but never once have I heard even a whisper of jealousy . . . with the help of a few British officers, all senior to himself and professional soldiers, who willingly placed themselves under his general guidance, he galvanized the Arab revolt into a coherent whole.'[12]

Allenby, the only man without whose support the Lawrence legend would not have gone far, was always careful when asked to write or speak about Lawrence, and he did so as little as possible, while at the same time associating himself with Lawrence's less eulogistic admirers. After the war, Lawrence was anxious to see his hero again, but did not like to call on him unless bidden. The two men did not meet for many years.

As for Lawrence's part in the Palestine campaign, Allenby's careful words—from a man of unquestionable integrity—are among the most unbreakable and valuable tendons of the legend that surrounds that extraordinary, brilliant, troubled and unhappy man. When asked by Robert Graves if Lawrence would have made a good General, Allenby replied: 'A very bad General, but a good Commander-in-Chief, yes. There is no show that I would believe him incapable of running if he wanted to, but he would have to be given a free hand.' Allenby said of Lawrence:

He was perhaps the most interesting product of the Great War; yet, withal, a character difficult to know. Not that he was unsociable; the reason for his apparent aloofness was his way of reserving judgement on those he met until he had formed on them a mental diagnosis. But when Lawrence did give his friendship, he gave it freely; and, in return, no man has had more faithful friends. . . . His exceptional intellectual gifts were developed by mental discipline; and the trained mind was quick to decide and to inspire instant action in any emergency. Hence his brilliance as a leader in war.

Lawrence was, in manner, quiet and unassuming; his figure, slight and unimposing; but a high forehead and a clear eye betokened a brain of unusual power, a mind dominant over the body. Lawrence, by will power rather than by physical strength, could compete in endurance with the Arabs themselves. His fiery energy amazed and delighted them, and those children of the desert were drawn to him in almost fanatical devotion.[13]

When first I met him, in the summer of 1917, he had just returned from a venturesome raid behind the Turkish front. . . . Lawrence was under my command, but, after acquainting him with my strategical plan, I gave him a free hand. His co-operation was marked by the utmost loyalty, and I never had anything but praise for his work, which, indeed, was invaluable throughout the campaign.

He was the mainspring of the Arab movement. He knew their language, their manners, their mentality; he understood and shared their merry, sly humour; in daring he led them, in endurance he equalled, if not surpassed, their strongest. Though in complete sympathy with his companions, and sharing to the full with them hardship and danger, he was careful to maintain the dignity of his position as Confidential Adviser to the Emir Feisal. Himself an Emir, he wore the robes of that rank, and kept up a suitable degree of state. His own bodyguard, men of wild and adventurous spirit, were all picked by Lawrence personally. Mounted on thoroughbred camels, they followed him in all his daring rides; and among those reckless desert rangers there was none who would not willingly have died for their chief. In fact, not a few lost their lives through devotion to him and in defence of his person. The shy and retiring scholar, archaeologist-philosopher was swept by the tide of war into a position undreamt of . . . and there shone forth a brilliant tactician, with a genius for leadership. Such men win friends—such also find critics and detractors. But the highest reward for success is the inward knowledge that it has been rightly won. Praise or blame was regarded with indifference by Lawrence. He did his duty as he saw it before him. He has left, to us who knew and admired him, a beloved memory.[14]

CHAPTER 11

Peace: Egypt and the Middle East

*I work on the principle that the business of a
government is to govern.* ALLENBY

Allenby's greatest influence was as a soldier, but his greatest
work was as an administrator. During much of his time in
Egypt after the war he wielded the power of a mighty pro-
consul, for which he had no previous training whatsoever.
Apart from his service in South Africa, he had no experience
of imperialism or nationalism, having, unlike most of his
contemporaries, never served in India. Allenby, however, was
to develop into one of the most notable, and one of the
last, of the great British administrators and statesmen abroad.

At first, he saw his task as the comparatively simple one
of carrying out, unquestioningly, the instructions of the
Government in London. Unversed in the ways of international politics, he took it for granted that such instructions
would be equitable and honourable; and so, on the 7th of
November, 1917, he pledged that the only aim of the Allies
in the entire area was to set up governments based on free
choice of the inhabitants. Although this was to provide his
critics later with the charge of cynical insincerity, in fact
it only showed that Allenby at the time still had an un-
sophisticated view of French ambitions in the area, and
especially of the ramifications of the Sykes–Picot Agreement.
But in time he found that instructions from London were few
and impracticable, and that British policy in the Middle

East was indistinct; he was to find himself, by no means joyfully, with greater scope for his particular talents than he had enjoyed as a soldier.

At the end of the war, Allenby was the single authority for a vast territory stretching from Egypt, where the base area was still under martial law, right round the Levant to southern Turkey. His difficulties were not only political. There was the question of the Australian troops, who were becoming unruly, and whom he wished to repatriate as soon as possible.[1] There were great problems of supply, prisoners-of-war, health and civil administration, but he more and more left these to his able staff and concentrated on the political ferment, which frothed up over the entire area at the end of hostilities. Associated with this there were primarily three factors: the ambitions of the French, the ambitions of the Arabs, and the furtherance of British efforts to please both sides while retaining influence in the area themselves. At times Allenby must have thought his efforts to ward off disaster were like that of a Dutch boy with his finger in a dyke. Establishing himself at Haifa, Allenby, as was his practice, motored about the area, dealing with crises himself, on the spot, as they occurred. During December and January he thought nothing of forty-eight-hour journeys to some trouble spot at which he would spend only an hour or so before returning. Dusty, but apparently inexhaustible, he was always greeted with warmth; as a victor in war, if not as a saviour:

On arrival at Hama today, I was again escorted through the town by wild Arabs on horseback. Rifles and pistols cracking off in the air, spears brandished, and horses galloping round the car.[2]

Gifts were lavished on him. On one occasion he was presented with:

A brass tray and an earthenware drinking bowl; and I had to buy a silver and amber necklace and a heavy silver ornament, worn, as a mark of virginity, around the neck. Virgins are, I believe, scarce.[3]

Immediately after the war, the worst of the problems was that concerning the French, but before he could attend to it, Allenby had first to deal with the Turks. North of Aleppo some of the Turkish forces were disregarding the armistice, and, encouraged by this, politicians at Constantinople began to show signs of haggling with the Allies. Allenby, accompanied by Wavell, boarded a French warship and went to the Turkish capital himself, while the Turkish government prepared a number of arguments and proposals. A two-man delegation was sent to voice these opinions to Allenby at the British Embassy. Unfortunately for them, Allenby was in his most dominating mood, and the two men, considerably shaken by Allenby's manner, left the Embassy without saying hardly a word between them.

I met the Minister of Foreign Affairs and the Minister of War. I gravely told them why I had come, and, refusing to hear any arguments, I left them the text of my demands in English and in Turkish. They were taken quite aback; and I do not think they will forget it while they live.[4]

Allenby immediately re-embarked and returned to Haifa. This interview marked the end of Turkish ambitions as an imperial power; the two ministers were so impressed that they put under way the measures of the armistice, and those demanded by Allenby, 'with all haste'.

Arab–French bitterness in Syria had already made that area explosive, and, while other leaders of the war were taking part in victory celebrations and riding through the crowded streets of European capitals, Allenby was fully engaged keeping the peace. The French Government still based its claims on the Sykes–Picot agreement, and both men were now in the area. Sykes himself had never been enthusiastic about the 'treaty' which bore his name.* French forces and administrators had entered Syria from Beirut, and the

* Sir Mark Sykes, diplomat and Middle East expert; father of Christopher Sykes, who wrote the definitive biography of Orde Wingate.

Arab army was preparing, outside Damascus, to push them back again. Allenby deployed British troops to keep both sides apart, thus, in the same rigmarole that was to heap curses on Britain for the next half-century, bringing accusations of treachery and favouritism from both sides. As early as the 30th of January, 1918, the French Ambassador in London, M. Cambon, had called at the Foreign Office to complain of Allenby's apparent unwillingness to allow the French full scope, although he admitted 'that French interests in the country were possibly rather sentimental than material and that French feeling in regard to them was exaggerated'. Sir Ronald Graham, Permanent Under-Secretary of State, forcefully defended Allenby, pointing out that he was responsible for law and order in the entire area, and if he considered the arrival of French troops a danger to such order, he was right to insist upon his point. The future settlement of the Middle East would be decided by the Peace Conference.

Allenby was not always to receive such support from the Foreign Office.

In Paris, Allenby was considered a blatant supporter of the Arab extremists. Clemenceau himself attacked him. Allenby wrote to a friend: 'I am keeping my end up, so far; but there is need to walk warily.'[5]

Feisal, with his able and ambitious aide Nuri-as-Said, had gone to Europe to plead his cause, largely as a result of Allenby's pressure on London[6] and Lawrence's on Hussein of Mecca. They were escorted by Lawrence, who was given a special grant of £1,000 for the purpose, and who ostentatiously associated himself with the Damascene cause by wearing his Emir's robes. Wavell, now a Lt.-Colonel of thirty-five, was on leave in England, and Allenby wrote to him:

Feisal wires that he is receiving sympathetic treatment. I am just back from Aleppo and Beirut, and have seen both Picot and Sykes; Sykes is all for soothing the Arabs and giving them a port.[7]

In Palestine, Allenby's task was a little easier. The full effect on Arab opinion of the Balfour Declaration was still not being felt, and Allenby refused to accord any Jewish privileges on the strength of it until after the Peace Conference had decided the fate of the country. His case was that Palestine was still an enemy territory occupied in war, and as such no alteration could be made to the political structure of the country until a peace treaty had been announced. Despite this, he managed, remarkably, to retain the trust and goodwill of the Jewish population; more so, perhaps, than that of the Arabs, although he was naturally criticized by the more militant Zionists. His attitude was also severely criticized in London, and even on his own staff.

Allenby's Political Officer in Palestine was Meinertzhagen. He believed that the Commander-in-Chief, and his deputy, Bols, were not ruling Palestine in accordance with the Balfour Declaration, which had stated a clear British policy of supporting Jewish claims. He wrote to the Foreign Office complaining about this, and was promptly sent home. The two men parted on the best of terms. They had a common love of birds, Meinertzhagen being one of the leading ornithologists in the Middle East. Allenby was in a difficult position, with his staff and advisers coming increasingly out in the open as Arab supporters. These men, who included Wavell, Storrs, Deedes and Lawrence's protégés, appeared to be in the ascendancy, but not long after Meinertzhagen's departure responsibility for Palestine was taken out of Allenby's hands. Lloyd George and his Foreign Secretary, Balfour, were both sympathetic to the Jewish case, and Herbert Samuel, himself a Jew, was made Chief Administrator for Palestine. Allenby's impartiality in all this is illustrated in the fact that Wavell thought Allenby pro-Jew, and Meinertzhagen believed he was pro-Arab. However, Allenby did strongly advise against Samuel's appointment, believing it to be 'highly dangerous'.

In Egypt, Allenby's responsibilities were at first few, but the seeds of his future discontent were already well sown. The country had been declared a British Protectorate a few months after the outbreak of war, although much of its domestic affairs had continued to be administered by Egyptians. This move was considered essential in order to safeguard the vital links of Empire. The only Ministry that had been taken over by the High Commissioner, McMahon, was that of Foreign Affairs. The Commissioner prior to McMahon, Lord Kitchener, had before this kept British power paramount in the country.

At the time of the proclamation of a Protectorate a 'puppet' Sultan had been installed, in the belief that an amenable figurehead would satisfy the Egyptians and be no bother to the British. On his death in 1917 he had been succeeded by his brother Fuad, later styled King of Egypt, the father of Farouk.* Fuad had little practical experience of Egypt, and in speech and outlook was Italian. During the war all had gone well, and many Egyptians, and the country as a whole, had profited from the British Army. The price of cotton had been high, and there were a number of cases of Egyptians who had owned about £5 in capital before the war having amassed a quarter of a million Egyptian pounds. Most British people in Cairo, civil and military, believed that British rule could be extended indefinitely. In fact, however, the Egyptian populace vastly resented this arrogant assumption; their aspirations had, indeed, only been curtailed for reasons of personal economics. The Legislative Assembly, which had been set up by Kitchener in 1913, burst into bitter activity at the end of the war, and there was much indignant talk of self-determination and the ideas of Theodore Roosevelt and even more those of Woodrow Wilson.[8] The Premier, Rushdi, lost control of the situation; a rival emerged in the person of an emotional, shrewd and not unworthy nationalist called Saad Zaghlul, who led the Wafd† party.

* Allenby: 'Farouk is a good-looking little lad 2½ years old, very fair, with blue eyes—talks English quite well.' (A.P. 23.9.22.)

† Arabic for delegation; a reference to the delegation to the Peace Conference which the Egyptians believed was their right.

Many of the events which now occurred were to be repeated again and again, in the coming decades, in other British territories, such as India, the Gold Coast, Cyprus and Kenya.

It was becoming evident to many Egyptians that they were not being represented by their real leader. With the ending of the war, there was a great urge throughout the world for a new order, and Rushdi was not seizing the opportunity. It was Zaghlul who called on Sir Reginald Wingate and, claiming to speak for the Egyptian people, demanded independence. Wingate was not totally unaware of the dangers and trends of the day and, instead of clapping Zaghlul in jail, he suggested to the Foreign Office that the nationalist should go to London and put his case before the British Government. This the Foreign Office curtly refused to accept. Wingate then suggested that Rushdi should go, but this was also turned down. At this same time, Feisal, who did not even represent a nation, was being politely listened to in London and Paris. In Cairo such a situation was intolerable. Wingate went to London himself. As Balfour, the Foreign Secretary, and much of the Foreign Office, had settled in Paris for the Peace Conference, current foreign affairs had been put in charge of Lord Curzon, who had moved into the Foreign Office and taken over considerable power there. Wingate waited in London for fourteen days before Curzon agreed to see him. Then, on his own authority, Curzon again made the disastrous and unimaginative decision to refuse an audience for Zaghlul. In February, 1919, a further decision of Balfour's to receive Rushdi came too late. (In a series of letters to Wingate, Balfour later said all decisions had been taken by Curzon, but Curzon said they had been taken in Paris.[9]) Zaghlul was the acknowledged leader of Egypt, and his political agitations were bringing the country to the brink of serious disorder. On the 8th March he was arrested and taken to Malta. This action, naturally, made the situation ten times worse for the British, and assured Zaghlul of victory in the end. Within days Egypt was in revolt, as Wingate had predicted.

Allenby had just left Haifa for the Peace Conference in Paris, where he was airing his views on the Syrian question. He most strongly advised against imposing the French on an unwilling Syria: 'there would be war,' he said.[10] Meinertz-hagen was also at the Conference: 'General Allenby arrived here today from Egypt to give his opinion on the future of Syria, which our plenipotentiaries have been unable to decide. I am glad to say that Allenby's views in no way differed from those of the General Staff, namely that we cannot divide up Syria as we would an apple, but must place it under one mandatory power, and that that mandatory power cannot be France owing to the intense local dislike towards her. . . . Allenby is really a most remarkable man, and his personality is most contagious.'[11]

This was Allenby's first entry into the world of statesmen and high diplomacy, and by all accounts he acquitted himself well: even the French were impressed with him. But as a newcomer into this stratosphere, his ambitions went no farther than faithfully and solidly backing up the views of the military hierarchy in London; he had been away long, but he still knew what was expected of him. The view of the General Staff was mostly sound, but Lloyd George was not interested in the views of soldiers on any subject, even war, and he believed that he himself understood the Middle East best. Despite the report of an American Commission, appointed by the Conference, that a French mandate would not be feasible in Syria, Lloyd George later agreed to trade Syria (to say nothing of a considerable slice of Turkey) for British influence in Iraq and Palestine, the latter to be mandated under British rule with the mission of making it a national home for the Jewish people and reconciling the Arab inhabitants to the process. The British thereby gave the French the ambition they had harboured, but had been unable to satisfy on their own account, since Louis Quatorze, and took on for themselves the most thankless task that existed at that time in the world.

While this argument and bargaining over Syria was going on, the situation in Egypt deteriorated; and the unfortunate

Wingate was still kicking his heels in London. It appears to have been tacitly decided that Wingate should be offered to the public as a scapegoat, although his advice, consistently ignored, had been consistently proved sound. Ruthless and determined action was clearly needed, or so it seemed in Whitehall, and who better to do so than the man widely known in London and Cairo as 'the Bull'? If anyone was likely to stand for no nonsense, and to enforce the benefits of British Protection on an ungrateful and ignorant people, then surely it was this tough, domineering soldier. Allenby was immediately appointed Special High Commissioner for Egypt, and instructed by the Cabinet to leave Paris for Cairo immediately.

On arrival in Cairo, he found the situation already under control, thanks to the use of the remaining British forces in Egypt under Bulfin. He immediately called for an assembly of leading citizens at the Residency. He addressed them in the following terms:

It is my desire and duty to assist in bringing to the country peace, quiet and contentment. My intentions are: first, to bring the present disturbance to an end; secondly, to make careful inquiry into all matters which have caused discontent in the country; thirdly, to redress such grievances as appear justifiable. It is you who can lead the people of Egypt. It is your duty to work with me in the interest of your country. I cannot believe that any of you will not assist me in every way, and I am prepared to rely on you to set to work at once with a view to calming the passions now set loose. After quiet has been restored, I feel confident that you will trust me to inquire impartially into all grievances, and to make such recommendations as may seem to be desirable for the content and well-being of the people of Egypt.

The effect of these resounding and obviously sincere words was to pacify for a while the entire country. Here was a man who not only held out a promise for the future, but who looked and sounded as if he really meant it. Allenby's prestige in the Middle East as conqueror of the Turks was great. This generous declaration was read in

Britain, however, with some concern. Could these be the words of a reliable and uncomplicated soldier-imperialist? The *Manchester Guardian* commented: 'There is good reason to expect an important change of policy towards Egypt. General Allenby's speech the other day sketched a programme which implies a very different temper from the temper in which Mr Balfour received the studiously moderate and proper requests of the Egyptian Ministers.'[12]

Allenby's first promise was complete within a week of his arrival. He devoted himself, therefore, to his second and third promises. Within seven days of his arrival in Cairo he telegraphed London recommending the immediate return of Zaghlul from Malta.

This telegram was greeted at the Foreign Office with amazement, astonishment and dismay. Allenby had replaced Wingate in order to lay a firm hand on Egypt, but now he appeared to be more 'soft' than Wingate himself. The discarded Wingate was, no doubt to his surprise, consulted about his successor's request, and he advised against the return of Zaghlul on the grounds that this would appear a capitulation to the forces of disorder. But Allenby had specifically been given the unprecedented post of 'Special' Commissioner, with extraordinary powers; the Government now could hardly ignore his advice, however distasteful. After a week's hesitancy, the release of Zaghlul was announced. This decision was greeted with hysteria by Egyptians, but with confusion by the British colony in Egypt, who branded Allenby as pro-Egyptian, an attitude which he considered an essential qualification for any High Commissioner of the country. His relations with one section of the local British community were never good. It had previously been the custom frequently to invite to the Residency British officials on loan to the Egyptian Ministries and other administrators; Allenby reduced these invitations, and in some cases stopped them altogether. Egyptians, and members of the non-British foreign communities, were asked more often.

So began Allenby's remarkable career in Egypt. Sent out

to preserve the *status quo* until the British Government had found the time or inspiration to attend to the Egyptian problem, he had reversed the situation within fourteen days of taking up his post. It was announced that a Mission of Inquiry, to be headed by Lord Milner—who had been an influential High Commissioner in South Africa throughout the Boer War, who was now Colonial Secretary, and who had written an authoritative book on Egypt—was to go to Cairo; it would study the situation and make recommendations to the Government as to Egypt's future. The clear indication was that independence was in the offing. The country settled into a short period of comparative calm.

*   *   *

Since the ending of the war, Allenby had missed most of the pageantry and gaiety, the victory rides and the brave speeches which had accompanied that event. In July, 1919, however, he attended a thanksgiving ceremony at the Alhambra Theatre, Alexandria, and there he gave one of his rare, and one of his first, carefully composed speeches:

It is nearly five years now since the war began, and we are here tonight to celebrate peace. . . . We have shattered that Power that for over a generation terrorized Europe, and we have been the means of bringing about the peace of the whole world. We see, besides that broken Power, boundary walls and fences broken down everywhere. Empires dissolved and crowns shattered. Is this the end? Are we to see civilization breaking up? No. We can and we shall build up a new and better world. We must face the difficulties, which are tremendous. We must face probably greater tasks than human beings ever had to face before, and we must work wholeheartedly and unitedly. Not only individuals, but nations, must work together, sinking their own differences and recognizing their duties and the sacrifices which those duties will inevitably involve. Winning the war is only the beginning of peace. During the last five years we have been destroying wealth and building engines for destroying property, and in many cases this has brought countries to the verge of ruin. We have to reverse that state of things now. Not to destroy, but to construct. You know what is required in creating wealth. Wealth is not silver and gold, it is food and clothing. We shall have now to erect a glorious monument to those who have died in the cause of justice and humanity. Our brothers and sons have given their lives by the hundreds of thousands, and we now have to erect a monument worthy of them. There is hardly a part of the world—civilized or uncivilized—which is not the scene of the burial of our glorious dead. We have got to be true to their memory. They have given all, and we have got to see to it that they have not given their all in vain. Their work is ended—ours is beginning. It depends on how we do that work whether we shall be judged worthy to share in the triumph which they have won.[13]

A few days after delivering this address, Allenby received a letter from Lloyd George informing him that a Viscountcy was to be conferred on him, and that he was to be awarded a grant of £50,000.* This latter news was particularly welcome, as the expense of being High Commissioner required substantial private means, which Allenby had not possessed. Wingate, who had also been without private resources, had already discovered this to his dismay. Allenby had known about the peerage for eight months before the official announcement.

It would not do to refuse it. I love to know, however, my sweetheart, that I shall be always your own knight. This is Michael's birthday. He is 21 today.[14]

For his title, Allenby chose 'Allenby of Felixstowe and

* Haig, having held out for a 'substantial' grant, and having turned down a Viscountcy, received an Earldom and was awarded £100,000. He also accepted a large country house, bought by public subscription from a branch of his family. Other grants were: Beatty—£100,000; Jellicoe—£50,000; Byng, Horne, Plumer, and Rawlinson—£30,000 each; Birdwood, Keyes, Robertson, Trenchard, Wilson—£10,000 each. After the Second World War, Montgomery and other commanders, on being approached by the Government, indicated that such grants would not be accepted by them. No commanders were given an Earldom for military services.

Megiddo': the first to please his mother and the second for its historical associations, which did not displease him. After the second breakthrough in the Palestine campaign, his excited staff had dubbed titles on each other in anticipation of the great victory; Allenby had then chosen Megiddo for himself.

I don't think I can do better than Allenby of Megiddo—Megiddo was the crucial point of last year's campaign; and is the base of the name Armageddon, which means 'place of Megiddo'. Alternatives are Esdraelon and Aleppo; and I like neither.[15]

It was also at this time that Allenby learnt he was to be promoted Field-Marshal. Warm congratulations flowed in from such old friends as Birdwood, Plumer, Clayton, Baden-Powell and the Duke of Connaught; the latter, with Baroness de la Grange, whom Allenby had visited again when at the Peace Conference, his old padre of the Boer War, Father Knapp, General Lord Horne, General Barrow, Herbert Lawrence, the second Lord Rothschild, and Dalmeny, was among Allenby's close personal friends. The Duke of Connaught had served under Allenby in the 4th Cavalry Brigade in 1905. In later years, they had struck up a firm friendship together; during the war, Connaught had visited Allenby in Palestine. One telegram of congratulations came from Feisal's Governor of Damascus: 'The Syrians will never forget your patronage and interest in them.'[16]

After more than two years, Allenby was at length granted a few weeks' home leave. He arrived at Victoria Station, London, on the 16th of September, 1919, and entered on a triumphal series of personal tributes, which in their warmth and spontaneity had been accorded no other British commander of the war, not even Haig or Beatty. This was all the more surprising as the public might reasonably have been well sated with official functions in honour of war leaders; but the entry of Jerusalem still captured the public imagination, and the Lawrence legend was just reaching the full flush of its first bloom. Honours were lavished upon him. Both Houses of Parliament accorded him a vote of thanks. He received the decorations of eleven Allied nations. He was made Colonel of the Life Guards. He was offered degrees by Oxford, Cambridge, Edinburgh, Yale and Aberdeen Universities.

On his arrival at Victoria Station, he was greeted, among others, by Douglas Haig and Lady Haig. The two men spoke together briefly and Allenby was seen to laugh; later in Allenby's tour, Haig invited him to a gathering of Scottish veterans in London. Another waiting for him on the platform was General Sir Archibald Murray, whom Allenby had recently praised in his despatches. Newspapers, at least one with the inevitable headline 'The Bull Returns', watched Allenby's every movement on his leave. Rumours were rife, particularly that Allenby, and not, as generally expected, Haig, would be given the coveted post of Commander-in-Chief in India. His visit to his mother at Felixstowe, which took place in an ocean of photographers, gave the old lady, now aged eighty-eight, great pride, but was not what Allenby himself had wanted for so long; he still wrote to his mother nearly every day.* In his Field-Marshal's uniform, he sat for a group portrait of the senior British military commanders by the leading American painter, Sargent. The one curious feature of this otherwise unexceptionable but enormous painting is, as has often been remarked, that Allenby has almost his full back on view, and appears to have turned round and to be staring straight at Haig, whereas the remainder of the group are nearly all painted in full face.

King George V was at Balmoral, and Allenby and his wife were invited to spend a few days there. But the greatest honour was always, rightly, considered by Allenby to be the Freedom of the City of London, bestowed on him at a glittering banquet at the Guildhall. Among those present were Haig, Herbert Lawrence, Birdwood, Chetwode, Ian Hamilton,

---

* Mrs Allenby, spry and formidable to the last, died in 1922, well content with a son whose character she had done so much to shape. George V wrote to Allenby of 'your dear mother—I know how devoted you were to her'. Felixstowe House was pulled down, and there is now a recreation ground on the site.

Trenchard, Shea, Dalmeny and Feisal—not to mention the
Archbishop of Canterbury, a Cardinal, the Chief Rabbi, the
Lord Chief Justice and the Prime Minister, with most of the
Cabinet, including the Minister of War, Winston Churchill.
In a resounding speech, the latter asked those present not to
forget, when speaking of 'the deadly blows struck at the
military fabric of the Turkish power', the contribution of
the Gallipoli campaign. Lloyd George said: 'Lord Allenby's
victories in Palestine will always be regarded as one of the
most brilliant military feats in the history of the world.'
It was Churchill who had been largely responsible for the
Gallipoli campaign, which, if properly conducted, would
have rendered the Palestine campaign superfluous; and it
was Lloyd George who had backed Allenby and the Palestine
affair, too late for much effect on the war at large. Even
among themselves the 'Easterners' did not always see eye to
eye.

In an eulogistic address, the City Chamberlain said:
'The Field-Marshal was not originally intended for the
military profession, as from Haileybury he successfully
passed the very difficult examination for the Indian Civil
Service. The love of the Army proved too great, so he threw
over the coveted opportunity he had won by his talents and
industry. . . .' Despite the pomp and ceremony of the occasion,
Allenby, typically, could not allow this error to pass:

I must begin by correcting a slight error the Chamberlain
made in his address. He told you I passed for the Indian Civil
Service. I did not. (Loud laughter.) I tried to, but I failed. (Renewed laughter and cheers.) I am happy now that I did fail.[17]

He went on to praise the men of twelve nationalities who
had fought under him: 'I had such an army as no other man
has ever commanded.' And he praised, particularly, Feisal's
Arabs: 'I am glad to call the Emir Feisal one of my greatest
friends.'

The liberator of Jerusalem, the victor of a dramatic and
romantic campaign, was one thing: the High Commissioner

of Egypt, it seemed, was another. In all the speeches of welcome, Egypt was barely mentioned. Most people in Britain were barely aware of the troubles there, and certainly did not want to hear anything further concerning them. It was the brink of the Jazz Age. The Charleston, the flapper, the punt and the 'boater' hat, the bound breast, the shingle—all were to become fashionable; foreign affairs and problems of Empire were to become unfashionable. There were troubles enough at home; the promised jobs for heroes were not always forthcoming; there was labour unrest, and rail and steel strikes. Egypt was a long way off; if Britain had obligations there, then the Government was no doubt attending to them. While everyone was delighted to meet Allenby, and confer honours on him, no one wanted to discuss Egypt and the Middle East. Allenby made a number of fruitless visits to 10 Downing Street, to determine from Lloyd George what, if anything, was immediate British policy in Egypt and the Middle East. On one occasion he was accompanied by Feisal and Lawrence. Milner himself was deeply engaged on other duties, and there was no sign of his departure for Egypt. Curzon was always busy. However, Allenby found a useful ally in Henry Wilson, who was sympathetic to his views; the two men, both with interests outside purely military affairs, still got on well together.

Back in Egypt, Allenby found that the political situation there had deteriorated. Zaghlul, in Paris, had ordered a boycott of the Milner Mission. Resignations from the Egyptian Government took place. Allenby's first care, as High Commissioner, was to secure a Ministry and the continuance of government in order that the administration of the country could be continued without serious break. As resignations in Cairo were frequent, this was a continual worry to him, particularly as he was of the belief that, once having appointed Ministers, it was useless for him to meddle in their departments if they were to be prepared for full self-government. It was work for which Allenby had little taste, but some natural aptitude. Always true to his word, he was

able to act as the one constant, solid cornerstone of the confused Egyptian political scene.

The lack of definite policy continued to embarrass Allenby,
a soldier trained to expect orders. A man with more political
training would have realized and accepted more easily the
day-to-day 'stop-gap' role that was required of him. He himself, however, was already convinced that the continuance of
the Protectorate was an impossible relationship between
Britain and Egypt.

From time to time he visited the Cairo Zoo to study the
beasts there. His celebrated stork at the Residency became
the best-loved pet of his life. This handsome bird, which became a legendary part of the Allenby story, had, in fact,
belonged to Lady Wingate, having been given to her in 1901
when Wingate was at Khartoum. Allenby inherited it,
according to Wingate's son, 'together with much else'.[18]
Other pets were two cranes and a parrot. Allenby, naturally,
took a great interest in the extensive gardens of the Residency, and also in the progress of archaeological work in
Egypt. He was friendly with Lord Carnarvon and was one of
the privileged group present at the opening of Tutankha-
men's Tomb, and among the first to see the treasure inside it.* But, in general, he had less time for his personal
interests than ever before in his life. One chore he had to
undergo was to sit for an as-yet-little-known artist, Eric
Kennington.[19]

I have had my portrait done in pastel, at the request of Lawrence, by a Mr Kennington, whom he brought out with him to
make portraits for a book which Lawrence is writing. I think the
likeness good.†

While in Cairo, Allenby was visited by his friends Feisal,
the Duke of Connaught and Baden-Powell, and, to his great

* Both Carnarvon, and his brother Aubrey Herbert, who had been in
the 'Arab Bureau' with Lawrence, died not long afterwards.

†This portrait was reproduced in *Seven Pillars of Wisdom*.

pleasure, the Baroness de la Grange. The Prince of Wales also stayed with him for a short while.

One of Allenby's A.D.C.s at this time gives a picture of a typical Allenby day: 'Mornings generally on administrative work, diplomatic, Egyptian affairs, receiving Egyptian notables, an occasional visit to King Fuad's palace, luncheon parties. The afternoons varied very much; attending the races, when he was driven down the course, going for walks, when he was driven across country, visiting the Zoo, and visiting exhibitions. From time to time there were musical afternoons at the Residency. In the evening; large dinner parties, visits to the opera house. When he was late for the opera on one occasion, there was a tremendous scene, and even his brother Claude, who was on a visit at the time, was alarmed. Once a week they dined alone, apart from one A.D.C. at their table.

'He was fond of walking, and I found that this was his opportunity for deep thinking. Several times he turned towards me and trod on my right foot, apparently oblivious of having done so, and then he came out of this trance with some interesting remarks. One was: "They sacked me from France, but it was a damned bad thing for the Turks."'

Among those of his war-time colleagues who remained with Allenby in Cairo for a while were Wavell, Dalmeny and Clayton. Wavell figured in an odd affair concerning Lawrence. Allenby was warned that Lawrence had disappeared from Feisal's side in Paris; the French were alarmed and believed it possible that Lawrence was on his way to Syria to organize Arab resistance to the French there. The Foreign Office did not take this seriously, but Allenby was advised to keep a close watch on Lawrence. The task of having a watch put out for him at the ports was entrusted to Wavell. Some weeks later, Lawrence was seen in Shepheard's Hotel— much to the surprise of Wavell; he was not on his way to Syria, and all passed off without incident, the two men being good friends. In 1920 Wavell rejoined his regiment, the Black Watch, in the Army of Occupation at Cologne.

Allenby continued his interest in the Syrian and Palestine problems, although he was no longer directly concerned with the second. It has recently been revealed[20] that Allenby played a much larger part in the Syrian affair, while High Commissioner for Egypt, than had been thought. He acted for some time as 'go-between' for the British Government and Feisal, and frequently supported the latter. On one occasion he transferred £100,000 to Feisal without authorization, indeed having been told not to do so; this resulted in an understandably cold telegram from Curzon.[21] Feisal always believed that Allenby would save him from the French.[22] Balfour told Allenby, categorically, in a telegram, that under no circumstances could Great Britain undertake a mandate for Syria, and that Feisal should be brought to appreciate the fact.[23] But Allenby seems to have found it difficult to stress this with Feisal, once a close ally in war; especially after his statement of the 7th of November, 1919. He wrote:

The French are, I fear, having bad trouble in Cilicia and Syria. They have had much fighting and heavy losses. Feisal is keeping Damascus quiet, but if he goes [back] to Paris the extremists will probably make trouble in his absence.[24]

Samuel will have difficult and trying work before him. Curbing the extreme views of his Zionist supporters and placating the hostility of the Moslems and Christians, who are shocked and angry at the appointment of a Zionist Jew as the first Governor of Palestine. However, he is an honest and moderate man, and I hope all will go well.[25]

I am glad to say that Samuel has had a good reception in Palestine, and seems to have won the support of all parties; and I hope that he will have great success. . . . Feisal wires me to, today, that he has conceded all the French demands, but that they are still assuming a hostile attitude. I have sent this on to the Foreign Office without comment.[26]

Herbert Samuel has returned to Jerusalem. I think he has quite the right ideas; and he should do well with luck. Not much more news from Syria, and what there is is not very certain; but I am afraid that Feisal and the French are at war. It is not Feisal's fault, but I don't think he can control the wilder spirits in Damascus, and the French have lost patience. [27]

This evening's wires say that, after much fighting, the French have entered Damascus. We have no details yet. I fear that this will be only the beginning of a lot of trouble. It is very disappointing to me, but I had not much hope of a peaceful outcome of the quarrel. [28]

I had a nice letter from Feisal today expressing his constant friendship for me. I have replied in similar terms.* [29]

The Milner Mission will go home again next month. I hope it has done good, but nothing very tangible has been achieved. [30]

I see that the Northern boundary of Palestine has been fixed. I don't think that the Zionists will be satisfied. They hoped for much more than has been allotted to Palestine, including the waters of the Yarmuk and Leontes, which they have not got. . . .

* The British obligingly installed Feisal as monarch in Iraq, much to the annoyance of the French, at a cost of £30 million a year, and with the backing of 40,000 British troops. [31] He died in Switzerland in 1933. His brother Abdullah was made King of Transjordan. This setting-up of two Hashemite Kingdoms was Lawrence's doing. The Hejaz continued first under Hussein until 1924, and then under another of his sons, Ali; in 1925, it was conquered by Ibn Saud of the Nejd and incorporated in Saudi Arabia. The British deserted Ali and Hussein and compacted with Saudi a triumph over the Lawrence–Hashemite faction for the Mespot-India faction, who had supported and subsidized Ibn Saud from the Persian Gulf during the war, although he had shown as much desire to fight Arabs as Turks (among the Lawrence-type figures of their sphere was H. St. J. Philby). Relations between the ruling descendants of Ibn Saud and those of Hussein have often been less than cordial. The Iraqi kingdom ended in revolt in 1958; Feisal II and Nuri-as-Said were assassinated. King Hussein of Jordan is the grandson of Abdullah. In 1941 it was Wavell who relieved the Vichy French of Syria, after four weeks of bitter fighting between French and British troops, in which a bridge across the Yarmuk featured once again. In 1945, despite the landing of a French Army and more Arab-French fighting in Damascus, America and Britain at last insisted on Syrian independence.

My Egyptians are behaving well, but anxious for some declaration of policy from His Majesty's Government. The Sultan [Fuad] is beginning to make tours in the provinces, and this will, I think, have a great effect towards making him more popular. The extremists, of course, are trying to create opposition to his travelling about the country. A decision by His Majesty's Government, as to the future status of Egypt, is eagerly awaited here. However, we can't expect anything definite just yet, as Milner does not seem, so far, to have presented his report—this, after a year's delay.[32]

*   *   *

The Milner Mission had been overflowing with good intentions. Liberal in composition, it had seemed to the British Government liberal in its intent. To the Egyptian politicians it had seemed an insult, as its terms of reference expressly stated that any changes in Egypt should be *within* a Protectorate. Milner himself was worn out by his work during the war, which he had finished as War Minister. He wrote: 'I am perfectly well physically—but *stale* mentally. I never so much wanted to be turned out to grass for quite a long time. The war was one thing—a perfectly tremendous strain, but one was carried along by the bigness of the thing. Everybody was working above his or her usual capacity. Now comes the inevitable slump. We are all tired to death. . . . [I] go out to Egypt, as Head of a Mission which is to try and straighten out the tangle into which affairs have got in that country. . . . If the high gods are gracious, I may perhaps get out of harness altogether on my return.'[33]

The Mission was greeted with nationalist and student riots and demonstrations. Having commanded their followers to boycott the Mission while it was in Egypt, Zaghlul and others changed their minds and raced after it to London, from Paris. Allenby, meanwhile, had gone on a long visit to the Sudan, to leave the stage clear for Milner. Protracted negotiations continued in London, while Allenby and Egypt waited impatiently. In the autumn, Allenby went home on leave, and strongly advised that Milner's proposals, to many of which Zaghlul seemed to agree, should be announced at once as the solution to the Egyptian problem. Although he did not himself agree with all of Milner's recommendations, he was in agreement with the main principles. These were that the Protectorate was to be abolished and an Anglo-Egyptian Treaty signed, which would safeguard British interests, particularly the Suez Canal and the Sudan. These suggestions had caused some dismay in the Government, which had not expected such revolutionary proposals from the Mission, and which had delayed its report as long as possible. Allenby wanted to get Egyptian independence first, and to discuss the other questions later. The Protectorate should be ended, as it had been initiated, by unilateral action. He pointed out that with naval command of the area, and the military base by the Canal, Britain had *de facto* power in Egypt if all points of the Treaty were not later met. This was his basic position throughout his time in Egypt, although few politicians were inclined to take very seriously the views of a soldier inexperienced in such affairs. There was a section in London, however, which was bitterly opposed to any withdrawal of British influence from Egypt, believing that the Suez link, vital to the Empire, was too important to risk; negotiations could proceed for ever, and Egypt could be given many concessions, but British influence must remain paramount.

The leader of this group was Winston Churchill. While anxious to set up pro-British and British-backed kingdoms to the east of the Suez Canal, in Palestine and under Hussein's sons, he had no desire to see the west of the Canal under an unreliable and probably anti-British independent Egyptian state. He had some influence with the Press, and as soon as Allenby's views became known, 'the Bull' once more became the victim of an intense campaign in the newspapers, as he had been, in different circumstances, at Ypres and Arras. But now he was criticized for being not firm enough.

I am still hanging around waiting to be interviewed by the

Cabinet. So far I have received no summons. Now they will be busy with this coal strike, and will, I fear, have little time for other affairs. It is a nuisance, as I must have instructions, before I go, as to what their policy is to be in Egypt.[34]

The Cabinet met at 4 p.m., and we sat till 6.30 p.m. Then it was adjourned till Thursday morning, when, I hope, something definite may be settled.[35]

At length it was decided that the Mission should officially submit its report, although practically everyone now knew, after the long delay, what it contained; and negotiations on its proposals should be discussed between the British Government and a representative delegation from Egypt. Allenby's advice that the Government should accept the proposals without more ado was, therefore, disregarded. However, the announcement of the pending negotiations did much to pacify opinion in Egypt; but the failure of Britain and Egypt to act immediately on the Milner proposals was the greatest tragedy of Egypt's long journey to independence.

I'm up to my neck in politics, watching the efforts of the Sultan to form a delegation which shall go home to discuss an agreement with H.M. Government. It is not easy; there are so many jealousies and policies.[36]

The Sultan, the Prime Minister and Zaghlul all wanted to lead the delegation. Allenby himself got on well with the Sultan, and was often inclined to favour him, although aware that Fuad was seeking almost despotic powers for the post-independence period; he disliked Zaghlul, although the latter had some respect for Allenby. It was his inability, or disinterest, in creating permanent good will with Zaghlul, who spoke for the mass of the people, if not for the educated few, that was one of Allenby's major failings in Egypt. Zaghlul, who still had not returned to Cairo since his deportation and release, now decided to do so, fearing that he was losing ground to Adly Pasha, the Prime Minister.

Zaghlul is due to arrive. He will have a tremendous reception, and there is almost certainly trouble to be expected. It will be a critical time . . . however, I have hopes that Adly Pasha, the new Prime Minister, will be able to keep mastery of the situation.

Zaghlul arrived in Cairo yesterday. I kept all officers and soldiers out of the streets, and left the whole management to the Egyptians. There was a gigantic and enthusiastic, but quite orderly, crowd, and not a single mishap occurred. Now we await developments, which will depend on whether Zaghlul is quite un-compromising or open to reason. The bulk of moderate opinion is on the side of the Adly Ministry and against Zaghlul, but the moderates never shout like the extremists.[37]

Shortly after the return of Zaghlul, disturbances broke out again and the nationalist leader spoke in open conflict to the Prime Minister. It seemed that the composition of a delega-tion would never be agreed upon. There were serious casualties, including fourteen Europeans killed and sixty-nine injured, during riots in Alexandria.

My politics are not going too well. Zaghlul's attitude has hardened, lately, and as he is a man devoured by self-conceit, I fear it will be unlikely that he will become tractable. I had a long talk with the Sultan this morning, and tomorrow I shall see Adly, the Prime Minister, when I hope to find out what his prospects of getting together a delegation may be.[38]

At length Zaghlul agreed to support a delegation led by Adly, while he himself remained in Cairo. Accompanied by Allenby, the delegation departed for London on the 1st of July, 1921. Allenby informed the Foreign Office that, so long as the Government insisted on putting the cart before the horse, negotiations between Adly and Curzon, who was now Foreign Secretary, would have no greater chances of success than the negotiations between Milner and Zaghlul had done. He was correct. After about three months of continual talk-ing, agreement was still not reached on one of the points which the British Government insisted on being written into a treaty: the location of British troops in Egypt. There was also the question of the Sudan, which was of no strategic or imperial consequence to Britain, but which the Government, with some reason, believed it could administer better than the Egyptians, and to which it felt morally bound, despite the objections of many Sudanese. All this meant a lengthy period in London for Allenby, who was meant to be advising the British Government on policy, but which, in fact, seldom met with him. He met the King ('He talked a lot about Egypt, but said nothing new'); talked to Raymond Savage, who had once been on his staff, was now Lawrence's literary agent, and who wanted to write a biography of him; attended the service in Westminster Abbey for the placing of the American Congressional Medal of Honour on the tomb of the Unknown Warrior ('The Battle Hymn of the Republic was a failure—played too slowly on the organ, and the choir was too far from the organ, and so were always out of tune'); and dined with the Asquiths ('I sat next to Margot, and she talked incessantly'). And, apart from a few visits to Curzon, he waited while the negotiations continued fruitlessly and apparently endlessly.

The negotiations collapsed. On his return to Cairo, Allenby was instructed to deliver a foolish and admonitory letter to the Sultan, in which Britain impatiently berated him and his country, and which immediately inflamed public opinion, already disappointed at the breakdown of the London conference. Adly Pasha resigned, and Allenby had the greatest difficulty in forming a new Egyptian Ministry. Zaghlul seized on the opportunity for causing further trouble. Fresh rioting broke out, this time in Cairo, and Allenby was advised to prohibit a great meeting planned by Zaghlul, who immediately challenged Allenby's authority.

Allenby, convinced that no progress could be made while Zaghlul made his inflammatory speeches, took the controversial decision to have the nationalist arrested, much to the delight of the British colony in Cairo and some of the London Press, but to the deep concern of more moderate Egyptians. Zaghlul was deported to Aden and then, like Makarios, four decades later, to the Seychelles Islands. At the same time, Allenby put strong military forces into the streets of Cairo and sent warships to Alexandria and the Canal to suppress the disturbances his critics warned him would result from his drastic action. Zaghlul himself, having owed his freedom to Allenby in the first place, was first astounded and then embittered. Allenby wrote:

The arrest of Zaghlul caused a considerable flare-up, but the fire has now almost burnt out, and I have great hopes for the future. I don't expect to be able to form another Ministry for a week or so, but am carrying on, for the time, without one. It won't do to hurry things. I want a stable and sound Ministry, when it comes. . . . I am making no concessions to my opponents, but am conciliatory to those who are inclined to be friendly. . . . The unrestrained tone of some of the English Press has done and is doing considerable harm here. I have had to suspend one or two newspapers here, temporarily—one an English paper—for articles subversive of authority, and calculated to create disturbances. The rioting in the towns has been easily dealt with and, so far, has not spread to the Provinces as it did in 1919. In fact, all my reports from the Provinces are to the effect that the *fellahin* are taking no interest in politics, but are busy farming.[39]

Throughout this time Allenby struggled to find 'someone strong enough or brave enough' to try to form a government. But no one was forthcoming; the country was administered by the permanent secretaries at the various departments, all but one of whom were British, and who were thus placed in an impossible position with their predominantly Egyptian staff.

A situation had now arisen in which the Egyptian leaders, like Adly, found themselves in an excellent position. Resorting to political blackmail, they indicated that they would only agree to take part in a new administration if certain conditions regarding independence were met. Allenby's tactics had not been successful.

Allenby now decided to resort to the only device left to him; having reached deadlock in Egypt, he would have to obtain concessions in London. It was in London, in 1922, that he struck, and where, by sheer force of character rather than by diplomatic skill, he enjoyed his finest hour as a statesman.

* * *

During all these crises, Allenby had kept a close watch on other affairs, particularly the Irish problem, with its lessons for Egypt, to which he constantly referred in his letters; to Feisal's career; and to the progress of Britain's seemingly impossible policy in Palestine:

I think that, after all, Feisal stands a good chance of being made King of Mesopotamia. If he is accepted by the people, and if he has good advisers, he ought to do well.* I hope, too, that his brother, Abdullah, will be established in Transjordania.[41]

Lawrence and Haddad Pasha are in Egypt, on a mission to the Hejaz. Both have lunched here, and now they leave for Jeddah. They will have a warm time in the Red Sea, and Jeddah is pretty hot at this season. Haddad, who was Feisal's right-hand man, will go later to see Abdullah in Transjordania, and then to Meso-potamia—by air, probably. He is hopeful as to Feisal's prospects; but Percival Landon, the *Daily Telegraph* correspondent, who has just come here from Mesopotamia, is of the opinion that the Arabs there won't accept him.[42]

The handing over of Cilicia to Kemal, by the French, is causing some trouble. Shiploads of Armenian refugees are arriving here. I refuse to let them land, and they are insisting, so there's a possibility of a row. I don't propose to give in. If I did, we should be flooded with thousands of undesirable paupers. I'm very sorry for them. They've been badly let down by the French. Many of them were repatriated by me two or three years ago when I was administering Cilicia. They think, with some reason, that they will suffer robbery and murder at the hands of the Kemalists, despite any guarantees.[43]

* When Feisal did arrive at Baghdad, he complained almost as bitterly about the British as he had done about the French in Damascus.[40]

Lawrence lunched here today. He is just back from Transjordania, and is on his way home to report to Winston Churchill. He gives a fairly hopeful report of Transjordania, but he sees possibility—even probability—of trouble in Palestine before long.*[44]

Samuel's problems in Palestine are not easy, and he will have as much trouble with his own Zionists as with the Arabs or Christians. I see that the Zionists have been smuggling revolvers, hidden in beehives, into Palestine.[45]

* * *

On the 12th of January, 1922, Allenby was informed by the Egyptian politicians of the conditions under which they would agree to form a government, and this formula Allenby telegraphed to London, demanding an immediate reply. The tone of his cable annoyed Curzon and the Foreign Office, and he was accused of presenting an ultimatum. Allenby was, indeed, intent on forcing the issue one way or the other, as Egypt was drifting into an ungovernable position. He appealed to Curzon, Foreign Secretary, to explain to the Cabinet the seriousness of the position in Egypt, which had been without a government for more than a month. Curzon promised to do so, but wilted before strong criticism of Allenby in the Cabinet, and appears not to have supported him to any great extent, thus making Allenby's position *vis à vis* the Prime Minister extremely difficult. Allenby was informed that the Cabinet could not agree to the proposals, and asked him to send two of his staff home for consultations. This Allenby refused to do; once more he appealed for a sense of urgency, and offered his resignation. Curzon, however, was not giving the support he had promised. To

---

* Lawrence at the height of his influence; of the visit to Transjordania, Churchill wrote: 'He had plenary powers. He wielded them with his old vigour. He removed officers. He used force. He restored complete tranquillity.'

Allenby he declared that he was supporting him 'up to the point of resignation', but to the Cabinet he suggested that Allenby's letter had been drafted by the Egyptians and not by Allenby at all (which, to some extent, was true).[46] Allenby was again ordered to persuade the Egyptians to agree to the British terms first, on which agreement the Protectorate would be ended. Again Allenby said he would attempt to do so, but pointed out it was a futile task. Again Adly and his supporters refused to countenance the procedure. At this the Cabinet sent a denunciatory telegram to Allenby, the gist of which was that Allenby had consistently misinformed the Cabinet and was hindering their liberal intentions in Egypt. Allenby was ordered home for consultations.

The Cabinet had, in fact, decided to dismiss Allenby, and then publish the telegram it had sent to him by way of explanation. It seemed that the Churchill faction had won the day. Churchill had succeeded Milner as Colonial Secretary, and had won Lloyd George to his view. The situation was complicated by the fact that Churchill and Curzon were engaged in a battle for power.[47] Thus any support that Curzon could give to Allenby would probably weaken his own position in the Cabinet. The Press was still mostly against Allenby, but he had found a useful ally in Lord Northcliffe, proprietor of *The Times*, which came out strongly in his support after Northcliffe had met and been much impressed by the Bull. Northcliffe had gone to Cairo at the suggestion of Allenby, and had found him 'direct, simple, honest—with very little frills or "Your Excellency" about him'.[48] Allenby told Northcliffe that he was probably not going back to Egypt. Northcliffe reflected: 'This British Empire business is no easy job.'

Allenby left Cairo on the 3rd of February; his opponents, however, had apparently forgotten that they were despatching not a lamb to the slaughter, but a bull, which is a different proposition altogether.

Allenby arrived at Victoria Station seven days later. There was no official car and no senior Foreign Office official to meet him. This was strange treatment for a ruler of the Empire second only in importance to the Viceroy of India. His friend Chetwode, however, was there, and offered him a lift in his car. Allenby, still thoroughly aroused by the Cabinet's telegram, had, together with his staff, written a cold, logical and clever reply. Quoting his past communications and presenting his case with great effect, he demolished one by one each sentence of the telegram. This was not a difficult task, as the telegram—a fatal move on the Government's part—had been carelessly put together and was, indeed, the almost exact opposite of the truth. This despatch, twenty-nine pages of type-written foolscap, Allenby had with him in his briefcase. Although it was pointed out that no one would be at the Foreign Office to receive it that early in the morning, Allenby insisted on driving there from Victoria Station and delivering it himself. This he did.

Curzon read the despatch on arrival at the Foreign Office later in the day, and he did so with some alarm. For not only was Allenby's logic correct, the wording was very much stronger than usual in official exchanges. In the evening he had an interview of an hour and a half with Allenby. Curzon complained that the despatch was not a document that could fittingly be circulated to the Cabinet, as it was couched in terms which the Cabinet could not possibly accept from one of their own representatives abroad. Allenby, however, would not budge. He said he did not know what the Cabinet were accustomed to, but charges had been made and he insisted on the right to reply. He was in his most intimidating mood, and a fascinating battle ensued in which a brilliant politician used all his experience and considerable guile to get Allenby to withdraw his despatch, and in which Allenby remained stern and totally unmoved throughout. Henry Wilson heard that at the end of the session the exhausted and frustrated Curzon was in tears. Allenby insisted on his despatch going through normal channels, and would not withdraw his threat to resign.[49]

Next day was a Saturday, and little could be done,

although Curzon had said that the Prime Minister would have
to be brought into the affair. Nevertheless, Allenby called
at the Foreign Office to ensure that his despatch had been
circulated to the Cabinet. This action, and Allenby's obvious
intention to stand firm, was a sensation among those in the
know in London. Henry Wilson wrote in his diary: 'Winston
took me to one side to ask me what the Bull was going to do.
I said he was going to stand fast on his proposals. Winston
said that he would never agree and would fight to the end. He
said the Cabinet was evenly divided.'[50] . . .'Allenby came to
see me on his way to the Cabinet. I told him of my little talk
with Winston yesterday. Allenby remains quite immovable.'[51]
. . . 'I had a long talk on the telephone tonight with Allenby.
He told me he was going to see L.G. tomorrow and was
going to put very plainly before him that he must choose at
once between his advice and his resignation. He said he was
going to refuse any longer to be kept hanging about being
made a fool of and, what was much worse, losing any
possible chance of coming to some arrangement with the
Egyptians.'[52]

The interview with Lloyd George duly took place. Both
factions of the Cabinet looked to the Prime Minister, who had
a great reputation both as charmer and cunning negotiator,
to get them out of the very awkward situation in which they
found themselves. For if Allenby either resigned or was
dismissed, as was the original intention, there was nothing
to prevent him reading his damaging despatch in the House of
Lords; it was clear from his determination and mood, which
had impressed everyone who had met him since his arrival in
London, that this he would indeed do.

Lloyd George began by firing off a great many questions
at Allenby, no doubt to put himself in authority from the
start. This did not please Allenby, who eventually said
(there were three others present): 'Well, it is no good disput-
ing any longer. I have told you what I think is necessary. . . .
I have waited five weeks for a decision, and I can't wait any
longer. I shall tell Lady Allenby to come home.' On this
Lloyd George, never one to resist a turn of phrase, said:

'You have waited five weeks, Lord Allenby; wait five more minutes.' He thereupon capitulated and agreed to Allenby's proposals, with only a few minor amendments. With the Government in danger, Lloyd George was not the man to mistake the lesser of two evils. The interview was at an end.

In the debate in Parliament, it was inferred that agreement had been reached only by Allenby accepting the Government's liberal proposals for Egypt, instead of the other way round. The Government spokesman was Austen Chamberlain.

What came to be known as the 1922 Declaration terminated the Protectorate and left the way open for the Egyptian moderates once more to co-operate in the Cairo government. Only four matters were 'absolutely reserved to the discretion of H.M. Government until such time as it may be possible by free discussion and friendly accommodation on both sides to conclude agreements in regard thereto'; namely: the protection of the Canal, the defence of Egypt, the protection of foreign residents in Egypt, and the Sudan.

Allenby stormed out of London as he had arrived. Instead of being dismissed, he had won a notable victory and the surprised respect of even his enemies. Almost on his own, with few, apart from Northcliffe, he could call powerful allies, he had at last got the British Government to commit itself to Egyptian independence without further ado. It was a considerable achievement, arrived at by character rather than skill. The Middle East was never to be the same again. And all modern history of Egypt, including the Nasser régime, can be traced to that week when 'the Bull' exploded on London, and when sheer integrity won, for once, over political intrigue.[53]

* * *

Although he returned in some triumph, Allenby's troubles in Egypt were by no means over. As his greatest critic, Lord Lloyd, put it: 'It now remained to be seen whether he was justified in the confidence with which he had repeatedly asserted that such action [i.e. recognizing independence] would successfully lead to a lasting settlement.'[54] The old factions, between Sultan, Prime Minister and Zaghlul's Wafd party, remained, indeed increased, as the prospect of power and independence advanced. It remained to frame a Constitution, abolish martial law, provide for the compensation of foreign officials who would lose their jobs on independence, and ensure the defence of the Canal. However, there was at first a general feeling that these problems were not now insurmountable, and there was a confident mood in Egypt. The Constitution that was eventually agreed on provided for two-fifths of the Senate being appointed by King Fuad, thus ensuring grist for more revolutionaries at some future date. In order to show good will on the Sudan question, Allenby suggested that the Commander-in-Chief of the Egyptian Army, mostly posted to the Sudan, should be an Egyptian. This suggestion was treated at the Foreign Office as if it were frivolous. In solving the remaining problems, the British Government was quite as undecided as it had been before the Declaration, and the Egyptian Governments were quite as confused.

Parallel with these discussions, which continued for many months under a succession of Prime Ministers—Sarwat, Nessim, Yehia Pashas—were other problems, of which the most important were a series of murders against British residents by a group of fanatics impatient of all negotiation.

Meanwhile Zaghlul had been languishing in the Seychelles, and suffering from bronchitis in the damp climate. He had been watching events, and later told Reuter's correspondent in Cairo that he would have accepted the 1922 Declaration without discussion if he had not been transferred from Aden to the Seychelles. After a delegation of fifty women had petitioned Allenby, Zaghlul was transferred to the more amenable climate of Gibraltar:

They were very ardent politicians, and were here nearly three-quarters of an hour, pressing their claims and smoking cigarettes and drinking coffee. Women here are taking a great interest in politics nowadays, and are tending to move towards emancipation; some are demanding the vote.[55]

On the abolition of martial law in Egypt, Zaghlul's banishment automatically ceased, and he returned in September, 1923, after nearly two years' absence. After studying the political scene he became convinced, with reason, that the Sultan had seized more and more power from the weak, liberal governments of Cairo, and that Allenby, undoubtedly aware of the fact, had been unable or unwilling to prevent this development.

At the beginning of 1924 the first elections to the new Egyptian Parliament were held, during which time Allenby diplomatically went on a tour of the Sudan. In a chamber of 214 members, 190 declared themselves supporters of Zaghlul, who became the first Prime Minister of the new Egypt. He was the idol of the populace. At the same time, Ramsay MacDonald had become Prime Minister of the first Labour Government in Britain.

On his return from the Sudan, Allenby, who had little confidence in Zaghlul, nevertheless made the sensible gesture of calling on him, although it was customary for a new Prime Minister to call on the High Commissioner. This did something to soothe Zaghlul's sensibilities; he respected Allenby personally, although he was suspicious of his intentions.

Before Britain could leave Egypt, described as 'Independent', there were still some outstanding differences, of which the Sudan question was one. In an effort to solve this, Zaghlul and Ramsay MacDonald, who knew each other and had frequently expressed a mutual admiration, agreed to meet in London. To the surprise of both men, their conversations were a complete failure. MacDonald found Zaghlul more intractable then he had suspected, and Allenby, of whom he had previously had a prejudiced idea, more liberal. Allenby himself later said that he got on better with MacDonald, who was his own Foreign Minister as well as Prime Minister, than with either of the two other administrations under which he served. Zaghlul, who always carefully studied, and played to, his popularity with the electorate, had committed himself to getting Britain out of Egypt with practically no privileges at all in the four 'reserved matters' of the 1922 Declaration. MacDonald, on the other hand, insisted on adequate safeguards for the Canal, which he explained was a prime responsibility of any British Government, no matter of what political party. Allenby was thus approaching a crisis in his career, for now his critics, who had said the Protectorate should remain till all issues had been settled, could place the blame for all failures to reach agreement squarely on to his insistence on the 1922 Declaration.

Meanwhile, murders of British subjects had continued in Egypt, and while Allenby was criticized in some quarters in London for being 'soft', among the British in Cairo he was criticized for being not harsh enough in his measures to stamp out the wave of crime. Matters came to a head on the 19th of November, 1924, shortly after 1.30 p.m.

The Governor-General of the Sudan, Sir Lee Stack, was shot at and wounded three times while his car was in a traffic jam at a busy Cairo street junction. The wounded chauffeur drove to the Residency, which was not far away, and where Allenby was in the middle of lunch with his guest, Herbert Asquith. Stack was carried in to a drawing-room, and Allenby and Asquith rushed in to see him. There was little that could be done for him, and he died the following day in the Anglo-American Hospital.

The news was flashed across the world, and suddenly the Egyptian problem was the talk of the day. The British people were stunned by the assassination, and the Lee Stack murder became one of the traumatic events of the 'twenties.

There was a great deal of speculation, especially in Egypt, as to what the reaction of the British Government would now be to Egyptian claims. It was widely accepted in Britain that the murder had in some way been inspired by Zaghlul, although this was not so.

Allenby himself was outraged. But he believed he could use the situation to force a settlement on the Egyptians. For years he had struggled to play the diplomat's game, although all his instincts revolted from it; and his natural temper had been bottled up inside him to the point of a vast explosion.

Before taking punitive action, he was determined first to see the funeral properly conducted. The 22nd of November, 1924, was the most crucial day of Allenby's life. At the funeral of Sir Lee Stack, on that day, he insisted that places should be reserved for Zaghlul and his Ministers, which, in the tense atmosphere of the day, brought forth all the venom and criticism of the British and foreign population in Egypt. The Bishop called on Allenby and protested in the strongest terms during a most electric interview. Zaghlul and his Ministers attended the funeral, to the open hostility of the predominantly British congregation. All this was lost on the Egyptian populace; they did not see it as a humiliation, which Allenby may well have intended, but as the right and proper reaction of their elected representatives.

After the funeral, Allenby returned to the Residency, where he waited impatiently for an answer to a cable he had sent to the Foreign Office. In this he had detailed a note he intended handing Zaghlul, which was couched in extremely strong terms and made many demands, including withdrawal of Egyptian troops from the Sudan and a fine of half a million pounds. Permission to deliver this note had not arrived by 4.15 p.m. The Egyptian Parliament was due to meet at 5.0. There was a possibility that the Cairo Government might resign, and that Allenby would thus have no one to whom he could deliver his note. As Allenby left the Residency, where an entire cavalry regiment, the 16th/5th Lancers, with which he had such close associations, was waiting to escort him, an aide ran out and told him that an answer from London had arrived. It was in code, and it would not be possible to decipher it before 5.0 p.m. From its length, it was obviously not a mere acceptance of Allenby's proposals.

Allenby now found himself facing the most difficult decision of his life. If he acted with the firmness and severity in which he knew he had no peer in Cairo, and for which he believed he had every justification, he might be able to force the Egyptians to settle all outstanding differences within a few days. On the other hand, he could not be certain whether he had the backing of the British Government. He was never a man to shirk a decision, and, dressed in a grey lightweight suit and a soft brown hat, he entered his car and was driven to the Prime Minister's office.[56]

He was not normally a man for pomp and display, and this, apart from purely ceremonial occasions, was the first time he had ever ordered a cavalry escort in his years in Egypt. It was the regiment of which he had himself once been Lt.-Colonel, and they were an impressive sight. Zaghlul was lying down in his office, half asleep, and resting before proceeding to the Parliament Building across the road. He was roused by the clatter of a large force of cavalry outside, by the calls of a mass salute, and a fanfare of trumpets. Within moments Allenby, unannounced, had burst into his office, and, before Zaghlul had enough time to fully collect himself, had read out his demands, left the note on a table and walked out again. More salutes outside, and then escort and car returned, before gathering crowds, to the Residency. Whether such 'gunboat' strategy, even when conducted in a lounge suit, could still have an effect in the world remained to be seen.

On his return to the Residency and Chancery, Allenby read the deciphered message from the Foreign Office. It included considerable revision of his demands, and was much softened in tone. In particular, it deleted the demand for a fine. It was, it can now be agreed, a better balanced and wiser document, less open to counter-charges, than the one which the Special High Commissioner for Egypt had just delivered. Even Allenby's greatest admirers have considered his demands mistaken.[57] It looked all too obvious that the British had either lost their temper, or were taking indecent advantage of the opportunity.

Although he continued at his post in Egypt for another seven months, this marked the end of Allenby's career as a soldier-statesman.

*   *   *

Zaghlul's Government shortly resigned, but not before the Finance Minister had written out a cheque for £500,000. The money was used by the British Government to improve the medical services of the Sudan. The other demands, apart from an apology and the promise to set up an investigation into the murder, were not met, the Egyptian Government feeling it unreasonable to be penalized for a crime which was not theirs and for which they insisted they were not responsible.[58] The Government which followed proved to be less principled, but it did make an appeal to the League of Nations for intervention.

With this desperate effort to improve his position in Egypt, Allenby had completely lost the confidence of his superiors in London, and now there was no Lloyd George to appreciate his worth. To make matters worse, he ordered the seizure of the tobacco customs, again without authorization from London, and suggested that Egyptian hostages should be taken. The Conservatives having regained power, the new Foreign Secretary in London at this time was Austen Chamberlain, a man of capabilities, who had a good opinion of Allenby's importance in Cairo as someone whom the Egyptians could trust. He did not, however, have a good understanding of Allenby's nature. The events after the Lee Stack murder, particularly Allenby's independent action over the note, had convinced him that a professional diplomat, well versed in political affairs, should now be sent to Egypt to act as guide and brake to Allenby, whom he nevertheless wished, at first, to retain as an indication of the continuance and good will of British policy in Egypt. Chamberlain had been influenced by the fickle Press, which had for long claimed that Allenby, now once more a 'bullish' General and no longer the 'glorious' conqueror of the desert, was incapable of bringing a solution in Egypt. The harshest critic was Ward Price of the *Daily Mail*, thus revealing also the fickleness of Lord Northcliffe, that newspaper's proprietor. Other enemies, knowing Allenby's hitherto liberal views, the effects of which they resented, continued to spread the word that he was a reactionary holding up an Egyptian treaty. Chamberlain made the mistake of not discussing his decision with Allenby, and of not being frank with him when Allenby demanded an explanation. Allenby had mistrusted Chamberlain since the latter's half-truths in the House of Commons after the 1922 Declaration; Chamberlain, on his side, was astonishingly tactless, and blissfully unaware as to the conditions in Egypt and the effect the announcement of a new British Minister would have in that country. He was also probably unaware, not being party to the 1922 Declaration intrigue, of the reason for Allenby's personal coldness towards him, and was taken aback by Allenby's immediate distrust of his intentions, which he had naïvely hoped to hide successfully. He had been Foreign Secretary for less than three weeks. He had listened to Churchill and especially George Lloyd, who played an important part behind the scenes, as well as to the Press, and believed Allenby was a simple General, out of his depth, but one who might still be of some use as a figure-head.

Allenby, however, suspected all this, and was having none of it. He knew only too well, as Chamberlain never appreciated, that loss of face in the Middle East means immediate loss of authority. He was not deceived by Chamberlain's artless tone. Once Chamberlain had realized his mistake, he was not willing to climb down, and decided that Allenby must at last be forced out. As Allenby had a reputation in London for being a difficult man to unseat, he resolved to make a better and more subtle job of it than Lloyd George and Curzon had done. Thus Allenby found himself being manœuvred into a position from which he could not extricate himself with dignity.

On the 24th of November, 1924, Chamberlain made the opening move by telling Allenby that he had decided to send a Foreign Office official, Nevile Henderson, to Cairo, who would rank immediately under Allenby himself. Allenby suggested that Henderson, having communicated Chamberlain's plans, should leave within a week of arrival. He complained that Henderson's presence would seriously undermine his position in Cairo; he could not have authority if he had lost face. Chamberlain protested that Henderson's presence would not mean loss of face for Allenby, but reminded him that the demands made of the Egyptian Government after the Lee Stack murder were not approved by London, although he had nevertheless received full support.

On the 27th, Allenby tendered his resignation, to take effect as soon as conditions in Egypt allowed. Chamberlain insisted that the resignation would have to be delayed. This delay turned out to be fatal to Allenby's position. The core of Allenby's argument was: 'Either you have confidence in me or you have not. Since you have made a striking appointment to my staff in the midst of a crisis without consulting me, and published it without giving me an opportunity of expressing my opinion, I presume you have not. It is therefore my duty to resign.'

Two days later Allenby was told by Chamberlain that he would be informed when he could submit his resignation, which would be as soon as Egypt had fully recovered from the effects of the Lee Stack murder. On the 22nd of December, the Foreign Secretary wrote a long letter congratulating Allenby on his achievement in Egypt, but complaining of being kept short of information. He then made a long appeal for Allenby to withdraw his resignation, which Allenby declined to do. The correspondence became increasingly acrimonious. Henderson arrived in Cairo, with nothing to do, and contrived to keep himself as much out of Allenby's way as possible. Relations between the two men were cordial. Henderson wrote to a friend: 'I like Allenby . . . I have done my best by inaction. He has, I know, appreciated that and I am glad to think so. Anyway, I have a fairly clear conscience.'

Six weeks later Allenby wrote again, suggesting that the time was nearly suitable for his resignation. Since the announcement of Henderson's appointment, he had lost much authority, and in any new crisis he would have had great difficulty in exerting any influence. About this time reports appeared in the *Morning Post* and Reuter's that

Allenby was leaving. Chamberlain denied that the 'leak' had occurred in London, and Allenby seems to have accepted this. At the same time, the Press campaign against Allenby was stepped up in London, and was having an unsettling effect in Egypt, especially as it was suggested that he was the main obstacle to Zaghlul's return to power, although he now had no influence on the democratic process. He cabled to Chamberlain, suggesting that it would be advantageous for everyone if the attacks would desist until after the forthcoming elections, the peaceful conclusion of which they were imperilling. Chamberlain replied that he would arrange for an 'inspired' question to be asked in the House, to support Allenby, but does not appear to have done so. In the event, the elections passed off comparatively quietly. Zaghlul's power appeared to be eclipsed,* and the demands in Allenby's note had been met. Allenby's action after the murder had therefore met with some short-term success, and during 1925 the country returned to a peace and calm that it had not known for a long period. In April, Chamberlain wrote suggesting that the time was shortly coming in which Allenby's resignation could take effect. Shortly afterwards, another story appeared in the Press that Allenby was to leave Egypt; Chamberlain told Allenby the 'leak' was 'most regrettable'. Thus did the public politician neatly deal with the public servant. For Allenby it was the *coup de grâce*; he left Egypt on the 14th of June, 1925.

It was widely accepted that he had been asked to resign, and the Government did not deny it. Till his death, the true history of Allenby's career in Egypt, and the reason for his resignation, were never publicly known; apart from the Press reports on his resignation, and one short debate in the House of Lords in 1929, his achievement went unnoticed. Chamberlain ignored his request to make it clear that the resignation had dated from the previous November, although he instructed his Private Secretary and the Foreign Office

---

* Zaghlul never again formed a government; he died in 1927, aged 74. Fuad died in 1936, much to the relief of most of his subjects; the Anglo-Egyptian Treaty was signed four months later.

News Department to obtain good notices for Allenby in the Press, which they succeeded in doing, although, oddly enough, they had not previously been able to quell the inaccurate statements about his actions in Egypt. This was nothing, however, to the barrage of exaggerated praise which Allenby received in America on the announcement there of his retirement. The *New York Times* said Allenby was 'worthy to be remembered along with the greatest in the days of the Old Testament and beyond the greatest of the Crusaders in the Middle Ages'.

A large crowd saw Allenby depart from Cairo, the vast majority Egyptians, and there was no reason to doubt the sincerity of their good wishes and esteem; the special train to Port Said was stopped by request on several occasions for spontaneous tributes to the departing Allenbys.

Henderson, who had been in an impossible position throughout, had behaved well. He had no previous experience of Egypt, had been on holiday when suddenly called to go there, and had only had one interview with the Foreign Secretary before leaving for Cairo. Henderson was to take charge in Cairo until the arrival of Lloyd.*

Allenby's three great feats in Egypt were that he forced a reluctant British Government into publicly recognizing Egyptian sovereignty; that he found the country in turmoil under authoritarian rule and left it in peace with the structure of democratic rule; and that he did so without having to suppress a bloody revolution. Those at home who had glibly branded him 'the Bull in an oriental china shop' knew as little of Egypt as they did of Allenby. It is not beyond the bounds of possibility that Allenby might have negotiated the remaining points in the Treaty somewhat sooner than his successors were able to manage; it was not

---

* Lloyd, an old friend of Churchill's, had served under Allenby as Intelligence Officer in Palestine. There is little doubt that Lawrence was considered for the appointment behind the scenes, but his views were even more liberal than Allenby's. Henderson later became British Ambassador in Berlin, up till the outbreak of the Second World War, and worked closely with Austen Chamberlain's brother Neville.

signed for more than ten years after his departure. With the
advent of Lloyd as High Commissioner a period of less con-
cession began; it seemed that the Churchill faction had got
their way. But Allenby had, in Wavell's words, 'recognized
the awakened spirit of a people'. For six years he had been a
courageous, and occasionally enlightened, statesman. Even
Lloyd, one of his most severe critics, says: 'There was no
doubt that political Egypt owed him a debt—it was his hand
that had procured for her the measure of independence she
now enjoyed.'[59] However, his career in Egypt was far from
faultless. His handling of the Lee Stack murder was un-
characteristic, both of his previous policy and of the advice
of his staff; at a stroke he destroyed much of the good he had
already achieved. He may have known it. His resignation
was badly managed, leaving him open, as it did, to the ploys
of the British Government. Once Chamberlain saw Allenby's
determination, and realized his own blunder, he was not
sorry to see him depart. Allenby, certainly, would not have
wished to have stayed in Egypt much longer; he had been
there nearly six years. But he felt an unsatisfactory departure
had been forced upon him. Henderson's position was quite
unacceptable to him, as he knew it meant, rightly, that the
new Foreign Secretary no longer had faith in him.

Bearing in mind protestations of good faith in Chamberlain's cables, it is surprising that he did not brief Henderson
more fully and that he was content to have him loiter around
the Residency doing nothing, of which he must have been
aware, until Allenby was on the train to Port Said. Allenby
was a man who understood and trusted only plain, honest
communication between men. Employed as he was by men
who seldom worked in such terms, his end was bound to
come sooner or later; the most remarkable aspect of his
career, perhaps, is that it came later rather than sooner.

CHAPTER 12

Retirement

In common with the rest of his life, Allenby's retirement was ruled by common sense. He had no desire to remain in the public eye, and he was not often heard of in the last decade of his life. He devoted most of his time to those interests which had always been close to him: flowers and birds, travel, and the attentive and accurate acquisition of knowledge; in natural history, horticulture, science and poetry (for which, like Wavell, he had an extraordinary memory). He detested golf, but remained a keen fisherman. Two clouds were the absence of his only child and the misunderstanding of his policy in Egypt. For the first time there was a touch of bitterness in him.

On his return from Egypt, he was given, probably through his friendship with the King, the honorary post of Captain of Deal Castle. Allenby was not a very wealthy man, although he had his pension and what remained of his gratuity, and the upkeep of a castle, together with an expensive taste for travel, was beyond his means; moreover, he found the castle draughty and too cold for comfort. Although he loved the countryside, he believed he could not afford to live the life of a country squire, and he bought a modest London house at 24, Wetherby Gardens, South Kensington. A red-brick, semi-detached Victorian dwelling, remarkably lacking in beauty, it was only just on the fringe of Kensington, being on the borders of the less-fashionable Fulham.*

* The house stands, and a plaque commemorates Allenby's residence there.

It was his home for the remainder of his life. In the small courtyard at the rear he built an aviary in which, by means of artificial lighting and heating, he contrived to make comfortable his collection of rare Australian, American and African birds, to whose feeding and general welfare he attended daily when at home. He became a member of the Zoological Society, and had something to do with the new buildings at the Zoo in that period; his friend in this field was Lord Rothschild, who had formed a great private zoological collection. Allenby travelled the world with his wife, studying birds, animals and plants: Australia, New Zealand, South Africa, Canada, Rhodesia, East Africa, India (for the only time in his life), Egypt, Burma, Jamaica, Brazil, Malaya, the Dutch East Indies. Allenby's taste for travel was inexhaustible.

Of flowers, Allenby once wrote: 'The joy of flowers is, to the ordinary individual, beyond power of expression.' He was modest:

We seem to detect in certain flowering plants a consciousness resembling intelligence. The delight exhibited by a plant in the enjoyment of good soil and congenial environment, its happiness in sunlight and fresh air, are so obvious that one can with difficulty believe the feeling to be sub-conscious. The ingenuity with which the orchid ensures fertilization in the interest of its race, the cunning of the sundew, of Venus's fly-trap, and others in snaring insects for food, the shrinking from rough contact of the sensitive plants, entitle them to be considered as on a par with, at least, some of the lower forms of animal life. Flowers know slumber and waking, they know health and sickness, they riot in wilderness, yet live contentedly in confinement, they endure discipline, they profit by education.[1]

Thus spoke 'the Bull'.

He confined his public work to the schools cadet force, and an institute for old soldiers, to which he gave his name and much time; his work for these was not nominal, but carried out with typical thoroughness. After the death of

Haig in 1928, he associated himself with the Douglas Haig Memorial Homes.

The most notable of the Allenbys' tours abroad was that to the United States in 1928. Raymond Savage wrote in 1925: 'I believe there is no Englishman living whose reputation stands so high in American estimation as does that of Lord Allenby.' The straightforward, no-nonsense character of Allenby was one to which Americans are customarily sympathetic. For many years a small group of his American admirers had been persuading Allenby to visit America, and he did so with some misgivings. America was the only country in which an 'Allenby legend' had taken hold of the public with almost equal intensity to that of the 'Lawrence legend'. At the end of the war, a great Victory Gathering at the Coliseum, in Chicago, was brought to a halt by the cheering when a speaker, relating the achievements of various Armies of the Allies, said: 'I now will tell you of Allenby.' At a meeting in New York, when the chairman had put the question 'What is the greatest event that has happened in the world since the death of Christ?' the answer was: 'The entry of Allenby into Jerusalem.'[2] The Palestine campaign, which had completely caught the imagination of the American public, was widely known as 'The Last Crusade'. Legend and rumour were constructed into a fallacious edifice on the simple facts. Some dozens of poems about the Victor of Jerusalem were published. One account held that Allenby had entered Jerusalem with a crucifix in his right hand and a Bible in his left. Another had it that he had prayed on his knees, in mud, on entering the city. A large fan-mail from America and Canada continued through the years, and many of them congratulated Allenby for having knelt with his staff before battle, and for holding Bible classes every morning. In fact, Allenby was not a religious man, and seldom attended church, although all his life he had a curiosity about religion, especially in the Catholic faith, to which two friends belonged: Father Knapp, his Boer War chaplain, and the Mother Superior of a French convent, whom he got to know in France during the First World War.

The *New York Times* was always Allenby's most fervid admirer. This was no doubt partly due to Dr John Finley, of the New York State University, who was associated with the newspaper and wrote a number of editorials about Allenby.* Finley, who also wrote an admiring book on his hero, had been in command of the American Red Cross in Palestine during the campaign, and organized an annual dinner for veterans. At one time Finley tried to launch the idea of Allenby being appointed Ambassador to the United States. He went on a pilgrimage to Felixstowe in 1921, and dedicated his book to Allenby's mother. He published a song of sacred verses extolling his hero, to be sung to the tune of *Maryland, My Maryland*.[3]

> And God has led thee on, O Knight,
> Allenby, O Allenby!
> In thy great battle of the Right,
> Allenby, O Allenby!
> The earth's free nations now will bring
> Their genius to its glorying,
> And they who sat in darkness sing
> Fore'er of thee, O Allenby!

On arrival in New York, Allenby was met by a reception committee. A band played martial music, and guns boomed. At a somewhat hectic Press conference, he was asked to comment on the possibility of chemicals being used in war. 'You can't stop progress,' he said. 'As one of your poets said— "Civilization must go on, even if sometimes on a powder cask."' After the conference the photographers commanded, 'Wave your hat at the ship, your Lordship.' Lord Allenby took off his old grey hat and lifted it high, revealing a head slightly bald, with iron-grey hair over his ears. 'Now turn

---

* Professor of Politics, Princeton, 1900–3. President, State University of New York, 1913–21. Associate Editor, *New York Times*, 1921–37. Editor-in-Chief, 1937–8. Died in 1940.

around. . . .'[4] It is doubtful if Allenby had received so many orders in thirty years, but he obeyed them all with humour and alacrity. He spoke modestly at a 'Meeting of Welcome' in Carnegie Hall.

In Los Angeles the Allenbys made the inevitable visit to the Hollywood film studios; they heard the first talking film, and apparently did not think much of it. They also spent some time in Washington, San Francisco and Chicago. The primary reason for their visit was to attend the Convention of the American Legionaries at San Antonio, Texas, to which they had been invited by General Pershing. Allenby and Pershing were old acquaintances, having first met accidentally at Allenby's tailor, immediately after the latter's arrival in London, in June, 1917. Pershing was on his way to France; Allenby to Palestine. With Pershing, at that first meeting, was his A.D.C., Captain George Patton, later the Second World War General.

The *New York Herald Tribune* was usually more sensible in its comments on Allenby than the *New York Times,* and during Allenby's visit there appeared in the former newspaper the first cold appraisal of the Allenby–Lawrence legend in America; a brilliant and critical analysis entitled 'Lawrence and the Myth-Makers'.[5] It was prompted by a recent book on Lawrence by Robert Graves; the author of the article pointed out that Graves claimed that Lawrence had read the best part of 50,000 volumes in six years, which meant an average of not less than eleven books a day during that period.

In his home country Allenby was practically forgotten, except among those who still rankled under the controversies of his time in Egypt. Two books appeared which were highly critical of his policies, including one by his successor, Lord Lloyd. The other, by E. W. P. Newman, which was published at almost the same time as the *Herald Tribune* article, claimed that Allenby's régime was one of rigid militarism. This charge, and others of the book, were demolished in a logical examination of the facts by R. A. Furness, who had been on

Allenby's staff, in a long letter to the *Manchester Guardian*.*[6] But most people still found it impossible to believe that the policy of 'the Bull' had been one of the velvet glove rather than of the iron hand. In 1934 the first book which gave a sustained attack on Lawrence was published.[7] Austen Chamberlain wrote the Foreword to it, and Allenby thereupon defended Lawrence in an article in a Sunday newspaper.

*　　*　　*

In 1935 Allenby, having seen an article in *The Field* that there was some extraordinary fishing to be had in a remote part of Patagonia, packed his bags and went to the Argentine. The British Ambassador in that country was Sir Nevile Henderson, the key figure in his resignation from Egypt a decade before. Their meeting was extremely cordial, and Henderson helped in the arrangements for the unusual trip, a trip which many men of seventy-four might have considered, to say the least, strenuous. The element of adventure, the rough scenery, and the profusion of salmon combined to make it one of the most satisfactory of all Allenby's journeys.

In 1936 a number of things happened. The Egyptian negotiations, over the indigestible 'reserved matters' of the 1922 Declaration, were at long last nearing completion. C. S. Forester's realistic and documentary-style novel, *The General*, appeared. It was, and still is, one of the best books written about the First World War. In it, the unpleasant character of 'the Buffalo' was widely believed to be based on Allenby.† And then Allenby, quite suddenly and unexpectedly, broke into the news again. 1936 saw the casting of

---

* Later Sir Robert Furness, he remained in Egypt in various official posts until 1950. Died in 1954.

† C. S. Forester denies that he intended to portray Allenby, but says: 'Some of Allenby's characteristics were bound to appear in depicting the type of General I had in mind.'[8]

shadows in Europe which were to result in yet another great war. Allenby sensed this. He had been elected Rector of Edinburgh University, a position which involved little duty apart from an inauguration speech. At the end of his life, it was the only speech he made in which he gave public voice to private thoughts on world affairs. It was later printed as a pamphlet, under the title *World Police for World Peace*. It began apologetically:

Though I have not had the good fortune to enjoy a university education, I have been privileged to know men and women of intelligence and learning in all walks of life; and it has been my constant endeavour to profit by the association. . . . We soldiers are sometimes looked down on as below the average educational standard; especially so, perhaps, cavalrymen—of whom I am one.

He then spoke of the war and its lessons:

Some of our statesmen and leaders, enthusiastic and optimistic, as well they might be, acclaimed the termination of hostilities as the glorious and welcome conclusion of a war which was to end all wars. The golden age had arrived, to stay with us eternally. We have waited long. The golden promise has not yet materialized. . . . It is on all of you who belong to the young and rising generation that the future of our civilization depends. You have got to fit yourselves, now, for the enterprise awaiting you. The labour, though severe, is honourable in the highest degree; yet, remember that you cannot expect recognition by personal honours bestowed; you will have to set about the work in a spirit of altruism, and the reward for altruism will be the inwardly sure knowledge that so far as in you lies you have done your duty and have deserved success, even if success has not crowned your efforts. . . . During the protracted course of that grim period of international strife many deplorable acts were committed; [but] it should be recognized that human nature remains as it has ever been; kindly, on the whole, and well disposed; faithful in friendship; manifesting admirable qualities of self-abnegation and of superb courage, in support of high ideals, or defence of kith and kin.

Nationalism is commonly held up to admiration; praised as a

high—perhaps the highest—virtue; while internationalism is often branded as a crime, a surrender, a betrayal of our own peculiar interests and rights. . . .

Nations now maintain internal peace and good order by means of their own organized police forces. . . . To an unprejudiced and dispassionate observer there can be, however, no obvious reason why the national procedure which has resulted in the establishment of a happy social state by the fusion in amity of once hostile tribes should not be extended to the creation of a wide comity of nations. . . . What have availed the victories of Napoleon Bonaparte?

There is danger in delay, for it seems likely that, unless an effort in the right direction—a successful effort—is made soon, the present social system will crumble in ruin; and many now alive will witness the hideous wreck. At the present moment, many years after the close of the war which was to bring enduring peace to all, we find the cleverest brains everywhere busily experimenting with new inventions for facilitating slaughter. . . . The convention that non-combatants are respected no longer obtains.[9]

He finished by making an impassioned plea for a world police force, to prevent disputes turning into hostilities. The speech was quite well reported—but to no avail.

Allenby became chairman of the committee formed to provide a memoral bust of T. E. Lawrence in a niche in St. Paul's Cathedral. It was his last public service.

One day in May he went for his customary walk in the fetid, noisy London streets, for which he had no love, unnoticed and unrecognized as usual. Few people took any notice of the old but still erect man, with voluminous coat and felt hat, peering at the exhibits in the Imperial Institute. In Fulham he bought some additions to his aviary, walked home, and then went upstairs to his study. He sat at his desk; then, instantly, without struggle or fuss, he died.

There were the usual obituary notices, but the world was troubled by many affairs in 1936, and Allenby was a name from what seemed a distant past. Only *The Times* and the *New York Times* paid exceptional tribute: the **obituary** in the former running to over five columns, and the latter devoting its top editorial to 'Allenby of Megiddo'. ('In the history of the human race his name will be permanently written as Allenby, the deliverer of the Holy Land. It is likely that in the English-speaking world no name among those of all who held high command will be so long remembered.'[10]) There were a number of memorial services; that in Cairo was attended by his nephew, the new Viscount Allenby, who, appropriately enough, was serving in Egypt at the time.

Allenby's remains were cremated, and his ashes buried in Westminster Abbey on the 19th of May, 1936. It was the first anniversary of Lawrence's death. Allenby lies, not in the main body of the Abbey, but in a secluded Chapel, beside the grave of Herbert Plumer, the only other General so honoured. Both tablets are customarily half-hidden under a row of chairs, and the staff of the Abbey themselves cannot always direct the inquiring visitor to them; but it was some knowledgeable fate which placed the notorious 'Bull' beside the only widely loved and respected General of the First World War.

CHAPTER 13

Epilogue

While Allenby was spending his last years in Egypt, and during his retirement, the men whom he had encouraged and watched over were developing influential lives of their own; men like Lawrence, Gilbert Clayton, Hubert Young, Wyndham Deedes, Robert Furness, Alex Kirkbride, Ronald Storrs, Kinahan Cornwallis, Alan Dawnay, and many others. Of these members of Allenby's 'kindergarten', one in particular, Archibald Wavell, was greatly influenced by his years with Allenby. He spent the remainder of his career as a soldier perfecting what he had learnt in the Palestine campaign. Through Wavell, Allenby's influence as a military commander continued many years after his retirement and death.

After the First World War, service in the Palestine campaign was not considered to be a useful asset for a military career, and Wavell was not sent as an Instructor to the Staff College, as he had wished. There, progressives like Alexander, Montgomery, Brooke and Gort were quite openly hostile to the old régime, which had made such a disastrous mess of things, and, in particular, were critical of the General Staff's work in France; they struggled to discover what could be done to restore mobility to war, and tacitly vowed never to let a Western Front settle across Europe again if they were in command; this promise, despite the efforts of Eisenhower and Marshall, who had seen less of the First World War than they, they faithfully kept, until overruled at Presidential level in America in 1944.

Meanwhile, after the First World War, the success of Allenby's campaign was for long held up by conservatives as proof that the Army should return to the horse. Every effort, fairly successfully, was made to hinder the adoption of the tank. But in Palestine, and even more so in Syria, Rolls-Royce armoured cars had frequently gone many miles ahead of advancing cavalry scouts and flank-protectors. Despite the success of the cavalry, Allenby had sent a mission to France, in March, 1918, to plead for some of the new, quick Whippet tanks. The mission was unsuccessful. Such tanks as he had were considered so important that they were given more work to do at Third Gaza than they could cope with. The fact is that Allenby, who was enthusiastic, like his staff, at the possibilities of the armoured car, used his cavalry to such an extent because it was, quite simply, all he had available to retain mobility. He would have much preferred mechanized armour, although he certainly enjoyed the success of his horsemen. As Wavell later wrote: 'The true lesson is not so much the value of the horseman as the value and power of mobility. . . . Speed is armour. . . . Provided they could have been brought to the field of battle at the right time, there can be no question that armoured-fighting vehicles could have achieved victory more surely and effectively than did the cavalry.'[1] Such commonplaces were considered fairly revolutionary in some circles in the 'twenties, although Wavell was not always in the van with progressives like Liddell Hart and J. F. C. Fuller. He had a spell at the War Office, where he was in the Operations Directorate, and was concerned in the development of the fortress of Singapore, the inadequacies of which he was to have every reason to rue when Commander-in-Chief, South East Asia, twenty years later. His lucid book on the Palestine campaign began to be required reading, and he was asked to write a number of entries in the *Encyclopaedia Britannica*, including the entry on the Army. Also he lectured to the Royal United Service Institution. All his theories were based on Allenby's tenets. With the command of the 6th Infantry Brigade, he began to establish his reputation as a trainer of infantry. His controversial training schemes became the talk of the Army. He was, perhaps, slower than some in appreciating the possibilities of the parachutist, and at first preferred the armoured car to the tank; but on the whole he was among the most thoughtful and advanced commanders in the service.

Meanwhile, the splendid *Official History* of the Palestine campaign, by Captain Cyril Falls, had given publicity to Allenby's lessons of mobility, surprise and concentration of strength in front of immediate objectives. And the works of Captain B. H. Liddell Hart, the leading progressive, were influencing all thoughtful commanders, particularly those in Germany, where the lessons of Allenby's campaign were being learnt better than elsewhere, despite the efforts of Wavell and others. There are clear parallels between the breakthrough to Megiddo and the *Blitzkriege* in Poland and France. As Wavell put it: 'Defeat is a more fertile mother of reforms than victory.' The Palestine campaign was taught in the staff colleges of the Commonwealth; an account of it was issued by the Australian Staff as an aid to students for military history examinations.

When Wavell was given command of a division, he became at last a power in the Army. His contemporaries went to Aldershot to visit him and hear his views; the most frequent were Dill, Gort, Alanbrooke and Freyberg. Serving under him were Wilson and Giffard. A correspondent was Colonel Crerar of Canada.*

Wavell's unconventional exploits on manœuvres are still

* Later: Field-Marshal Sir John Dill, C.I.G.S. 1940–1; Field-Marshal Viscount Gort, C.I.G.S. 1937–9, and Commander-in-Chief B.E.F., 1939–40; Field-Marshal Viscount Alanbrooke, C.I.G.S. 1941–6; Lt.-General Lord Freyberg, Commander-in-Chief, Crete, 1941; Field-Marshal Lord Wilson, Commander-in-Chief, Middle East, 1943, Supreme Allied Commander, Mediterranean, 1944; General Sir George Giffard, Commander-in-Chief, 11th Army Group, South East Asia, 1943–4, and a supporter of Orde Wingate; General H. D. C. Crerar, Commander-in-Chief, 1st Canadian Army, 1944–5.

remembered in the Army;* and he gained a moral superiority over some of his brother officers, including some of those senior to himself. Spit and polish were notable by their absence from his scheme, and he was, as his A.D.C. later said, 'perhaps the worst-turned-out General in the Army'. In the desert campaign, during the Second World War, his favourite dress was a short-sleeved tunic over a long-sleeved khaki pullover. Nevertheless, with his glass eye, stiff arm and long, uncomfortable silences, he could be at times, by all accounts, almost as alarming a figure as Allenby himself had been. His ability to quote at great length from some hundreds of English poems was legendary, and true. He was asked to set examination papers for the Staff College, although he had never been an instructor there, and he rewrote Volume II of the *Field Service Regulations*, the tactical bible of the Army. His theory of the modern infantryman, deriving from his experience under Allenby, was developed in this, although some of it was too advanced for the War Office. He then rewrote Volume III, which dealt with strategy.

Discipline, Wavell said, derived from lecture room and playing field rather than from the barrack-square; this was so revolutionary that it has never yet been accepted. He took the greatest interest in Army education, and his only son later did important work with the R.A.E.C. He believed infantrymen should be able to work alone, and take initiative as well as orders. He thought ridiculous the idea of an N.C.O. overlooking three or four men at some task. An infantryman should have the qualities of 'cat-burglar, poacher and gangster'. These ideas later bore fruit in the informal Commando and U.S. Rangers groups.

Remembering the importance of air support in Palestine, he urged that every senior officer should have a thorough

---

* But not as unconventional as Meinertzhagen's, when, in September, 1924, he bombarded 'the enemy' with tennis balls from an aircraft. 'I witnessed what I had never seen before—panic on peace manœuvres. The infantry were terrorized and ran, fixing their bayonets.' (*Army Diary*.)

knowledge of the workings, limitations and potentialities of the R.A.F. The air weapon would mean that in a future war it would not be enough to interpose the Army between the enemy and the civil population. Thus the Army would have to study civil defence. After a visit to Russia, he at last became fairly enthusiastic about the use of parachute troops.

These are some of the many ideas which Wavell was airing from 1928. In 1937 he was appointed to the Palestine command, and thus returned to the scene of his work with Allenby.* But before leaving England, he asked that an infantry brigade be given to a Colonel Bernard Montgomery, of whom he thought highly. When war in Europe became inevitable, Wavell was recalled to help in the reorganization of the Army, and received the Southern Command. Commanding the Mobile, or Armoured, Division under him was Maj.-General Alan Brooke. In 1939, Wavell delivered the Lees Knowles lectures at Cambridge (of which Rommel kept a printed copy at his side during the desert campaign). These were translated into Russian, and published in America. In the same year General Wilhelm Keitel wrote of Wavell: 'In the British Army today there is only one good General, but he is incomparably good. The others have no proper conception of the direction of mechanized war, but this officer, from 1928 onward, has studied the subject, and he may well prove the dominant personality in any war within the next five years.'[2] The fact that Allenby, therefore, was one of only two Generals of the First World War to have any positive, rather than negative, influence on those of the Second World War (the other being Trenchard, founder of the R.A.F.) was very largely due to Wavell. Others, like Douglas Haig, had an influence only in that their successors, Montgomery in particular, were determined to avoid the pitfalls into which they had fallen.

---

* During his time in Palestine, Allenby's old rival Gough made a visit there, and was shown round the 1917 battlefields by Wavell. Gough found Wavell uncomfortably silent.

In 1939 Wavell was appointed Commander-in-Chief, Middle East, being the Army's acknowledged expert on that area. For Wavell it was a fatal assignment. He never commanded in the European theatre, and until March, 1947, he spent only a few weeks in England. He was thus not on the scene when the Iron Curtain descended on Europe in 1945; an absence which may perhaps be regretted in retrospect, as of all senior Allied Generals and, indeed, of statesmen, he was the only one who knew Russian intimately, spoke the language fluently, had lived in Moscow, understood the Russians, and had known personally the leaders of the Red Army. On the other hand, it may be that he had passed his peak even by 1939.

In the Middle East, his command was enormous: from the Syrian border to Lake Victoria, from Libya to Aden, from Cyprus to Somaliland. He found himself in almost exactly the opposite position to Allenby; outnumbered, unconcentrated, with inadequate air power, and with little means of massive mobility. He nevertheless based much of his campaign on Allenby's simple principles, which he knew from experience to be so effective. Wavell's great difference to his master was that he was prepared to gamble much more. Allenby took risks, but, like Montgomery, only if there was no alternative. Wavell took bold risks as part of his strategy, and thus when he lost, as any gambler is inclined to do from time to time, he risked losing all, including his place in history as one of the great captains. He once wrote: 'I have always been for unorthodoxy and for taking risks.'[3]

In the summer of 1940 the Long-Range Desert Group, consisting mainly at first of New Zealanders and Australians, began penetrating far behind the Italian lines, and attacked lines of communication, in much the same way as Lawrence had done. Like Lawrence, they were not always successful, but, again like Lawrence, they spread confusion and alarm among the enemy. This was a direct result of what Lawrence had wanted to do with armoured cars. After the First World War Wavell had continued his friendship with Lawrence, and had listened to Lawrence's theory of irregular

warfare. They had arranged to meet at Lawrence's cottage
for further discussion in May, 1935, but Lawrence's death
intervened.

One of the most notable L.R.D.G. exploits was the destruction of the isolated desert airfield at Murzuk, five
hundred miles south of Tripoli, which had been reached in
temperatures of 160° Fahrenheit and with water rationed to
a pint a day. Lawrence would have appreciated it. One of
Wavell's biographers wrote: 'The dummy horses in the
orange grove which were to delude the Turk in 1918, became the dummy tanks which deceived the Italians in 1940
in the Western Desert, and the false dust tracks which so confused Kress von Kressenstein's intelligence staff at that time
were used again, years later, to confuse the Italian intelligence.'[4]

Wavell's early success in Libya, magnificently carried out
by General Richard O'Connor, was the finest piece of
generalship, on the Allied side, in the first two or three years
of the war. Containing-attacks with infantry were supple-
mented by disguised flanking movements with armour. The
feint and counter-stroke used as Allenby had used them, but
in more extempore circumstances, were beyond the realms
of O'Connor's Italian adversary, Graziani—whose desert
blitzkrieg had at first met with dramatic success—either to
counter or even to understand. O'Connor took over 100,000
prisoners—more than were in his own attacking force.
Wavell was the General of the hour, but his hour was to be
short. In perfection of design and execution, the Cyrenaica
campaign rivalled that of Allenby's Syrian campaign. The
knowledge that this was so, and that Allenby's basic principles, especially the relentless, deep pursuit, had been followed, must have caused him satisfaction.

Before long Wavell found himself fighting five campaigns
at once—the Western Desert, Syrian, Eritrean, internal dis-
orders in Iraq, and Greece. Wavell's willingness to mount the
latter was his most controversial gamble. Allenby said:
Trust your luck. Wavell trusted his, and it led him to
disaster. Only one staff officer at G.H.Q., de Guingand,

repeatedly and consistently advised against it.* The best
that can be said for it, as another of Wavell's staff has
pointed out, is that it prevented the Germans supporting the
Syrian and Baghdad theatres (with the probable loss of the
Persian oil supplies), and delayed their attack on Russia.
The invasion failed and, against all expectations, including
even those of the German High Command, Rommel, only
half-prepared, struck a counter-blow in the desert. Wavell,
under-supplied and under-manned on every front, had been
asked to do the impossible; as is known, the impossible can
happen in war, but this was one of the more frequent occasions when the impossible proves to be impossible. There was
nothing in Allenby's principles which would answer such a
predicament. Wavell's reputation never recovered.

It was Allenby who once wrote of 'that friction seldom
absent when soldier and statesman have been closely associated in war'.[5] Wavell and Churchill were never congenial.
This was a most unfortunate business, and may have had
some effect on Wavell's later career. It was an unlikely
situation, as Churchill had always backed the progressives,
even, as in his profile of Haig in the *World Crisis*, when
ostensibly praising a conservative. (This was the profile
which Lawrence described to Liddell Hart as 'the most
deadly, if subtly veiled, indictment'.) Churchill, moreover,
continued the old struggle between 'Easterners' and 'Westerners' in the Second World War, on behalf, as always, of the
former. Churchill was exuberant and overbearing; he looked
for the extrovert type in his Generals. Wavell was reserved
and taciturn, and even less fond of discussion with any but
close associates than Allenby had been. Churchill was
acknowledged as a historian of the first rank. Wavell also
was a historian. Most important, Wavell always kept in his

* Later Maj.-General Sir Francis de Guingand, Chief of Staff to
Montgomery in North Africa and Europe, and author of a book
critical of Wavell. Frankly admitting his own disloyalty to Wavell, de
Guingand indicates that he was not aware of the political implications
of Greece and Crete. Wavell told him later: 'There was more in the
Greek business than you knew.'

mind the Churchill who had intrigued around Allenby in the 1920s. That kind of great, master politician has always been the antithesis of the great professional soldier. But Churchill as a national leader was no longer basically a politician, and he was determined, as a progressive in the military sphere, to avoid the mistakes of the First World War by keeping a firm hand on his Generals. The irony was that Wavell should have been, before the war, continually warning that a greater understanding between the military and the government was essential. However, on the 3rd of April 1941, Wavell's own decisions helped his downfall; they were not sufficiently demanding of an adversary of Rommel's calibre, and they heightened confusion among his own forces.

In 1941, when his reputation was at its height, Wavell sent a staff officer to London with a secret and still little-known message for the Chiefs of Staff. It was about one of his favourite subjects, Deception, and is highly relevant to the Greek campaign. He held that deception, to be effective, could not just be enacted in one theatre. It had to be considered overall; every operation, in every part of the world, however distant, and however different in conditions, would have its effect on all the others. Therefore if there was deception in one area, that ruse might not be effective in the overall scheme, and it might even be dangerous in its overall effect unless its relation to other operations elsewhere was foreseen and controlled. The Chiefs of Staff should therefore co-ordinate all such plans. This suggestion, as has been revealed by Sir Ronald Wingate, a General Staff Officer with the Chiefs of Staff secretariat, was adopted.[6] Wavell had, in fact, already adopted this theme, many years before, with regard to Allenby's Palestine campaign, which he had put forward in the *Army Quarterly* as part of 'one continuous battle on a single front, a front which extended across Belgium . . . to the frontiers of India.'*[7]

When Churchill sent Wavell to India, it was widely imagined that he was sending him away to peaceful pastures.

* Guy Dawnay was editor of the *Army Quarterly* after the Great War.

Few, not even the Prime Minister, foresaw Pearl Harbor and Singapore. Once again Wavell found himself fighting in an enormous area with totally inadequate forces. The most up-to-date 'fighter' aircraft in India were a squadron of old artillery-spotting planes. In 1939 Wavell could hardly have expected to have had the two worst commands of the war. On both occasions, as soon as he was relieved of his command, supplies and men poured in, and others gained the glory. Wavell, of course, like Allenby, was the type of Englishman who did not complain about such things, either privately or publicly, by word or in print; he considered it part of a life dedicated to service and duty.

In India he made use once again of his Allenby training. He became more keen than ever on the idea of planting inaccurate information on the enemy. One of those who had to repeat the Meinertzhagen haversack ruse on the Japanese in 1942 was the author Peter Fleming. And once more Lawrence's shadow was cast, in the shape of Major-General Orde Wingate, the remarkable, bearded, sun-helmeted expert on guerrilla warfare, who led, with Bernard Fergusson* and others, including Michael Calvert and Wavell's son,† the dramatic raids across the Chindwin river, behind Japanese lines. Wavell was the very commander to support such a scheme, and in so doing he had the fullest support of Churchill, who was equally enthusiastic.

It was only in the later stages of their acquaintance that Wavell discovered that Orde Wingate was related to T. E. Lawrence, but he had long known that this was a cousin of his old friend Sir Reginald Wingate of the Sudan. The world of the progressives in the British Army has never been extensive. It was Sir Reginald Wingate's son, Ronald, who helped his cousin into the Sudan Defence Force, from where

---

* Brigadier Sir Bernard Fergusson, who spent much of his Army career working with Wavell. Appointed Governor-General of New Zealand in 1962, a post once held by Lord Freyberg, another close associate of Wavell.

† Major A. J. Wavell; killed in action against the Mau Mau in Kenya, the 24th of December, 1953.

he eventually found himself in Allenby territory and became a fervent Zionist. Wavell had first met him when he was on his Intelligence Staff, and had taken an interest in him, having known and admired Sir Reginald. He was extremely impressed: 'I carried away in a corner of my mind the impression of a notable character who might be valuable as a leader of unorthodox enterprise in war, if I should ever have need of one.'[8] Wavell closely supervised the preparations and planning for the Wingate expeditions, in the second of which Wingate lost his life. Wingate himself detested being referred to as a second Lawrence; as an ardent Zionist, he abhorred Lawrence's Arabist policies. He was always quick to point out the essential difference between his own and Lawrence's theories of guerrilla warfare: using highly trained invading troops, rather than supplying and leading local insurgents.[9] Nevertheless, there were similarities between the two men, and both preferred to work behind the enemy lines, striking near his heart, than in front of them.* It was an exasperated conservative commander who said of Wingate and his theories 'The curse of this war is Lawrence in the last'.

When the time came for Wavell to hand over to a commander with more luck than himself, he was tired after a long and mostly disappointing war. But, as he continued to follow his master's footsteps, as if fate, perhaps not too kindly, was determined upon his so doing, the parallel between his career and that of Allenby becomes wider. The High Commissionership of Egypt after the First World War was an unenviable task for a soldier inexperienced in diplomatic work; the Viceroyship of India was a wretched one. But Wavell conducted himself with the same unconquerable integrity, in a similar sea of suspicions, betrayals and intrigues, as Allenby had done before him; and both men were brought

---

* Before going to India, Wingate had been sent to help Haile Selassie against the Italians in Abyssinia. He is buried in Arlington Cemetery, Washington. It was Lowell Thomas who helped to popularize his campaign in America, as he had done that of Lawrence before. (*Back to Mandalay*: Greystones, New York, 1951.)

down, as is so often the fate of all great public servants, by their political masters.

Wavell may have been a greater General than Allenby, but Allenby was certainly a more successful one; and the task of Generals is to win their battles. Who was intrinsically the greater man? One officer had the unique experience of serving on the staff of both: with Allenby in the First World War, and with Wavell in the Second. His opinion was that Wavell was the greater man; and he was Allenby's nephew.[10]

Such is the brief history of one strain of the progressives from Colesberg to the Chindwin. Wavell has never been without his admirers; not only was he 'Adversity's General', he was also a most attractive personality. But it is stating too much to say, as his admirers do, that he was 'the greatest British General of this century'. There are certain requisites such a great commander must have. He needs more than a modicum of luck. He must happen to be in the right place at the right time. These Wavell never had. But it will not be forgotten that he found victory in the midst of defeat; that he clung tenaciously to the principles of waging battle propounded and employed by Allenby; and that he helped, with others, to improve them and install them in the military stream which had for so long been dominated by the conservatives.

Synopsis of Events in the Middle East

1. July, 1915. Exchanges begin between Hussein of Mecca and MacMahon regarding Arab rising against the Turks.

2. May, 1916. Sykes–Picot Agreement outlines Anglo–French influence in Middle East.

3. June, 1916. Hussein declares independence of the Hejaz. Turkish garrison concentrates on Medina.

4. 1917–18. Feisal and his brothers lead Arab forces against the Turks in North and South respectively.

5. November, 1917. Balfour Declaration promises British support for a National Home for the Jews in Palestine.

6. January, 1919. Feisal asks Paris Peace Conference for independence for the Arabic-speaking peoples.

7. July, 1920. French troops evict Feisal from Damascus.

8. August, 1921. British put Feisal on the throne of Iraq in Baghdad.

9. February, 1922. Allenby forces British Government to recognize Egyptian independence, subject to certain reservations.

10. September, 1922. Transjordan detached from Palestine, and given to Abdullah, Feisal's brother. Lawrence considers his work is done, and retires from public life.

ALLENBY

11. December, 1925. Hussein's son Ali evicted from Mecca
    by Ibn Saud. Hussein flees to Cyprus; Ali to Feisal.
    Britain supports Ibn Saud.

12. 1925. The Syrians revolt against the French.

13. September, 1933. Feisal dies.

14. 1936. Second revolt against the French in Syria. Arab–
    Jewish disturbances in Palestine begin on a large scale.

15. June, 1941. Wavell's troops enter Syria and defeat French
    forces.

16. May, 1945. Britain and America force France to evacu-
    ate Syria and Lebanon together.

17. May, 1948. State of Israel proclaimed.

18. July, 1951. Abdullah assassinated in Jerusalem.

19. July, 1952. Officers of Egyptian army depose Farouk.

20. February, 1954. Nasser gains power in Egypt.

21. November, 1956. Britain joins with France in Suez
    venture, in effort to curb Nasser and secure Canal.

22. February, 1958. Formation of Hashemite Union of Iraq
    and Jordan, in reply to United Arab Republic of Egypt
    and Syria.

23. July, 1958. Feisal II of Iraq and Nuri-as-Said assassi-
    nated in Baghdad. Jordan alone remains of the British
    attempts to set up pro-British states in the Middle East.
    French influence virtually non-existent.

Notes

CHAPTER 1 Early Life

1. *Highways and Byways in Nottinghamshire*, J. B. Firth (Macmillan, 1916). Extensive notes on the Allenby family tree, compiled by Mrs. C. A. Allenby (mother) and Mrs. H. H. Porter (sister), are in A. P.
2. *Allenby: Soldier and Statesman*, Lord Wavell (Harrap, 1940, 1944, and 1946).
3. Letter, A.P. 10. 9. 01.
4. J. E. C. Welldon, one-time Headmaster of Harrow, quoted in Wavell. A.P.
5. *Haileybury Past and Present*, L. S. Milford (Fisher, Unwin, 1909).
6. Rev. H. Dunkin, A.P.
7. *Haileybury Register*, 7th edition, 1946.
8. Wavell and A.P.
9. *Allenby of Armageddon*, R. Savage (Hodder & Stoughton, 1925).
10. Wavell and A.P.
11. Notes by Edmonds and Barrow in A.P.
12. A.P.
13. Family Tree, A.P.
14. Letter, A.P. 24.5.97.
15. Introduction by J. F. C. Fuller to *In Flanders Fields* (U.S., 1958; Longmans, 1959).
16. Telegrams, A.P. 11.99.

CHAPTER 2 War: South Africa

1. Letter, A.P. 6.11.99.
2. *Goodbye Dolly Gray*, R. Kruger (Cassell, 1959), for this and other background.
3. Letter, A.P. 15.12.99. To his wife, as all the following unless otherwise stated.
4. Letter, A.P. 29.12.99.
5. Letter, A.P. 7.1.00.
6. Letter, A.P. 8.1.00.
7. Letter, A.P. 10.1.00.
8. Letter, A.P. 13.1.00.
9. Letter, A.P. 16.1.00.
10. Letter, A.P. 20.1.00.
11. Letter, A.P. 31.1.00.
12. Letter, A.P. 31.1.00.
13. Letter, A.P. 7.2.00.
14. Letter, A.P. 10.2.00.
15. Letter, A.P. 19.2.00.
16. *Lord Roberts*, D. James (Hollis & Carter, 1954).
17. An unidentified Australian newspaper cutting, A.P.
18. Wavell, op. cit., and A.P.
19. Letter, A.P. 8.3.00.
20. Letters, A.P. 18.3.00 to 1.5.00.
21. Letters, A.P. 18.5.00 to 14.6.00.
22. Letters, A.P. 29.6.00 and 3.7.00.
23. Letters, A.P. 11.7.00, 14.7.00 and 19.7.00.
24. Letter, A.P. 31.7.00.
25. Letter, A.P. 9.8.00.
26. Letter, A.P. 12.7.00.
27. Letter, A.P. 19.7.00.
28. Letter, A.P. 21.7.00.
29. Letters, A.P. 23.8.00 and 14.9.00.
30. Letters, A.P. 6.9.00 to 12.10.00.
31. Letters, A.P. 14.10.00 to 29.10.00.
32. Letter, A.P. 7.11.00.
33. Letters, A.P. 13.11.00 to 29.11.00.

34. Letter, A.P. 1.12.00.
35. Letter, A.P. 4.12.00.
36. Letters, A.P. 6.12.00, 7.12.00 and 12.12.00.
37. *The Inniskilling Dragoons*, E. S. Jackson (Humphreys, 1909), and *A Very Gallant Gentleman*, L. C. Bernacchi (Butterworth, 1933).
38. Letter, A.P. 6.1.01.
39. Letter, A.P. 25.1.01.
40. Letter, A.P. 31.1.01.
41. Letter, A.P. 11.2.01.
42. Letter, A.P. 3.3.01.
43. Letter, A.P. 23.3.01.
44. Letter, A.P. 6.4.01.
45. Letter, A.P. 30.4.01.
46. Letter, A.P. 4.5.01.
47. Letters, A.P. 15.5.01 and 25.5.01.
48. Letter, A.P. 11.6.01.
49. Letters, A.P. 11.6.01 to 16.7.01.
50. Letters, A.P. 29.7.01.
51. Letters, A.P. 28.8.01 and 29.8.01.
52. Letter, A.P. 1.9.01.
53. Letter, A.P. 14.9.01.
54. Letter, A.P. 4.10.01.
55. Letter, A.P. 27.10.01, to his father-in-law.
56. Letters, A.P. 28.11.01 and 4.12.01.
57. Letter, A.P. 5.12.01.
58. Letters, A.P. 9.4.02, 15.4.02 and 14.5.02.
59. Letters, A.P. Father Knapp and Major Yardley to Allenby's wife. Yardley wrote a book on the campaign.
60. Wavell and A.P.

CHAPTER 3 Peace: Cavalry

1. *A History of the 5th Dragoons & 5th R.I. Lancers*, J. R. Harvey (1923).
2. Letter to Royal Humane Society, A.P. 15.12.05.
3. From an unidentified cutting.

ALLENBY

4. Wavell, op. cit.
5. *Lessons from the Varsity of Life*, Lord Baden-Powell (Pearson, 1934). Miss Loveday's own account of the episode is in A.P., also a letter concerning it from B.-P. A letter from one of his masters at Wellington described Michael as 'an exceedingly pleasant and sociable boy whom everyone liked'. Michael was in the College Hockey XI.
6. Letter to his wife, A.P. 4.10.01.
7. *Soldiering On*, H. Gough (Barker, 1954).
8. *Through the Fog of War*, B. H. Liddell Hart (Faber, 1938).
9. *Journal of the Royal United Service Institution*, 11.10.
10. Review of an article by Col. D. Frobenius in *Kriegstechnische Zeitschrift*, 1909, *R.U.S.I. Journal*, 9.09.
11. *Alfred Lord Milner*, J. E. Wrench (Eyre & Spottiswoode, 1958).

CHAPTER 4 War: Retreat

1. Letter from Lord Roberts, A.P. 11.8.14. Early in the war, Allenby's sister, Mrs. Porter, wrote to Roberts with a suggestion that may have seemed frivolous, but was to be only too sensible. Roberts replied (24.9.14): 'I am afraid it would not be possible to supply the troops with fishermen's waders, as the amount of baggage of an army has to be strictly limited, and the waders would not be often required, as the fact of the trenches being full of water is exceptional and not I hope likely to recur often.'
2. Letter to his wife, A.P. 15.8.14.
3. Ditto., 20.8.14.
4. Memo. from Henry Wilson, Sub. Chief-of-Staff, 21.8.14. *Official History of the War, Military Operations*, France and Belgium, 1914, Vol. I, Appendix 12.
5. *Official History*.
6. *Soldiering On*.

7. *Brasshat*, B. Collier (Secker & Warburg, 1961).
8. Wavell letter, quoting Edmonds, A.P. 13.7.38.
9. *1914*, Lord Ypres (Constable, 1919).
10. Letter, A.P. 20.6.38.
11. Letters and Notes, A.P. The italics are Edmonds's own.
12. Letter to his wife, A.P. 30.8.14.
13. An officer who witnessed the event. Quoted in Wavell.

CHAPTER 5 War: Frustration

1. Letters to his wife, A.P. 16.9.14 and as follows:
2. 22.9.14.
3. 23.9.14.
4. 26.9.14.
5. 28.9.14.
6. 12.10.14.
7. *1914*, op. cit.
8. Letter, A.P. 31.10.14.
9. Letter, A.P. 4.11.14.
10. Letter, A.P. 8.11.14.
11. Letter, A.P. 15.11.14.
12. Letter, A.P. 18.11.14.
13. Letter, A.P. 20.11.14.
14. Letter, A.P. 2.12.14.
15. Letter, A.P. 15.12.14.
16. Letter, A.P. 18.12.14.
17. *The Private Papers of Douglas Haig* (Eyre & Spottiswoode, 1952), 11.4.15.
18. Introduction by J. F. C. Fuller to *In Flanders Fields*. Fuller was on Allenby's staff, Third Army, for six months. 'Of the Generals I have served under, in my opinion he was out and out the best.' A.P.
19. Letter, A.P. 17.6.15.
20. Letter, A.P. 26.8.15.
21. Letter, A.P. 6.1.16.
22. Letter, A.P. 22.10.15.

CHAPTER 6   War: Arras

1. Letter from General Plumer, A.P. 10.15.
2. *The World Crisis*, W. S. Churchill (Odhams, 1938).
3. Letter to his mother, A.P. 3.1.16.
4. Wavell, op. cit.
5. S. E. Holland. A.P. 16.10.38.
6. Letters, A.P. 26.8.15 and 17.2.16.
7. *The Tanks*, B. H. Liddell Hart (Cassell, 1959).
8. *From Chauffeur to Brigadier*, C.D.B.S.B. Carr (Benn, 1930).
9. *Official History*, 1917, Vol. I.
10. Letters, A.P. as dated.
11. Letter from French, A.P. 4.17.
12. Australian *Official History of the War*, Vol. IV, C. E. W. Bean (Angus & Robertson, 1935).
13. *War Memoirs*, Vol. II, D. Lloyd George (Odhams, 1936).
14. Ditto.
15. Ditto.
16. *Daily Telegraph*, 30.6.17.
17. Unidentified cutting, 6.17.

CHAPTER 7   War: The Taking of Jerusalem

1. *Seven Pillars of Wisdom*, T. E. Lawrence (Jonathan Cape, 1935).
2. *Army Diary*, R. Meinertzhagen (Oliver & Boyd, 1960), 15.7.17.
3. Transcript of statement made by Shea on the B.B.C. News, A.P. 14.5.36.
4. Official Despatch, General Murray, 11.17.
5. Letters, A.P. 9.7.17 and 28.7.17.
6. Australian *Official History*.
7. British *Official History*, Palestine, Pt. II.
8. *Soldiers and Statesmen*, W. Robertson (Cassell, 1926). Memo. 9.10.17.

9. Lloyd George, op. cit.
10. A.P. and quoted in Wavell.
11. Meinertzhagen. Diary entry: 10.10.17.
12. Letter, A.P. 20.8.17.
13. *Parliamentary Papers*, 1939, Misc. No. 3, Cmd. 5957.
14. Newcombe was adamant about this to J. B. Villars, author of *T. E. Lawrence* (France, 1955; Sidgwick & Jackson, 1958), a by no means uncritical biography.
15. *Seven Pillars of Wisdom.*
16. Letter, A.P. 3.10.17.
17. T. E. Lawrence: articles in *The Times*, 27.11.18, 28.11.18; article in *Army Quarterly*, 10.20.
18. *Five Years in Turkey*, Liman von Sanders (Germany; U.S. Naval Institute, 1928).
19. Letter from T. H. Sebag-Montefiore, T. Batt., R.H.A. In A.P. 29.7.17.
20. Ditto, 4.8.17.
21. Letter from Haig, 8.8.17.
22. Letter, A.P. 26.8.17.
23. Letter, A.P. 1.8.17, from an officer.
24. Letter, A.P. 29.8.17.
25. Letter from Lady Allenby, A.P. 15.8.17.
26. Letter, A.P. 31.8.17.
27. G.O.C. 16th Division, A.P. 29.10.33 (Turkish year).
28. *Army Diary*, 31.10.17.
29. *With Lawrence in Arabia*, Lowell Thomas (new ed., Arrow, 1962). Lawrence's view from *Lawrence to his Biographers* (Cassell, 1963).
30. Letter, A.P. 7.11.17.
31. Letter, A.P. 8.11.17.
32. Letter, A.P. 9.11.17.
33. *Army Diary*, 10.11.17.
34. Savage, op. cit.
35. Letter, A.P. 20.11.17.
36. Letter, A.P. 26.11.17.
37. Letter, A.P. 10.12.17.
38. Letter from Wingate, A.P. 20.11.17.
39. *Advance of the E.E.F.*, H. P. Gordon (Cairo, 1918).

40. Letter from French, A.P. 25.12.17.
41. Telegram from War Office, A.P. 13.12.17.
42. *Official History*, Pt. II, Vol. II, Appendix I.
43. *Army Diary*, 10.11.17.
44. Letter, A.P. 11.12.17.
45. *Seven Pillars of Wisdom.*
46. Letter, A.P. 11.12.17.
47. Letter, A.P. 14.12.17.
48. Letter, A.P. 17.12.17.
49. Letter, A.P. 20.12.17.
50. Letter, A.P. 30.12.17.

CHAPTER 8 War: Armageddon

1. *Army Diary.* 3.1.18.
2. *Balfour,* K. Young (Bell, 1963).
3. Liman von Sanders, op. cit.
4. *Memoirs,* F. von Papen (Deutsch, 1952).
5. *Reputations,* B. H. Liddell Hart (Murray, 1928).
6. A letter from P. Rutenberg, A.P. 27.4.33, contains the following: 'I am proud to state now the fact, known to few, that I am the author of the idea of the Jewish Battalions to fight with the Allies during the Great War. To redeem with Jewish blood Jewish Palestine. That was in August 1914. The idea was so contradictory to all Jewish traditions and conceptions of life that the then powerful authorities in Jewry intended, as I was told, to excommunicate me publicly from Jewish life. It was the privilege of Jabotinsky to make the dream a reality. As to myself, I was deprived of the privilege of joining them, I was enjoying a doubtful rest in the notorious dungeons of St. Peter and St. Paul's Fortress, as one of the first prisoners of the Bolshevik Government.'
7. Sir J. Barrett, A.P.
8. Savage, op. cit.
9. Wavell, op. cit.

10. Figures are controversial. These are from the British *Official History*.
11. Force Order No. 68, 9.9.18.
12. Wavell, op. cit.
13. Savage, op. cit.
14. Letters, A.P., as dated.
15. Letter, A.P. 24.9.18.
16. *Seven Pillars of Wisdom*.
17. Letter, A.P. 3.10.18. This letter was incorrectly dated September by Allenby.
18. This account is taken from a long memorandum on the meeting by Chauvel, in A.P. It differs to some extent from the two published accounts by others present: *Seven Pillars of Wisdom*, and *The Independent Arab* by H. Young. Chauvel wrote to Allenby and Wavell after the war, complaining bitterly of *Seven Pillars of Wisdom* and the acceptance of the *Official History* of much of Lawrence's account: 'The official historian seems to have swallowed it whole.' Chauvel described Allenby (*Daily Telegraph*, 16.5.36) as: 'The greatest soldier since Wellington, with the exception of Lord Roberts.'
19. Letter, A.P. 17.10.18.
20. U.S. Consulate General, Cairo. A.P. 4.12.18.
21. Lloyd George, op. cit.

CHAPTER 9 Allenby the General

1. Note, A.P.
2. *Seven Pillars of Wisdom*.
3. *The Times*, Dr. H. H. Thomas, F.R.S. 5.36. Thomas, who became a leading Cambridge botanist, conducted an aerial survey of Palestine under Allenby.
4. Despatch, 31.10.18.
5. Speech in Cairo. *The Times*, 16.12.18.
6. *New York Herald Tribune*, 27.5.28.

CHAPTER 10   Allenby and Lawrence

1. *Middle East Diary*, R. Meinertzhagen (Cresset Press, 1959), 24.12.21.
2. *Lawrence to His Biographers.*
3. Wavell, op. cit.
4. *Middle East Diary.*
5. Both quotations from *Seven Pillars of Wisdom.*
6. *Army Quarterly*, 10.20.
7. *Wingate of the Sudan*, R. Wingate (Murray, 1955).
8. *The Nation*, 20.9.19.
9. Letter, A.P. 10.10.19.
10. J. B. Villars, op. cit., and *Lawrence of Arabia*, E. Lönröth (Sweden; Valentine, Mitchell, 1956).
11. *Great Contemporaries*, W. S. Churchill (Butterworth, 1937).
12. *Safety Last*, W. F. Stirling (Hollis & Carter, 1953). A letter from Bartholomew in A.P. says: 'Lawrence played a useful part in increasing the difficulties of the Turks and the Germans. It suited Allenby to make much of Lawrence from that point of view and he did it legitimately. I personally did everything I could to help Allenby to use him in that way.' However, Meinertzhagen, a Zionist, told the author: 'I think Allenby saw through Lawrence; a charming little man, but a complete humbug. He had not the slightest effect on the campaign.'
13. Journal of the Central Asian Society, 7.35.
14. *The Times*, 20.5.35 (report of a broadcast).

CHAPTER 11   Peace: Egypt and the Middle East

1. Letter, *The Times*, 1964, A. F. Nayton, Military Governor in Beersheba, 1918. 'Lord Allenby had the Anzacs paraded at Gaza and addressed them. He had withdrawn his recommendations for decorations, and hoped to get the Anzacs out of Palestine as soon as possible. As

if rehearsed, the assembled Australian troops counted in unison, slowly from one to ten, and ended with a roar of OUT. General Allenby's anger can be imagined. Undoubtedly an uncomfortable moment in an illustrious career.'

2. Letter, A.P. 10.12.18.
3. Letter, A.P. 12.18.
4. Letter, A.P. 5.2.19.
5. Letter, A.P. 2.3.19.
6. *Nuri-as-Said*, Lord Birdwood (Cassell, 1959).
7. Letter, A.P. 15.1.18.
8. Two speeches by Theodore Roosevelt on Britain in Egypt, in which he called for strong British rule leading to independence. University of Cairo, 28.3.10, and Guildhall, London, 30.5.10.
9. *Wingate of the Sudan.*
10. Cf. *England and the Middle East*, E. Kedourie (Bowes and Bowes, 1956).
11. *Army Diary*, 19.3.19.
12. *Manchester Guardian*, cutting, A.P.
13. *Egyptian Gazette*, 18.7.19.
14. Letter, A.P. 7.1.19.
15. Letter, A.P. 23.8.19.
16. Telegram, A.P. 10.8.19.
17. *The Times*, 8.10.19.
18. *Not in the Limelight*, R. Wingate (Hutchinson, 1959).
19. Letter, A.P. 18.3.21.
20. *Documents on British Foreign Policy*, Vol. IV, Vol. XIII (H.M.S.O., 1952, 1963).
21. Ditto, Vol. XIII, No. 259.
22. *Orientations*, R. Storrs (Nicholson & Watson, 1937).
23. *Documents on British Foreign Policy*, Vol. IV, No. 206. 26.6.19.
24. Letter, A.P. 28.5.20.
25. Letter, A.P. 7.20.
26. Letter, A.P. 22.7.20, to his mother.
27. Letter, A.P. 25.7.20.
28. Letter, A.P. 26.7.20, to his mother.

29. Letter, A.P. 26.8.20.
30. Letter, A.P. 17.10.20.
31. *Great Contemporaries* (essay on Lawrence). *The Hashemite Kings*, J. Morris (Faber, 1959) for background.
32. Letters, A.P. 8.12.20 and 28.12.20.
33. *Alfred Lord Milner.*
34. Letter, A.P. 17.10.20
35. Letter, A.P. 2.11.20.
36. Letter, A.P. 12.3.21.
37. Letter, A.P. 3.21.
38. Letter, A.P. 29.4.21.
39. Letter, A.P. 29.12.21.
40. Particularly in his unpublished letters to Lawrence, deposited in the British Museum.
41. Letter, A.P. 6.4.21.
42. Letter, A.P. 17.7.21.
43. Letter, A.P. 30.11.21.
44. Letter, A.P. 13. 12.21.
45. Letter, A.P. 8.1.21.
46. Unpublished section of diary of Henry Wilson, 25.1.22.
47. *The Decline and Fall of Lloyd George*, Lord Beaverbrook (Collins 1963).
48. *My Journey Round the World*, Lord Northcliffe (John Lane, 1923).
49. Diary of Henry Wilson, 11.2.22. Allenby reported the gist of this interview to Wilson, Sir Walford Selby and Wavell, all of whom have it on paper in the A.P.
50. Diary of Henry Wilson, 12.2.22.
51. Ditto, 13.2.22.
52. Ditto, 14.2.22.
53. The account given of this affair in *Curzon: The Last Phase* by Harold Nicolson (Constable, 1938), pages 180, 181, in which it is suggested that the 1922 Declaration is the work of Curzon, is not entirely correct. An account less favourable to Curzon is given in *The Life of Lord Curzon*, Earl of Ronaldshay, Vol. III (Benn, 1928).

54. *Egypt Since Cromer*, Lord Lloyd, Vol. II (Macmillan, 1934).
55. Letter, A.P. 18.7.22.
56. According to the commander of the 16/5th Lancers, Col. C. Howard, Asquith gave some encouragement to Allenby in his attitude. Letter from Howard in A.P. Allenby had been previously thinking of an ultimatum. He wrote to his sister Nell: 'Stack's murder merely hurried a line of action, on our part, which had been inevitable. The attitude of Zaghlul would have necessitated my ultimatum anyhow.' A.P. 23.12.24.
57. For instance, *Egypt*, H. Young (Benn, 1927).
58. For the Egyptian attitude: *Independent Egypt*, A, Youssef Bey (Murray, 1940).
59. *Egypt Since Cromer*.

CHAPTER 12 Retirement

1. Speech in A.P.
2. Letters from American correspondents in A.P.
3. *A Pilgrim in Palestine After its Deliverance*, J. Finley (U.S.; Chapman & Hall, 1919).
4. Report in *New York Sun*, 10.28.
5. *New York Herald Tribune*, 7.10.28.
6. 29.10.28.
7. *Shifting Sands*, N. N. E. Bray (Unicorn, 1934).
8. Letter to the author.
9. Rectorial address, Edinburgh University, 1936.
10. *New York Times*, 5.36.

CHAPTER 13 Epilogue

1. *The Palestine Campaigns*, A.P. Wavell (Constable, 1928).
2. *Deutsche Wehr*. Quoted in *Wavell*, R. H. Kiernan (Harrap, 1945).

3. *Wavell : Portrait of a Soldier*, B. Fergusson (Collins, 1961).
4. *Lord Wavell*, R. J. Collins (Hodder & Stoughton, 1947).
5. *Sunday Referee*, 13.4.30.
6. *Not in the Limelight*.
7. *Army Quarterly*, 1.22.
8. *Soldiers and Soldiering*, Lord Wavell (Cape, 1953).
9. *Orde Wingate*, C. Sykes (Collins, 1959). Sir W. Platt, C.-in-C. Sudan, is quoted.
10. R. H. Andrew, to the author.

Index

INDEX

India, 10, 42, 110, 212, 218, 225, 256
Indian Army, 144, 175
Indian Cavalry Corps in France, 41
Indian cavalry in Palestine, 174
Indian Civil Service, 6, 18
Indian troops in Palestine, 175
Inniskilling Dragoons (6th), 7–8, 10–11, 12, 13–14, 20, 59; in South African War, 25 *ff*; and New South Wales Lancers, 32; at Bloemfontein, 34–5; E.A. to command (acting), 35; casualties (May, 1900), 35–6; in Barberton operation, 39–40; in isolated action, 40–1; refitting at Pretoria, 42; in Rimington's Column, 43
Inniskilling Fusiliers, 48
Intelligence, British, in Palestine campaigns, 126, 128, 132, 154, 180; Chiefs of, 128, 129. *See also* Deception.
Interests, E.A.'s personal, 7, 14, 16, 23, 54, 55, 82, 255–6. *See also* Botany, Ornithology, *etc.*
Internationalism, E.A. on, 261–2
Intrigue in B.E.F., 88
Iraq (*formerly* Mesopotamia, [*q.v.*]), 169, 208, 219, 231 *n*
Ireland, 19, 20, 62, 238
Is War Impossible? (Bloch), 20
Ismailia, 116, 120
Istanbul, *see* Constantinople

Jaffa, 155
Jaffa Gate (Jerusalem), 161
Jaffa Road, 158
Jazz Age, the, 227
Jeddah (*or* Jiddah), 134, 137, 238
Jenin, 184
Jericho, 170, 180
Jerusalem, 112, 114, 123, 125, 153, 165, 170, 205, 206; attack

on, 154–8; evacuated, 158; surrendered, 159; entered formally, 159–60, 161, 224; capture announced in London, 160; E.A.'s Proclamation in, 161–2; lunch to celebrate, 162; clash of creeds in, 168; water supply of, 168–9
Jerusalem, Mayor of, 158–9
Jerusalem-Beersheba road, Newcombe's raid on, 150–1
Jews in Palestine, 216, 219; battalions, 176
Jiddah, *see* Jeddah
Jodhpur Lancers, 175, 186 *n*
Joffre, General Joseph Jacques Césaire (French C.-in-C.), 84, 89, 90, 97
Johannesburg (Transvaal), 36, 41, 42, 52
Jordan, Kingdom of (*formerly* Transjordan, [*q.v.*]), 208, 231 *n*
Jordan, River, 169, 170, 180, 184
Jordan Valley, 170, 176, 179, 180, 184
Joyce, Lieut.-Colonel P. C., 134–5, 191; (quoted) 141; and Lawrence, 141
Judea, foothills of, 155

Kaiser, the (Wilhelm II, German Emperor, 1888–1918), 83, 160
Keir, General Sir John, 93
Keitel, General Wilhelm, on Wavell (quoted), 268
Kemal, Mustapha, Pasha (Ataturk), 181, 186, 194, 238
Kennington, Eric (artist), 228
Kenwick (Lincs.), 4
Kenwick Hall (near Louth), 2
Kenya, 218
Khartoum, 20, 135, 137, 228
Kiggell, Lieut.-General Sir Lancelot (Haig's Chief of Staff), 99, 107 *n*

305

INDEX